Where's a Good Church?

Donald C. Posterski
and Irwin Barker

Wood Lake Books Inc.

Editing: Michael Schwartzentruber, Jim Taylor, Tim Faller
Design and Layout: Tim Faller, Michael Schwartzentruber
Cover: Tim Faller, Jim Taylor

Canadian Cataloguing in Publication Data

Posterski, Donald C., 1942–
Where's a good church?

ISBN 0-929032-94-2

1. Protestant churches—Canada—Public opinion. 2. Canada—Religious life and customs—Public opinion. 3. Public opinion—Canada. I. Barker, Irwin Roy. II. Title.
BR570.P68 1993   280'.4'0971   C93-091306-x

Copyright © 1993 Donald C. Posterski and Irwin Barker
All rights reserved. No part of this publication may be reproduced—except in the case of brief quotations embodied in critical articles and reviews—stored in an electronic retrieval system, or transmitted in any form or by any means, electronic, mechanical, photocopying, recording, or otherwise, without prior written permission of the publisher or copyright holder.

Published by
Wood Lake Books Inc.,
Box 700, Winfield, BC,
Canada V0H 2C0

Printed in Canada by
Hignell Printing Ltd.,
Winnipeg, MB, R3G 2B4

Contents

Preface 5
Introduction 8

Section I: Surveying the Landscape
Chapter One
    Who Goes to Church? 13
Chapter Two
    Why People Like Their Churches 19
Chapter Three
    Why People Leave Their Churches 49
Chapter Four
    Why Denominational Walls Are Tumbling Down 73

Section II: Mapping the Canadian Context
Chapter Five
    Cultural Shifts 89
Chapter Six
    Canadian Religion Is Not American 117
Chapter Seven
    Contextualizing the Message 135

Section III: Charting New Directions
Chapter Eight
    Striving for Balance 151
Chapter Nine
    Effective Leadership Styles 171
Chapter Ten
    Marching Off the Map 189

Conclusion 215

Appendix A: Methodology 221
Appendix B: Survey 227
Appendix C: Survey Results 237

Endnotes 261

Preface

Taking things apart is easier than putting them back together. So we shouldn't be surprised that figuring out what will make life work better is more difficult than simply defining what's gone wrong.

This book is based on our conviction that we can learn more by figuring out what is going right than by critiquing what has gone wrong. Our strategy is to assess church effectiveness by focusing on churches that are healthy rather than on those that are sick.

We hope that by identifying what is effective and vibrant in church life in Canada, others will be able to pursue more effective ministry too.

The impetus for this project was generated within World Vision Canada's Department of National Programs. Functioning as a "national expression of World Vision's global mandate," one of the intentions is to put something back into the soil of the country that so generously supports international mission.

Using limited resources, World Vision's National Programs department commits its energies to responding to selective segments of the poor in Canada, and also to serving and complementing the church. Within the department's ethos of using research to enhance ministry, the project to define the characteristics of effective churches was born. The royalties from the sale of this book will go toward the costs of the research and the ministry commitments of World Vision Canada in the developing world.

The pages that follow are a collaborative effort.

Co-author Irwin Barker lives in Winnipeg, where he works as a senior research director for the Angus Reid Group. In the past year, we have spent many days and late nights together. We have discussed ideas, debated strategies, listened to each other, laughed a lot, prayed together, blinked back a few tears, and developed appreciation for each other. Irwin has repeatedly expressed his joy for being able to use his professional skills as a researcher to contribute to the well-being of the church in Canada. His experience and credentials allow us to withstand the scrutiny of research critics, but it is his warm spirit and fine mind that I hope you sense in the pages that follow.

Chuck Ferguson researched and wrote the first draft of Chapter Six. His graduate educational background in "Canada-U.S. relations" and his crafted competence qualify him for the task of comparing the role of religion in the two countries. Chuck is World Vision's Director of MARC Ministries. He serves as the associate editor of the quarterly publication *Context*, which uses "research to make religion relevant" and is especially designed for Christian leaders in Canada. Chuck's contribution to this project has been critical. Beyond critiquing our first draft efforts, his input has elevated the level of the final product.

Glenn Smith, the Executive Director of Christian Direction in Montreal, applied his gifts and energies to produce the first draft of Chapter Seven. Glenn recently completed his doctoral studies in urban ministry. His commitment to clear thinking and concern for the contextual expression of the church's mission in the modern world uniquely qualifies him to express that emphasis for the book.

I would be remiss not to acknowledge Reg Bibby's unspoken role in this venture. A friend and collaborator in other youth-related research projects over the past ten years, Reg willingly set aside a weekend to compare our findings with his on the subject of the "circulation of the saints." It is impossible to focus on religion in Canada without citing Reg's extensive work. The reality of that fact is evident in the chapters that follow.

David Adcock also made a valuable contribution. David is World Vision Canada's Eastern NeighbourLink Coordinator. He added to the literature review that strengthened the substance of the final text. Colleague and friend Dr. Ken McMillan read drafts of the chapters and offered his helpful input. Joan Morin serves as my adept administrative assistant. On this project she selected and compiled comments from the surveys as well as patiently responded to a myriad of requests for "help."

Irwin, Chuck, Glenn, Reg, David, Ken and Joan are more than just collaborators making a contribution to a project. They are my friends and I am grateful for each of their gifts and their commitment to our shared vision.

We, the authors and researchers, also want to extend a special thank you to the 761 respondents who took the project seriously enough to express their views on what makes churches vital and effective. In addition, numerous individuals cooperated by conducting interviews and arranging for focus group discussions. We are grateful for their contribution.

Preface

I know that it is often said that without competent editorial support, it is difficult to produce a book that can capture its potential. The reason the statement is often made is that it is true. We extend our thanks to Jim Taylor and Mike Schwartzentruber from Wood Lake Books for their counsel and skill.

Our joy will be complete if the following pages bring readers a sense of hope about the future of the church in Canada.

Don Posterski
Vice-President, National Programs
World Vision Canada

Introduction

Whether people have had a positive or negative church experience, when they move to a different city or just across town, one of their priorities is to find a good church. When young people leave home to begin their first full-time job or go away to school, they face a crucial decision: Should I even look for a church to attend? They often wonder whether there are any good churches out there.

The question keeps coming up—"Where's a good church?"

Perhaps you are someone who has recently sat in a Sunday morning worship service thinking to yourself,

"I like my church.
"I belong here.
"My family is cared for here.
"Quite often, I get in touch with God when I come here.
"The issues of life are dealt with in this church.
"And furthermore, I am ready to get involved with the world beyond myself.
"This is a good church."

But maybe this is not your story. Perhaps you are someone who attends church with reasonable regularity but you find yourself thinking and feeling,

"I'm not sure I like being here.
"The preaching is disconnected from life.
"The music is flat.
"Anyway, most of my friends have moved away.
"Our kids would rather stay home.
"Sometimes I feel like I don't belong here any more.
"Whether I want to admit it or not, I'm beginning to wonder, 'Where's a good church?'"

One of the convictions of the authors of this book is that if you are wrestling with discontent, you shouldn't feel guilty about asking the question, "Where's a good church?" Discontent can be a sign of spiritual hunger. And if honesty is a Christian virtue, we have to candidly admit that a sizable number of churches in Canada are pretty bleak places to belong. They can be damaging to your spiritual health. Although we do not want to demean the value of loyalty or depreciate the merit of perseverance, if one has to choose between long-term spiritual health and leaving a negative church situation, then leaving may be a legitimate option.

In researching the question, "What are the characteristics of effective churches?" we began by holding focus groups across the country. It was soon apparent that the prime players in creating alive and vibrant churches were clergy, academics (teaching in Christian colleges, universities and seminaries) and laity. Consequently, we spread our interviews among those prime players, with the strategy of talking to people across the Protestant spectrum. In several instances we spent evenings talking with groups of people who had switched churches in the past year. Our intent was to probe what prompted their dissatisfaction, what caused them to change churches, and what aspects of church life were especially satisfying to them in their new worship environments.

Using the input from 26 focus groups and approximately 75 individual interviews, the next stage in the research methodology was to design a survey instrument. We then distributed the survey to a national sample of clergy, academics and laity that included representation from both mainline and conservative Protestant denominations as well as independent churches. In the end, 761 individuals responded by completing and returning their questionnaires. The research design allowed us to utilize the strengths of both qualitative and quantitative methodologies. A detailed analysis of the methodology and sample is contained in Appendix A. The survey tool itself is contained in Appendix B. The detailed results of the survey are contained in Appendix C.

The responses in the sample group are from those who are "committed" to their churches. They are frequent attenders. They are the insiders. Not only do those in the sample represent the core of organized church life in Canada, in most cases they are best of the best. In other words, the 761 people who responded are representative of the fruit of what the Protestant churches have produced in the past two decades.

The book is more than a research report. The survey findings provide the data for the central conclusions and they are woven through the commentary. But the content also analyzes numerous aspects of contemporary Canadian life and makes recommendations designed to enhance the future of the church.

Several assumptions are implicit throughout the book.

We are convinced that we cannot understand what is happening to the church or find our way into an enhanced future without also having a solid grasp of the contemporary Canadian context. We agree with Thomas Oden that "Since the gospel addresses us in a particular here-and-now situation, rather than as a timeless abstraction, it is impossible properly to conceive of ministry apart from studied awareness of its current context."[1]

As authors, we have attempted to be conscious of and honest about our own belief biases and spiritual style preferences. We have tried to avoid making judgements about any one denominational way being superior or more correct than another. We believe deeply in denominational diversity and have endeavored to convey faithfully the various perspectives that represent the Protestant spectrum of churches who responded to the survey. To paraphrase C.S. Lewis, "There are many ways of bringing people into the kingdom, some of which I especially despise. I have therefore learned to be cautious in my judgments."

Much of the existing literature under the title of church **effectiveness** really deals with church **growth**. We have come to realize that church effectiveness and church growth are not the same thing. It is true that effective churches tend to grow as a consequence of what they offer their members. But there are also many churches in the country where congregational numerical growth is not the case, though individual members in those churches are growing in their personal faith.

We have listened to people tell us why they like their churches, and why they leave their churches. After studying the research results and analyzing what they mean, we are convinced that church effectiveness cannot be reduced to a precise formula. Nor are there any magic-wand solutions to the present predicaments facing the church in Canada. However, there are some specific ways to increase church effectiveness. The facts are simple—some churches are healthy and vital and involving increasing numbers of people; others are limping and lifeless and experiencing continual decline.

Our conviction is that all churches can benefit from looking at effective churches. We believe that life in the church is a divine-human partnership—a partnership that can implement creative correctives and express new initiatives that will make life "in Christ" both believable and desirable in the modern world.

Section I

Surveying the Landscape

Who Goes To Church?

Chapter One

A few years ago, the federal government announced that it would be cutting back its substantial $600 million subsidy to VIA Rail. The result would be a disruption or possible discontinuation of the transcontinental passenger rail service. The Canadian public was not pleased. Some were saddened, others were outraged. Was it because they would have to find some other way to travel across the country?

No. In fact, relatively few Canadians make the trek. They simply opposed the "idea" of not having passenger rail service because the transcontinental rail line was part of our Canadian heritage. Attitudes toward long-distance train travel were romanticized images, with no market value. In essence, Canadians were saying, "We want it, we just don't want to use it."

For many Canadians, the church is like the train. It is part of our history and identity. It is even on our list of "things to do someday." It has a place in our hearts, but not in our calendars and wallets.

Church attendance patterns

Religious affiliation is "extremely stable" in Canada, concludes sociologist Reginald Bibby in his detailed analysis of religion in Canada.[1] At the same time, Bibby and others continue to document declining attendance patterns.

This apparent contradiction springs from a series of developments which allowed identification to become separated from participation. People can identify with a church, but rarely attend or support it. Bruce Shelley and Marshall Shelley, in their analysis of the "consumer church," note that, for many people, the trend in recent years is to "consider church attendance a mere rest-stop on their religious pilgrimage… They consider the church a convenience, not a home."[2] There was a time in the history of the church when a separation of participation from identification was unthinkable. To belong meant to attend. But for many contemporary Canadian churches, the gap between who sits in the pew and who remains on the membership list grows continuously.

By contrasting affiliation and participation, we can create a rough portrait of types of linkage that remain between the population of Canada and the church. *(See Fig. 1.1)*

Participation

For purposes of simplicity, participation can be categorized as either "committed" or "conditional." Committed participation assumes regular attendance, support and involvement as well as holding formal group membership. Conditional participation includes regular attendance and involvement in a local church, but it stops short of full-status membership. Some denominations and local churches are presently re-writing their bylaws to allow increasing numbers of "conditional participants" to hold offices and function as full members.

Affiliation

Affiliation refers to people who limit their formal religious expression to special-event attendance and the use of the church for "rites of passage," such as birth, marriage and death. Although affiliation neither implies formal membership nor regular participation, it does include the subjective classification of oneself as "belonging" to a particular denomination or tradition.

Fig. 1.1

| | | Institutional Affiliation ||
		Yes	No
Local Church Participation	High	Committed Participants	Conditional Participants
	Low	Cultural Christians	Unchurched People

Committed participants
　　Committed participants are characterized by regular attendance, combined with a strong sense of group affiliation. These people represent the committed core group in today's churches. They both "identify with" and "belong to" the denomination and church they attend.

Conditional participants
　　Conditional participants are also characterized by regular attendance in their local churches but they do not hold formal membership at the church they attend. Neither do they necessarily identify with the denomination of their local church. Typically, they have switched churches and have a conditional commitment to the church they attend. They will likely continue to attend as long as their needs are being met and they are having a positive church experience.

Cultural Christians
　　Cultural Christians are characterized by affiliation with the church, but very limited participation. While they may identify themselves as belonging to a particular denomination or tradition, their religious identification is often rooted in their family or cultural history. They limit their religious activity to special occasions and expect to use the church for rites of passage ceremonies. Cultural Christians are "religious somethings" without participation.

Other people—unchurched
　　Unchurched people neither participate nor affiliate. This category includes a range of individuals. The confirmed atheist, agnostic or apostate would fit neatly into this category, along with those who are committed to religions other than Christianity. This category also includes those who profess no religious affiliation. From the point of view of the Christian church, these people are the unchurched.

　　Using the above definitions, most Canadians fall into the "cultural Christian" category and the relative number of "unchurched" is low. It is the "cultural Christians" who are the subject of Reginald Bibby's analysis of religious fragmentation in Canada. Concerning this group, Bibby writes,
　　　　Canadians are not attending religious services in numbers comparable with the past. But the overwhelming majority still continue to identify with the historically dominant groups.

It has been a major error to equate attendance drop-off with religious disaffiliation. The ties remain strong.[3]

But in a recent conversation, an Anglican minister commented, "I know some people who call themselves Anglicans who wouldn't attend church even if we offered frequent flyer points."

Religious consumers

By offering a selective menu to its constituents, the church has been, to a certain extent, the unwitting author of the separation between affiliation and participation. Why would the church plant the seeds of its own demise? As Bibby points out, "They have not provided a religion based on what religion is, but a religion based on what the market will bear."[4] The separation of affiliation from participation has given rise to a "market" model of the Christian church. This model portrays the church as responding to, or catering to, the needs of Christian "consumers." Consumers take what they need and leave the rest. They expect the products they consume to be permanently available.

Affiliation without participation is a manifestation of individualism. But the problem is not strictly one of individualism. Individualism has long been a driving force behind "modernity." The real problem arises when individualism, once inside the walls of the church, meets up with a longstanding tradition of measuring success by counting heads. Where church success is measured quantitatively, the tendency to respond to individualism with a marketing approach will be more pronounced. For churches to grow, a well-organized marketing strategy which identifies and then satisfactorily meets the needs of members must be implemented.

Viewed in this way, churches which attempt to discern and deliver what Christians "want" are accused of treating Christ as a product and Christ's ministers as merchants. Christian consumers of religion shop around and eventually find churches which, at least for the present, meet their needs. In this market model, loyalty is conditional on continued delivery, decisions are made on the basis of self-interest, and very little is sacrificed to the common good. Furthermore, the marketing model places churches in a competitive environment where only the innovative and responsive survive.

Limitations of the consumer model

The analysis of religious consumption patterns outlined in Bibby's

Fragmented Gods provides a useful portrait of the patterns of the majority of religious consumers in Canada. However, as a portrait of what is going on in our churches, it has limited value in that it focuses primarily on the "cultural Christians" who, although they identify themselves with churches, offer only minimal support and participation. There is no denying that this segment exists. But one must ask whether these people are a part of the church in any meaningful way, or whether the church's response to these individuals simply constitutes part of the inherited activity of the church in contemporary Canadian culture.

The limitation of the consumer model is that it applies to people who rarely "consume" and it ignores active participants. If the consumer model is used as a motif for the church, it should apply to regular participants as well. After all, **they** are the true consumers of what the church has to offer. However, if the active participant is also a consumer, we need to re-examine the negative value judgement frequently applied to the consumer church model.

Can we really criticize anyone for asking the question, "Where's a good church?" Committed Christians have a responsibility to find a place of worship where their spiritual needs can be met. There is nothing wrong with asking yourself, "Where's a good church?" The question implies that there are churches out there in which your needs for spiritual growth can be met, and that you should be attending one if you are not already doing so.

Segmenting the market

If we want to use a market model to better understand church attendance patterns, then it becomes necessary to segment the market into various consumer types based on their consumption patterns. The first and most basic distinction would be between loyal customers and convenience shoppers. Our description of committed and conditional participants, along with cultural Christians and unchurched people, provides a starting point.

It is not the purpose of this book to provide a detailed market segmentation. However, committed Christians who regularly participate in church life but for various reasons find themselves asking, "Where's a good church?" are not the same as people who rarely attend church but still expect to receive the sacred rites of passage and other religious benefits when they desire them.

This is not to say that we should deny religious benefits to cultural Christians acting as convenience shoppers. One reason the church continues to permit fragmentation is that it offers a way in the door. Nonattenders may have a fragmented relationship with the church—a daughter's soccer team, a local "environmental concerns" group, a desire to associate themselves with the church they were married in, whatever. Tenuous as it may be, that fragment is a link which they may draw upon in times of crisis. The church's compassionate response to the crisis could then lead to a life-transforming experience.

We believe that people should be given the benefit of the doubt. Many times, Christians who are asking the question, "Where's a good church?" are implicitly recognizing that their spiritual needs are not being met where they are. Our intent is not to give out permission slips to leave churches just because difficulties arise. But committed Christians, and those who are searching for a personal faith, will be wise to find a good church where they will be spiritually stimulated and nourished.

Why People Like Their Churches

Chapter Two

In the past, preachers could be heard proclaiming, "The church is the one organization in the world that exists to serve people who are not members. God's people live to serve others."

It may not sound spiritual or by past stands very virtuous, but "good churches" in Canada in the 1990s look after the needs of their members first, and then express their concern for others.

What today's committed Christians want

Our approach to the question of "Where's a good church?" examined the opinions, beliefs and preferences of those who have already found a good church and those who are genuinely looking for a meaningful expression of faith.

Our initial discussions with people took place in 26 focus groups and 75 interviews, where we asked the question, "What makes an effective church?" Several themes or key areas emerged from these discussions. For most of these people, effective churches are those which build on the strengths of four cornerstones:
- **orthodoxy**—in touch with truth
- **community**—in touch with personal needs
- **relevance**—in touch with the times
- **outreach**—in touch with the needs of others.

Using the input from the focus groups and interviews, we designed a survey to collect data from a national sample of Protestant clergy, academics and committed laity. We got 761 responses. What follows is not only the data itself, but our interpretation of its significance. (Detailed results of the survey, conducted by the Angus Reid Group, can be found in Appendix C.)

Orthodoxy

Orthodoxy sounds like an old-fashioned idea, but the message from the research results is clear. Church-attending Christians still believe in the basics of the faith. This orientation towards orthodoxy should not be confused with an invitation for ministers to launch into a series of sermons on the doctrinal distinctives of their particular denomination. In fact, there is little interest in the fine points of doctrine.

There is, however, a gravitation towards the historical framework that has sustained the Christian faith since the first century. People who faithfully and frequently attend church affirm the uniqueness of Jesus Christ and accept his resurrection as an event in history. They believe that the Bible is a special revelation from God, from which they can derive direction for their lives. They want to discern God's truth and apply it to the complexities of the age. The place of prayer and meditation remains as part of healthy spirituality. They believe in life after death and expect to live with God forever. Church-attending Christians continue to embrace the essence of what others before them have embraced.

As change swirls around them, those who go to church look to the church for stability. In the midst of Canadian pluralism and increased secularization, the people of God do not want to attend worship and hear sermons that dismantle the foundation of their basic beliefs. Instead, they view strong preaching and solid doctrinal teaching as an essential characteristic of an effective church. Conventional Christian doctrine is also a strong criterion by which people will decide what church to attend if they move to another city and are faced with finding a new church.

In our discussion groups with Christians across Canada, we asked participants what type of situation would lead them to select a church other than the one they currently attend. Orthodox teaching and preaching emerged as a major consideration. Members will leave over unorthodox preaching much sooner than over dull or lifeless preaching. Thus, orthodoxy has implications both for quantitative and qualitative growth, for drawing people to the church initially, and for retaining their participation. It should be pointed out that orthodoxy is not as likely to attract uncommitted Christians or those outside the church. It is, however, a major consideration among active Christians in terms of finding a church home.

A comment from a lay leader expresses the view of the majority of church attenders, both mainline and conservative: "Effective churches seem to be those that teach an uncompromising message based on the authority of Holy Scriptures."

The demand for orthodoxy reflects a desire for stability in a changing world. Biblical orthodoxy provides a basis for clear moral and ethical choices in a culture where relativism creates ambiguity. For many people, certainty, stability and order are attractive commodities. People who live in the world all week don't want to come to church on Sunday and deal with yet more divergence. That is not to say that church attenders are opposed to creativity and never want to be surprised. Rather, people who live with spiritual commitments find solace in the strength of the basics of the faith that have endured for generations.

Relate without compromising doctrine

In our survey of Canadian church attenders, a strong majority disagreed with the statement, "It is very difficult for churches to relate to the outside world without compromising their traditional biblical teaching." One-half of those surveyed disagreed "strongly," while just over one-third indicated that they "disagree" with the statement. The findings show that church attenders think that the church need not compromise orthodoxy to relate to the world. This commitment to biblical orthodoxy was equally evident in both mainline churches and conservative churches.

Christian academics and clergy were even more likely than lay members to support the idea that the church can relate to the outside world without compromising its traditional biblical teaching. Almost all academics who responded supported this idea. This finding is somewhat surprising given the amount of attention scholars and academics, especially in the mainline churches, have paid to the tension between cultural relevance and doctrinal integrity. Academics and clergy, in particular, do not want to be either irrelevant or unfaithful. Clearly, people in effective churches want to maintain a balance which allows them to relate biblical truth to the outside world.

Low tolerance for diversity in belief and practice

When asked whether churches today must "allow for a wide range of diversity in their belief and practice," two-thirds of church attenders disagreed. Again, mainline and conservative did not greatly differ, although the tolerance for doctrinal diversity was much lower among Pentecostal attenders. Clergy and lay members were much more opposed to permitting diversity in belief and practice than were academics. Almost half of those teaching in Christian seminaries and colleges thought diversity should be allowed.

This attitude item pertains to diversity in belief and practice **within a congregation**, not within the church as a whole. One can easily accept the fact that people in other churches may worship differently or subscribe to a set of behavioral norms unlike one's own, without condemning them. However, people select churches which reflect a pattern of belief and practice consistent with their own convictions and comfort level.

In our discussion sessions with Christians across Canada, lay members were quick to distinguish between those areas where compromise and flexibility is important and those areas where conviction should rule. People were also careful to point out that diversity in belief and practice is part of Protestantism and the church (universal). The existence of different religious traditions is what makes the church more inclusive. But denominations and particular congregations are defined in terms of "where they stand" on various doctrinal and behavioral issues. The pendulum swing of doctrinal and behavioral diversity becomes narrower at each level. By the time we reach the level of the local congregation in a particular denomination, the acceptable level of diversity is minimized. One of the pastors we interviewed noted that his church is "not for everyone."

> People who attend here have to know what to expect. If someone is not comfortable with the way we worship, then maybe this isn't the church they should attend. I'd be happy to recommend another church where the style is more to their liking, and I've done it! But we are not going to change.

Churches that have a clearly defined self-understanding offer their participants few surprises. They also run the risk of sending the signal that "unless you conform, you are not welcome here." Churches that know who they are but also embrace a healthy degree of diversity will be more adept at making new people feel like they belong.

Provide clear rules for living

Church attenders were also asked to indicate their preference for churches which "provide clear rules for how to live and behave" versus ones that "leave lifestyle decisions to personal choice." Overall, 45% wanted clear rules, while 27% preferred a wider range for personal choice. The remaining 28% would like to see a balance between the two. The survey found that lay members were significantly more likely to want clear rules than were either academics or clergy. *(See Fig. 2.1)*

Surveying the Landscape

Fig. 2.1

Clear Rules or Personal Choice

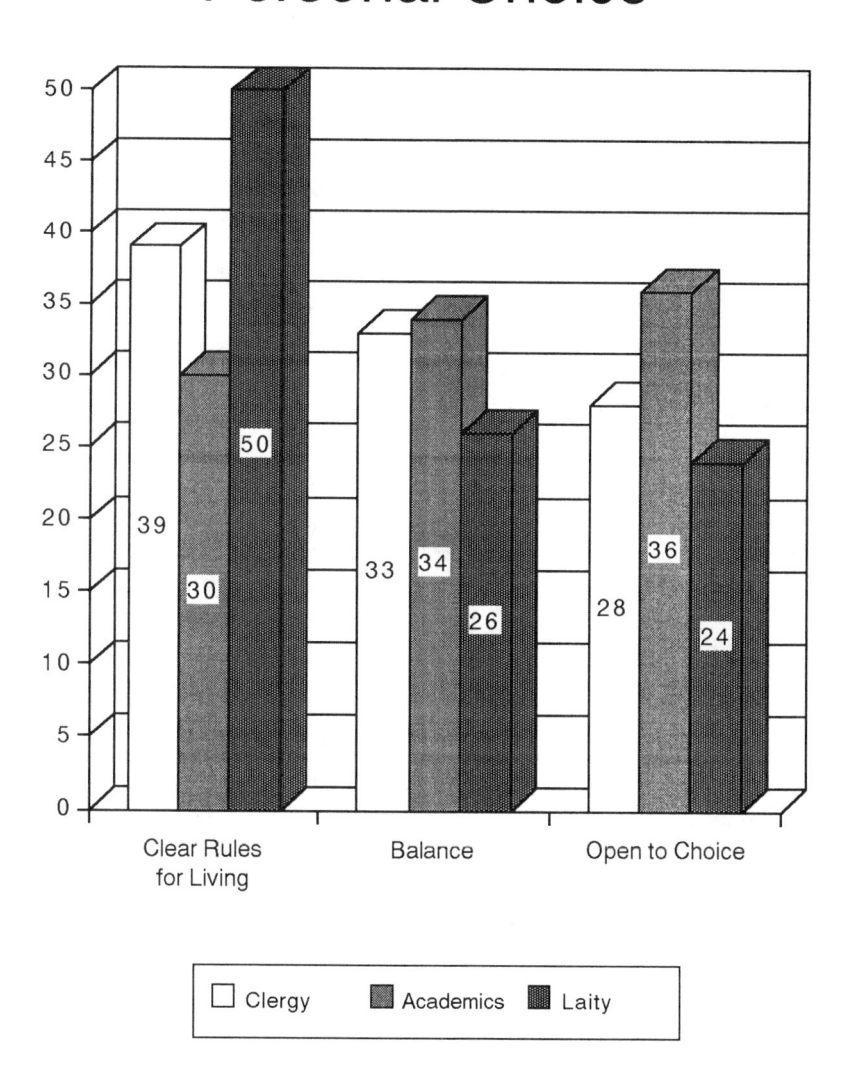

	Clear Rules for Living	Balance	Open to Choice
Clergy	39	33	28
Academics	30	34	36
Laity	50	26	24

Graph shows percentage of respondents who marked each choice as their preference in church emphasis.

Demand for orthodoxy is slightly higher among older Christians. Disagreement with the notion of diversity in belief and practice is highest among those aged 55 and older and those aged 35–54 compared to those aged 25–34 or those under 25 years of age.

On the issue of clear rules for behavior, the age differences are even more pronounced. More than half of those aged 55 and older think rules should be more important than personal choice. The percentage of respondents who felt this way dropped steadily with each age group, with less than one-third of those aged 25 and under preferring rules over personal choice.

The survey results support one further conclusion. Committed attenders are not about to give in to "consumerism." Orthodoxy is central and little room is made for "catering" to the uncommitted. While churches are willing to provide programs and activities designed to appeal to non-participants, they are not willing to compromise their biblical teaching in doing so.

The desire for orthodoxy on the part of Canadian Christians is a call for stability, certainty and conviction in a world where these are lacking. To be effective, churches must recognize that their committed members and the serious seekers who arrive at their door are not looking for a string of endless "ifs" and "maybes." The advice which Rev. Canon Herbert O'Driscoll gave in his 1991 convocation address at Wycliffe College expresses the sentiment of many Christians across Canada:

> We have lost the capacity to say "yes" as our first word in reply to the question "Do you believe...?" To questions of belief we have learned to reply tentatively and carefully. We employ such phrases as, "Well, it depends on what you mean by..." or "Are you asking me if..." or "Perhaps if I can reshape your question..." If this is at all true then I suggest that we very badly need to recapture a way of response that expresses what I will call the child of faith in us rather than the adult of ambiguity.
>
> Let me suggest a perfectly viable succession of questions and responses we might consider. Do you believe that Jesus Christ is the son of God? Yes, I do. Do you believe that Jesus Christ rose from the dead? Yes, I do. Do you believe that the blood of Jesus cleanses us from all sin? Yes, I do. Do you believe that the Bible is the word of God? Yes, I do.
>
> If we do indeed believe, then, without haranguing people or invading them, let us quietly communicate the fact that

our first word to God is not "maybe," not "perhaps," not "it depends on...," but a simple YES.[1]

Worship

Worship is situated at the intersection of orthodoxy and community. Among Christians, worship affirms both belief and community. The centrality of worship emerged as a critical concern both in the discussion sessions and in the open-ended comments provided by survey respondents. Yet there was considerable diversity in terms of style of worship. As a minister from an independent church in Manitoba wrote, "An effective church is a worshiping community with a strong sense of the holiness and transcendence of God—regardless of the form of worship."

Who should lead the worship? Lay members, especially those over 55 years of age, were more likely to prefer a worship service led by professional clergy than worship services which require extensive lay involvement. Those who attended mainline churches were more likely to want clergy-led worship than were those who attended conservative churches. The view that worship services should be conducted by professional clergy was expressed by few of the clergy themselves, and even less by Christian academics. *(See Fig. 2.2)*

The survey findings reveal some tension between the professionals who would like to see more lay involvement, and the lay people who feel that worship services should be led by the professionals. These differing attitudes toward worship reveal that a remnant of the clergy-laity separation still remains in people's perceptions. From our discussion sessions with lay people, these differing attitudes are stronger than mere "preferences in style of worship." They reflect belief structures concerning the notion that clergy have a special relationship with God. While they are unlikely to view the clergy as a mediator, there is a sense in which many lay people view the clergy as "bringing the congregation before God."

One of our discussion groups in Alberta had a particularly lively exchange about the nature of the relationship between themselves as congregation members and their pastor. Some of the parishioners felt "perfectly comfortable" addressing the pastor on a first name basis. Others in the same group felt that it would be "disrespectful" to address the pastor in any other way than with the formal title of Reverend. The issue was rather easily settled by the discussion group members as a matter of "preference," even though it really reflected a diversity in belief. For some, the priestly function of the clergy creates more sacredness and separation than it does for others.

Fig. 2.2

Who Should Lead Worship

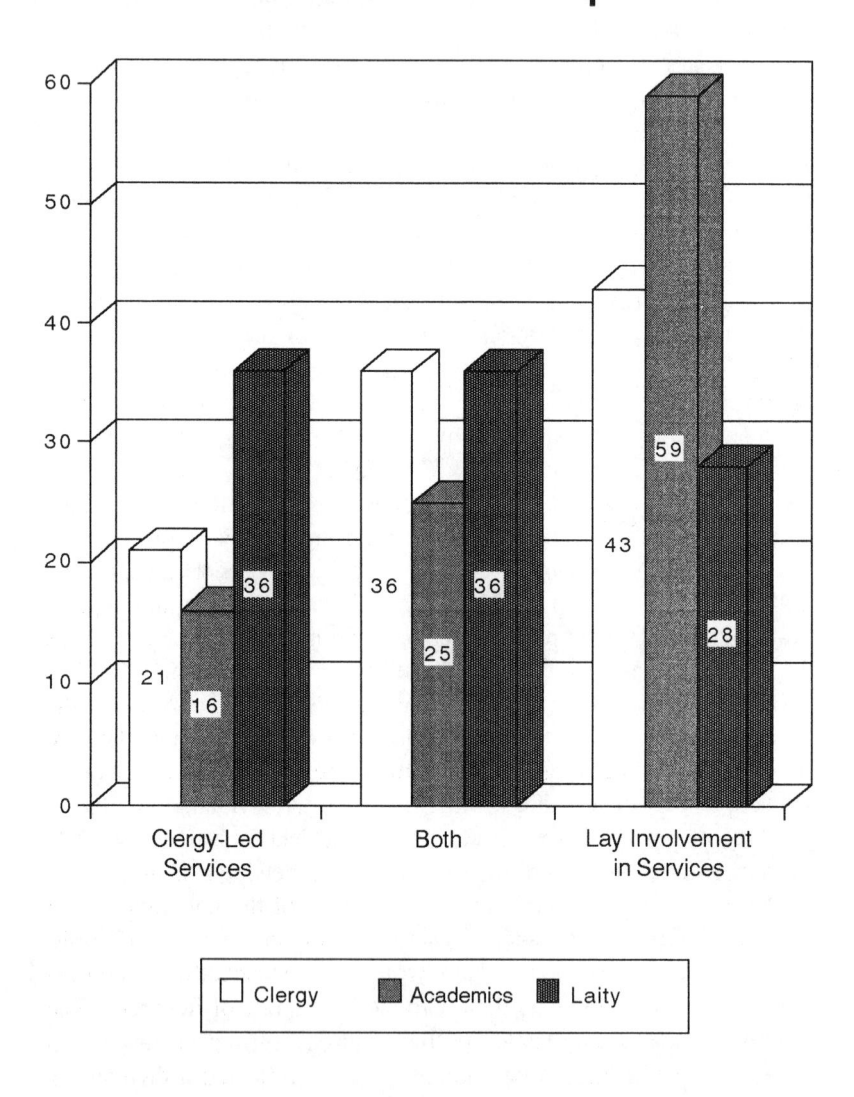

Category	Clergy	Academics	Laity
Clergy-Led Services	21	16	36
Both	36	25	36
Lay Involvement in Services	43	59	28

Graph shows percentage of respondents who marked each choice as their preference in worship leadership.

Room for preferences in worship

Survey respondents were asked to indicate whether they preferred traditional worship with hymns and liturgy, or contemporary worship involving choruses and experimental venues. Overall, 19% preferred traditional worship, while 40% preferred contemporary worship. A balance between the two was preferred by 41% of those surveyed.

Academics and lay members were more likely than clergy to express a preference for traditional worship. *(See Fig. 2.3)* A desire for traditional worship was also much more common among both those under 25 and those over 55, while it was less common among those in the middle age range.

Among those attending mainline churches, equal preferences were expressed for either traditional or contemporary worship styles. Conservative attenders and Pentecostals indicated a strong preference for contemporary worship over traditional worship styles. Pentecostals in the sample expressed a much stronger preference for contemporary worship than either mainline or conservative churches.

A similar questionnaire item asked people whether they preferred a church which was characterized by expressive worship or by quiet, contemplative worship, that is, worship that invites spirited participation compared to worship that is reflective and more ordered. Overall, 41% preferred expressive worship, 43% wanted a balance and 16% preferred quiet, contemplative worship. Young persons (under 25) were least likely to want expressive worship, while those aged 25–34 were much more likely to want a church where worship was expressive rather than contemplative.

Clergy in the sample were much more likely to prefer an expressive style of worship, while academics showed the opposite preference. Lay members were more likely to prefer expressive worship than contemplative worship. *(See Fig. 2.4)*

Expressive worship was more likely to be preferred among Pentecostals and conservatives than among mainline church attenders. Mainline church attenders were more likely to prefer a balanced approach to worship.

Whatever style of worship people prefer, most will undoubtedly agree with the amusing statement that, "Worship without creativity is like inviting a congregation to come and chew on Kleenex for an hour."[2]

Christians today want a style of worship that is both meaningful and recognizable. One of the benefits of the diversity of worship that tends to follow denominational lines is that it provides an opportunity

Fig. 2.3
Preferences in Style of Worship

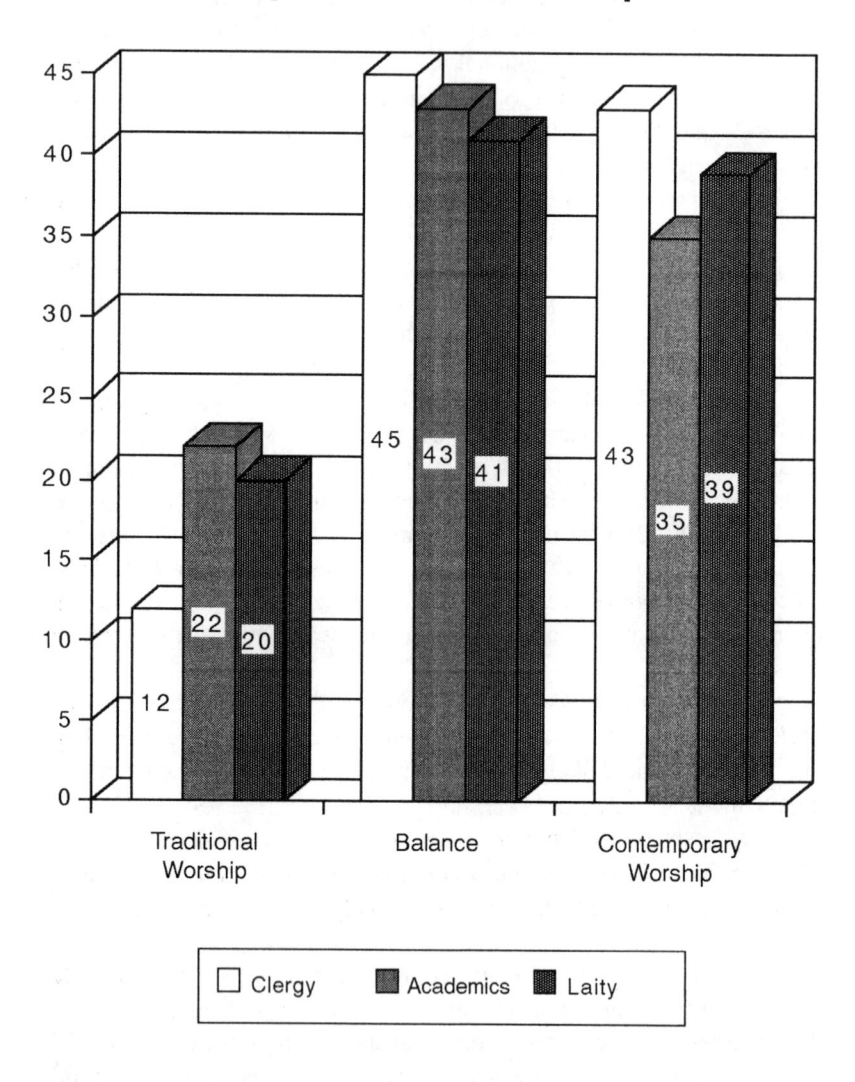

Style	Clergy	Academics	Laity
Traditional Worship	12	22	20
Balance	45	43	41
Contemporary Worship	43	35	39

Clergy ☐   Academics ▨   Laity ■

Graph shows percentage of respondents who marked each choice as their preference in worship style.

Fig. 2.4

Preferences in Style of Worship

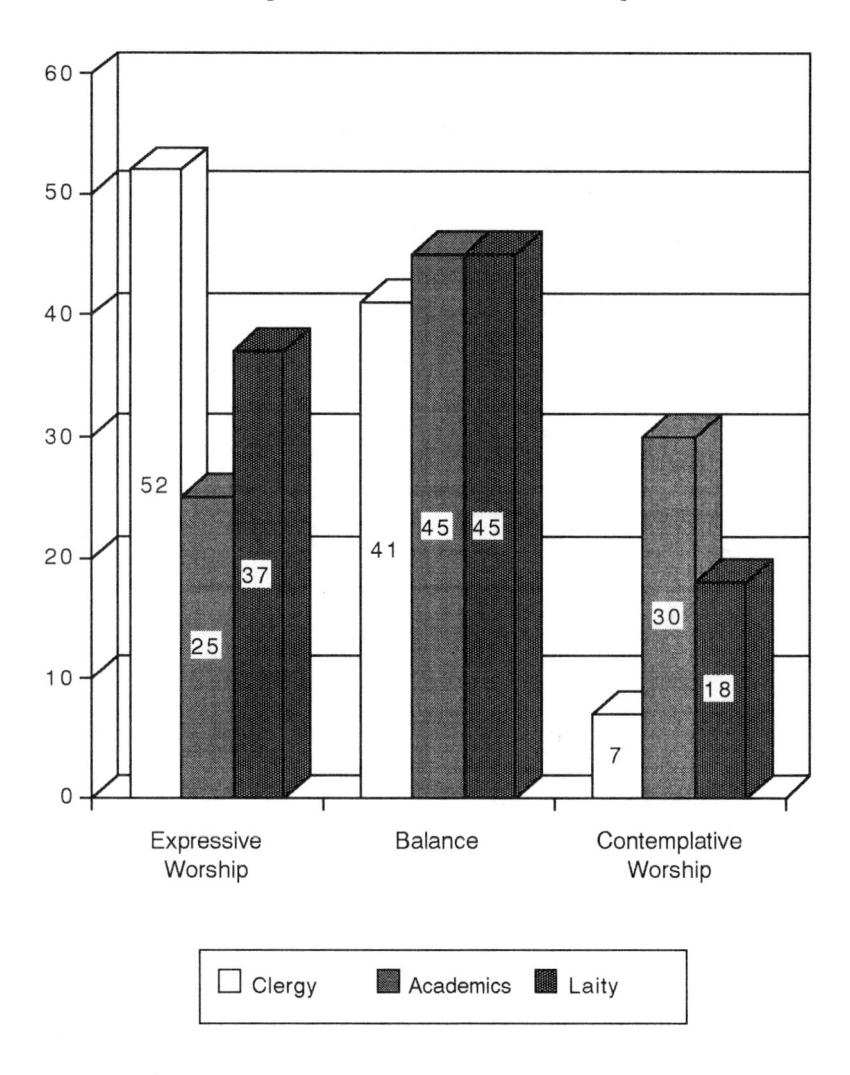

Style	Clergy	Academics	Laity
Expressive Worship	52	25	37
Balance	41	45	45
Contemplative Worship	7	30	18

Graph shows percentage of respondents who marked each choice as their preference in worship style.

for believers to find a style of worship which best fulfils their needs. A female respondent from a Presbyterian church in Ontario expressed concern over "radical young ministers instituting major changes in worship" such that it was "no longer recognizable as Presbyterian." She feared that a radical departure from the familiar style of worship would alienate many of the members, particularly seniors.

Selecting a church with a compatible style of worship is important because worship is one of those activities that is both individual and collective. It both engages and engulfs the self. As a collective activity, it reinforces the alignment between individual and community. Eugene Peterson views worship as collective activity which establishes a sense of common destiny. He writes:

> The act of worship rehearses in the present the end that lies ahead. Heaven is introduced into the present. It also, of course, conserves the past and so acts as a stabilizing force, but its dynamic function is anticipation; a community planning its future in the light of its charter.[3]

Community

In our discussion sessions with Christians across Canada, there was a strong sense that an effective church is a community of believers characterized by love, caring and warmth. Effectiveness, especially among lay participants, was closely tied to the availability of strong, personal ties within the group.

Clergy sometimes expressed frustration over members' inability to feel safe enough to express their personal needs. A similar sentiment was echoed among laity toward the clergy. Lay people want their pastors to "recognize that neither pastors nor lay people are perfect" and to "relate to people as they are." An effective church will address and meet people's personal needs. Lay members also expressed a critical need for a sense of belonging. This is especially important for retention. People may initially be drawn to a church because of the preaching or because of denominational affiliation, but they will continue to attend because of meaningful relationships with other believers.

For newcomers, a sense of community is like a wide open door into the church. Much of the literature on church growth, as well as the sociological literature on religious trends, notes that newcomers often attend because of close ties with family and friends.[4] The same is true of cult conversion. Relationships are the most common bridge to a new belief system. Sociologist Peter Berger notes that "to have a conversion is nothing much... The real challenge is to maintain a sense of its plausibility."[5] That, Berger says, is where the religious community comes in. The community provides the indispensable framework within which conversion makes sense.

The survey of church attenders isolated five aspects of community which were felt to be critical elements of effective churches:
- opportunity for involvement
- a sense of belonging
- emphasis on the family
- building self-worth
- meeting emotional needs

(See Fig. 2.5)

Opportunity for involvement

Most of the church attenders surveyed agreed with the statement that "to be effective, churches must provide an opportunity for members of the church to become involved in programs and activities." Participation is important in that it engages the member in the functioning of the church and creates a sense of responsibility, accountability and ownership. A female clergy from the Mennonite Brethren Church noted the need to "develop a sense of belonging by getting involved in programs and the lives of people, and to become participants as opposed to spectators."

At the same time, a caring community must be careful not to exploit its members. The survey results showed that over one-half of church attenders felt that switching to another church would be justified if their current church were to demand too much of their time, leaving them without enough time to spend with their families. Kennon Callahan, in his book on church effectiveness in the U.S., warns that "most people come to a local church looking for community... Instead we put them on a committee."[6] Participation is critical, but it must also be equitable. A woman from a Nazarene congregation in British Columbia makes this point:

> It is important that all church members share the work load. It is as dangerous to be over-involved as it is to be under-involved. The more a congregation takes ownership of the ministries of the church, the more effective they will be.

Fig. 2.5

Community Dimensions

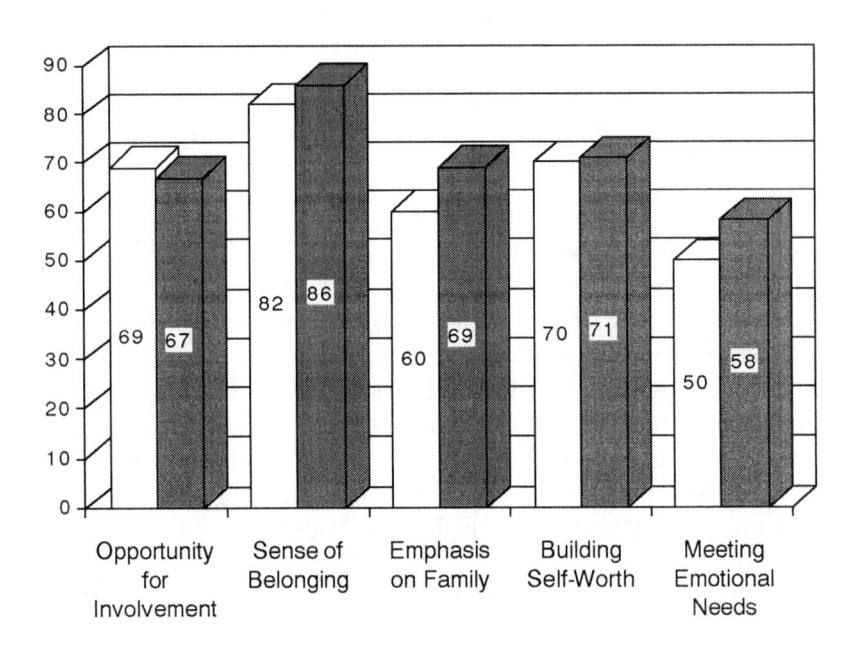

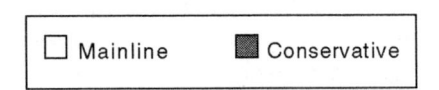

Dimension	Mainline	Conservative
Opportunity for Involvement	69	67
Sense of Belonging	82	86
Emphasis on Family	60	69
Building Self-Worth	70	71
Meeting Emotional Needs	50	58

☐ Mainline ■ Conservative

Graph shows percentage of lay members who ranked each community dimension as "very important."

A sense of belonging

When asked to rate the importance of various elements of church life, almost all of the Christians surveyed rated belonging as "very important." Findings were consistent across denominations. Academics were slightly less inclined to rate belonging as "very important" in comparison to lay members and clergy. A male Pentecostal pastor from Alberta commented on the need to foster a sense of belonging from the very beginning, as newcomers visit the church:

> Each individual needs to feel welcome from the first exposure to a church body. Each individual needs to be able to develop a network which includes others of like needs and which will allow them to grow spiritually with a view to developing ministry potential.

The ability to establish and sustain positive relationships with believers has important implications for retention. Regardless of the methods used to bring people into the church, they won't likely come back if they walk out without a friend. Church growth specialist Win Arn reported on a study which used a matched sample of 50 active members and 50 persons who had left the church. The study discovered that the number of friendships developed in the first six months is critical in maintaining and strengthening a relationship between the visitor and their new congregation.

Of the active members surveyed in Arn's study, all could name three or more friends made during the first six months. Thirteen new members could identify seven or more friends, and 12 could identify nine or more friends.

But of the 50 persons who had left the church, eight had established no such relationships, 14 could name only one friend, and eight could name three friends. Only one drop-out could name six friends.[7]

Emphasis on the family

Two-thirds of active church members stated that it was "very important" to them personally to attend "a church which places a strong emphasis on teaching about the value of the family." Lay members were more likely to view family as "very important" than were clergy, while academics were least likely to place a strong emphasis on family. Family values were slightly more important among conservative church attenders than among those active in mainline churches. Family values were also more likely to be viewed as very important among those aged 55 and older in comparison to those under 55 years of age.

The family, like the church, has experienced disruption and upheaval in the course of rapid social and cultural change. Its stability as an institution has suffered in the wake of changing moral values. In a sense, the emphasis on the family is as much a cry for stability as it is for community.

Although the definition of what constitutes a family continues to diversify, the family unit remains the basic building block for Canadian society. Neither the fracturing of the family, nor the emergence of new family forms is lessening the importance of the family in the eyes of Canadians. Like so many phenomena in these times, ideas about the family are changing, but the aspirations and ideals that revolve around the family remain entrenched.

Where the data send a clear message, however, is that families who go to church count on the church to meet the spiritual needs of the entire family. The Christian education of children is a concern for young families. The removal of religion from the curriculum of most public schools means that unless children attend a Christian school, the church is the only institutional source for teaching and coherently communicating the basics of the faith. It may not be in the Sunday school hour format of the past, but effective churches in the future will continue to contribute to the formation of young Christian minds.

The other specific area of concern for families relates to youth ministry. In the past, youth groups were an inherent part of almost every denominational structure. Today, one of the characteristics of healthy and vital churches is a strong commitment to an active youth ministry.

Churches that conclude that it is inevitable that young people will leave the church during their "traumatic" teenage years are abandoning their commitment to young people at a crucial time in their lives. Denominations that simply assume that after young people get married and start having their own children they will return to church should start planning for their own demise. Certainly, a few parents will be motivated to return to the church of their childhood for the spiritual benefit of their own children, but it will only be a few. The more fruitful approach for both the individuals who receive the spiritual nurture and for the long-term interests of the institution is a sustained ministry relationship from the cradle to the grave.

Academics and members of the clergy would do well to evaluate where they position the importance of the family in the life of the church and note the priority that laity give to ministry to the family. A miscalculation that leads to an absence of programming and emphases on the family will prompt parents to start looking elsewhere for a good church. Ministry to the family has become a key priority for many churches. The Evangelical Fellowship of Canada has set up a special task force on the family to assist churches in identifying areas of need within their own congregations and communities. Divorce, family disruption and teenage pregnancy, at one time an anomaly among Christian families, have become increasingly prevalent. The church has had to come to grips with parents and children struggling with the pain of divorce or the reality of emotionally empty marriages. While we preach an ideal for the Christian family, we must be careful not to add stigma and rejection to those for whom the ideal has turned into disappointment and failure.

Family ministry has also become critical to those who have been hurt by abusive relationships and who have turned to churches for counsel and support. For many, the family is no longer a haven of safety and protection. Violence, sexual abuse and abandonment have left deep emotional scars. When victims of dysfunctional families turn to the church for healing, adequate ministry must involve more than simply reciting the biblical prescription for forgiveness and salvation. For victims of violence and incest, the traditional language of a "loving Father" speaks of an entirely foreign concept.

The early church recognized the need for compassion in its treatment of widows (1 Timothy 5). In today's churches, the same compassion must be extended to a wider group. Divorce has become a road to poverty for many single parents, particularly women. Effective churches offer a model of healthy family relationships, and at the same time recognize the need for integration, support and healing among those who are hurting because of failed family relationships.

Building self-worth

A primary building block in creating a sense of self-worth is acceptance. Self-worth needs a safe place to grow. This sentiment was expressed by one of the academics who responded to the survey: "Effective churches allow people to express their struggles and inner thoughts without rejection or condemnation."

One crucial source of acceptance that can contribute to a positive self-image is involvement in a supportive community. This is a basic premise of Symbolic Interactionism in sociological research. The self is a "social object" which is continually defined and re-defined on the basis of the reflected appraisals of others.[8] How we look at others has an impact upon how they come to look at themselves. Thus, community plays a critical role in validating our self-image. In community, we find acceptance; in acceptance, we find identity. A female lay leader from an Evangelical Free Church in Ontario writes:

> Church effectiveness will begin when we stop looking at people through our judgmental attitudes and begin to accept them for who they are, faults and all. We're too quick to shoot our own wounded.

Attending a church which "creates a sense of self-worth among members" is viewed as personally "very important" to two-thirds of active church members surveyed. The survey data show that self-worth is more important to females than males and more important among older Christians than younger Christians. There is no difference between mainline and conservative Christians in terms of the high importance they attach to self-worth.

The role of the church in creating a sense of self-worth among its members is much more important to lay members and clergy than it is to academics. However, like their clergy and lay counterparts, the majority of Christian academics continue to feel that the church must address issues of self-worth.

I remember listening to a radio interview with Dr. James Dobson one morning while driving to the office. The interviewer asked Dr. Dobson to name "the most important thing a parent could give a child." He answered immediately: "Self-esteem." His words challenged me profoundly and affected my approach to my own teenage children. Perhaps one of the greatest equipping gifts a church can give its members is self-esteem. It is a prerequisite to ministering effectively to others.

Meeting emotional needs

Participating in a church "geared to meeting the emotional needs of people who attend" is viewed as "very important" among more than half the Christians surveyed. The ability of a church to respond to emotional needs is more likely to be viewed as personally "very important" among those under 25 and those over 55 than among middle-aged respondents. Females in the sample are also much more likely than males to rate this as "very important."

Responding to emotional needs was also more likely to be "very important" to conservatives than to mainline Christians. Christian academics were less likely to view emotional needs as an important personal priority than were either clergy or lay members.

In his book *Cages of Pain*, Gordon Aeschliman[9] notes that religion itself often creates emotional pain instead of offering healing and reintegration. Perhaps we "shoot our wounded" out of a sense of helplessness. A female Anglican lay leader in Quebec suggests that "a focus on 'causes' sometimes discourages those who are wounded." She continues: "Healing ministry is integral to meet people 'where they are' and support them through the necessary process toward a relationship with our Lord, and complete spiritual healing."

Although Dietrich Bonhoeffer's language may be dated, the ideas he presents in his book *Life Together*[10] remain as important as ever:

The Christian lives wholly by the truth of God's Word in Jesus Christ. If somebody asks him, Where is your salvation, your righteousness: he can never point to himself. He points to the Word of God in Jesus Christ, which assures him salvation and righteousness... But God has put this Word into the mouth of men in order that it may be communicated to other men... Therefore, the Christian needs another Christian who speaks God's Word to him. He needs him again and again when he becomes uncertain and discouraged... And that...clarifies the goal of all Christian community; they meet one another as bringers of the message of salvation. As such, God permits them to meet together and gives them community.

Relevance

Among respondents, the need for relevance was expressed both in terms of biblical preaching and teaching that equips believers to express their faith in the workplace, and in terms of providing Christians with the tools to respond compassionately to the needs they see around them. There is a strong recognition that laity are more "in touch" with the unchurched and the affiliated non-attenders than are clergy. The clergy work with and minister to Christians who, in turn, work with and minister to those outside of the church. In the discussion sessions, lay members felt that an effective church is one which provides its members with relevant tools to "bring the gospel home." Whether ministers like it or not, there is a prevailing perception among many laity that members of the clergy are so far removed from the realities of the world that they are not really able to equip their parishioners to live relevantly in today's world.

George Barna, an American public opinion researcher specializing in church trends, points out that, "It will be increasingly difficult to convince the unchurched that our faith is pertinent to the 21st century if the tools of our trade are from the last century."[11]

Still, there is an expectation upon clergy to teach their congregation how to care about and express compassion toward others, especially those outside the community of believers. Lay members also expressed the need for some experimentation with different venues and with methods for communicating the gospel message to people who would not ordinarily attend church. The church needs to "relate to people where they are," rather than "pigeon-hole" them or expect them to respond to our pre-defined way of doing things. A female lay leader from a Mennonite Brethren church in Alberta described the need for the church to be "contemporary enough, without compromising itself in order to create an exciting option to the community around it."

The demand for a church to be "in touch with the times" is measured in the national survey through three different attitude items. These included:
1. Openness about tough issues
2. Providing practical guidance for faith expression
3. Understanding today's culture.
(See Fig. 2.6)

Openness about tough issues

One-quarter of the Christians surveyed agreed strongly while an additional one-half expressed moderate agreement with the statement, "Effective churches are more likely than other churches to be open about addressing social problems such as domestic violence, child abuse, racism and alcoholism from the pulpit." There were no differences between mainline and conservative church members in terms of overall agreement levels. Christian academics were more likely to view effective churches as tackling tough issues than were lay members or clergy.

Providing practical guidance for faith expression

When asked whether "a church is not worth attending unless it provides practical guidance for expressing one's faith in the world during the week," 84% of active Christians agreed, either strongly or

Fig. 2.6

Relevance Dimensions

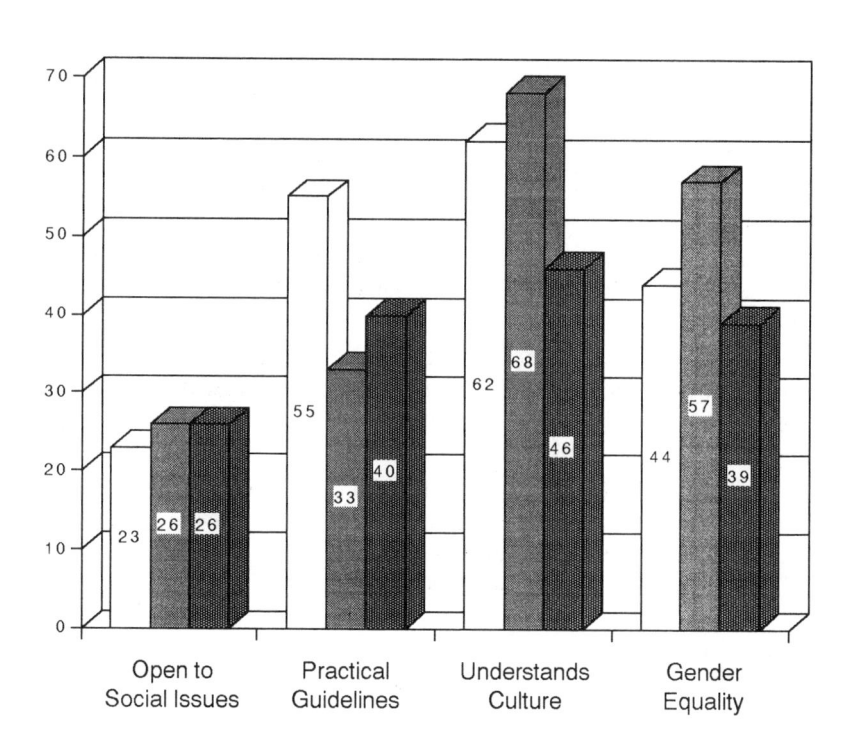

	Open to Social Issues	Practical Guidelines	Understands Culture	Gender Equality
Clergy	23	55	62	44
Academics	26	33	68	57
Laity	26	40	46	39

□ Clergy   ▨ Academics   ■ Laity

Graph shows percentage of respondents who ranked each relevance dimension as "very important."

moderately. Clergy were more likely to agree than were either lay members or Christian academics. Differences between mainline and conservative Christians were minimal. Interestingly, young people (under 25) were less likely to agree with this statement than were those aged 25–34, 35–54 or 55 and older.

Understanding today's culture

When asked how important it was to attend a church which "demonstrates a solid understanding of today's culture," 40% of survey respondents described it as "somewhat important" and 53% as "very important." The view that cultural understanding is "very important" was much more common among Christian academics and clergy than among lay members. Conservative church members were more likely to view an understanding of today's culture as "very important" than were those who attended mainline churches.

Those aged 25 or younger were, again, less likely to view cultural understanding as "very important," compared to those aged 25–34 or 35 and older.

Earlier we noted that most Christians, including clergy, believe that it is possible for churches to relate to the outside world without compromising their traditional biblical teachings. Yet, as John R.W. Stott explains,

> It is comparatively easy to be faithful if we do not care about being contemporary, and easy also to be contemporary if we do not bother to be faithful. It is the search for a combination of truth and relevance which is exacting.[12]

Outreach

Underscoring the importance of the fourth cornerstone for effective churches, a Presbyterian minister articulates a commitment to outreach: "Churches today must build bridges to the unchurched community." The parameters for outreach extend to the spiritual, social and justice needs of the community outside the church. The span of the vision is both local and global.

One of the key conclusions concerning outreach involves the need to balance external outreach with internal needs. Essentially, survey respondents view outreach as a consequence of participating in a faith community where one's needs are met, one's wounds are healed, and one's spiritual energy is revived in the common experience of worship. As one lay member in British Columbia commented: "The full needs of the Body must be accepted with attempts made to address them, and only then can the full needs of the surrounding community be embraced."

Balancing outreach with internal needs

A Christian Reformed minister, responding to the survey, wrote that "Effective churches balance outreach with nurturing opportunities." The majority of Christians surveyed feel that the church must provide a balance between ministry that focuses on the needs of congregation members and ministry that focuses on the needs of the community outside the church building. Lay members and clergy are relatively consistent in terms of supporting the internal/external balance. Two-thirds of academics think both emphases are important. *(See Fig. 2.7)*

While it is recognized that the church should be a "tight" community, the need for openness to those in need is equally important. Effective churches, according to lay members in the survey and discussion groups, strike a balance between a strong commitment to community and a commitment to embrace those outside the existing congregation. A lay leader from a Baptist church in Nova Scotia described effective churches as "encouraging members to love each other, even those outside its walls, thereby building a stronger society."

Diversity over targeting

In terms of outreach, Canadians are more likely to prefer diversity over targeting a particular age or ethnic group. Churches are expected to make the Bible relevant to diversified audiences. Effective churches are clear about their mission. They know who they are trying to reach and are ready to use a variety of forms of communication to have as wide an appeal as possible. As an Anglican lay leader from Quebec stated in his survey response, "we become an effective church when a common love of Jesus enables us to overcome the natural inclination to avoid people who do not think as we do."

Overall, 62% of Christians disagreed with the statement that "effective churches are more likely to focus on a particular ministry or target group, rather than on reaching a broad spectrum of people." Canadian Christians are also much more likely to want a church with a multi-ethnic mix than one that is ethnically homogeneous. *(See Fig. 2.8)*

Where's a Good Church?

Fig. 2.7

Balance of Internal Needs and Outreach

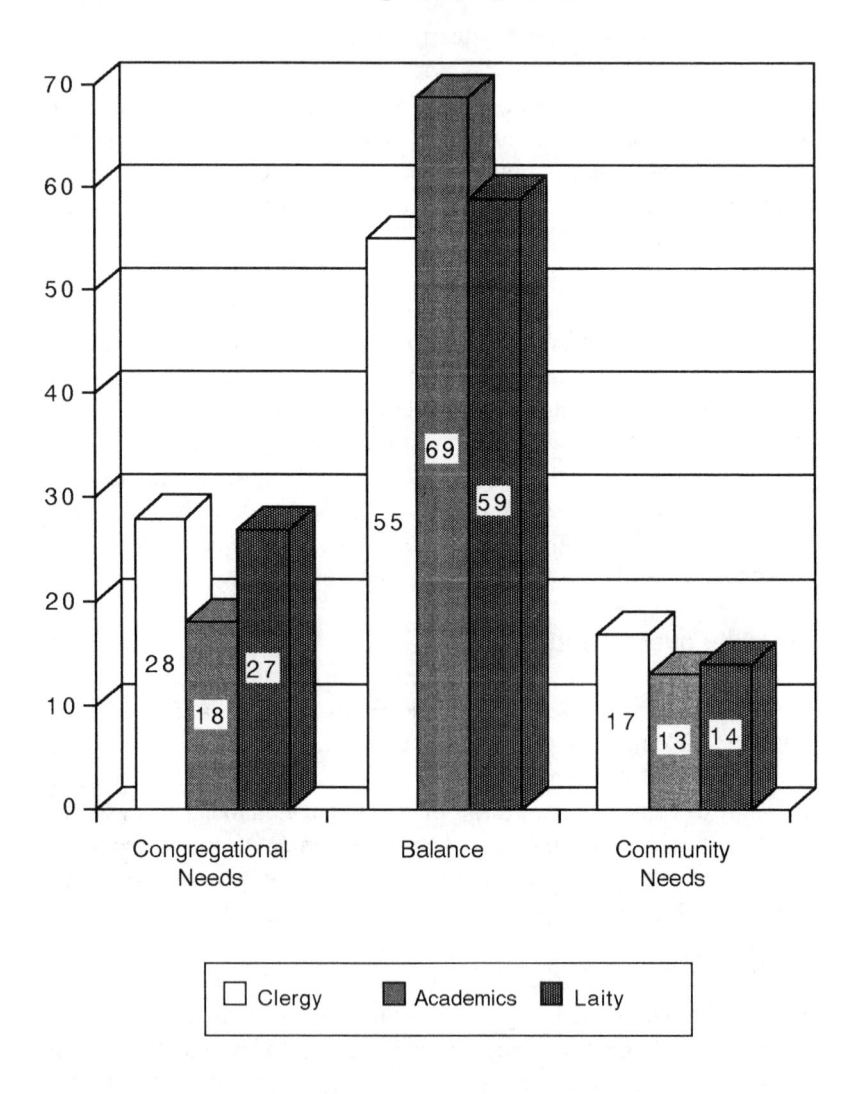

	Clergy	Academics	Laity
Congregational Needs	28	18	27
Balance	55	69	59
Community Needs	17	13	14

☐ Clergy ■ Academics ■ Laity

Graph shows percentage of respondents who marked each choice as their preference in church emphasis.

42

Fig. 2.8

Multi-Ethnic Mix

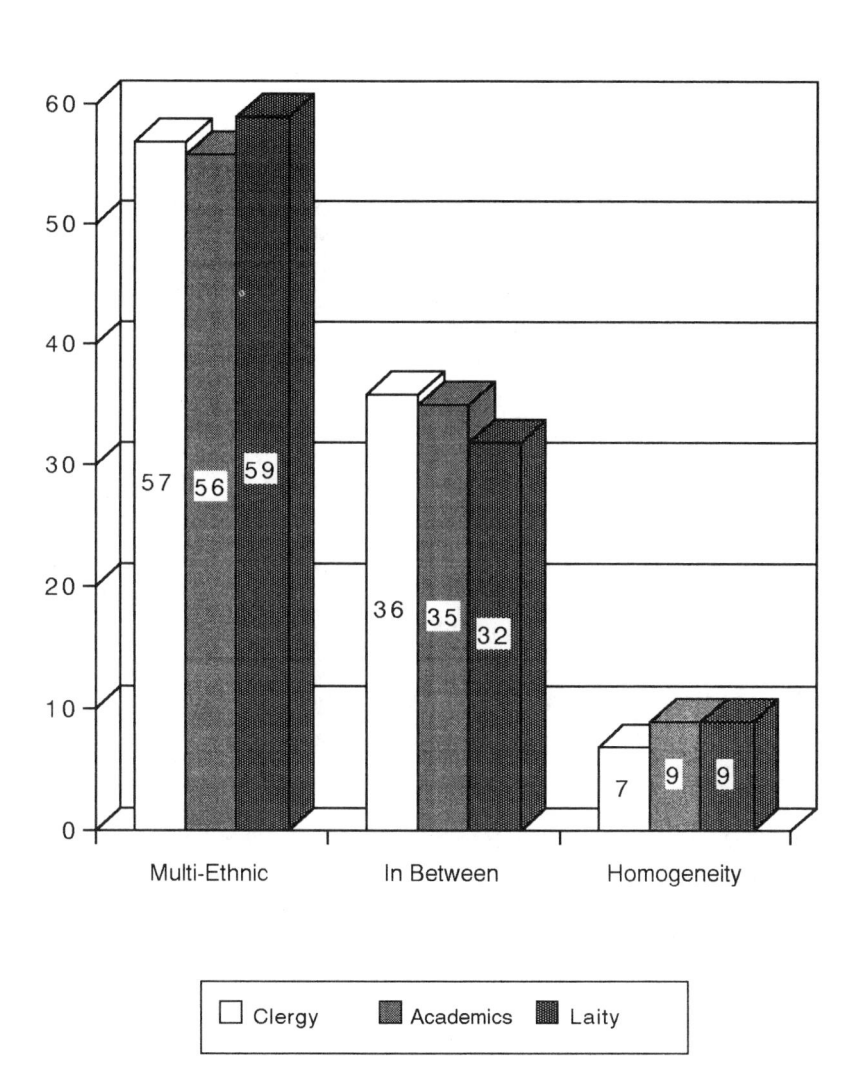

	Multi-Ethnic	In Between	Homogeneity
Clergy	57	36	7
Academics	56	35	9
Laity	59	32	9

Graph shows percentage of respondents who marked each choice as their preference in church emphasis.

Numerical growth as a consequence of other priorities

In the discussion groups, it was felt that while an effective church will be successful at both recruiting and retaining members, numerical growth should be a consequence, rather than a goal. Spiritual growth should be the paramount consideration. The national survey results show that Christians are not likely to view the emphasis on quantitative growth to be an effective strategy.

Attending a church which places a strong emphasis on numerical growth was considered not important among 55% of the respondents. Lay members were more likely to express this view than were academics, while clergy were least likely to view numerical emphasis as unimportant. *(See Fig. 2.9)* An emphasis on numerical growth was considered unimportant among 59% of mainline respondents and 53% of those attending conservative churches.

Similarly, 60% of mainline Christians and 54% of conservatives felt that leadership styles which place a strong emphasis on numerical growth are ineffective. Lay members were much more likely than academics or clergy to view the emphasis on numerical growth as an ineffective approach to leadership. Overall, only 4% said an emphasis on numerical growth would be "very effective."

In a series of items designed to prioritize various factors which Christians take into consideration when selecting a church to attend, the size of the congregation was the least mentioned priority.

Evangelism within the local community

For many church attenders, just hearing the word "evangelism" triggers negative emotions. Whether people attend mainline or conservative churches, they react to the term "evangelism" with as much enthusiasm as they would to the sound of a police siren behind them on the highway.

Numerous denominations have regular evangelistic emphases and call their people to involvement in projects like the "decade of evangelism." However, even though the language may be the same across denominational lines, the meaning is often different. For some, evangelism connotes verbal witness. For many, it means community service and the expression of Christian compassion. In the minds of others, evangelism is simply the natural expression of an integrated lifestyle of Christian words and deeds.

Whatever the meaning, the lower emphasis on numerical growth does not mean that Christians do not want their churches to grow, or that

Fig. 2.9

Perceptions on Numerical Growth

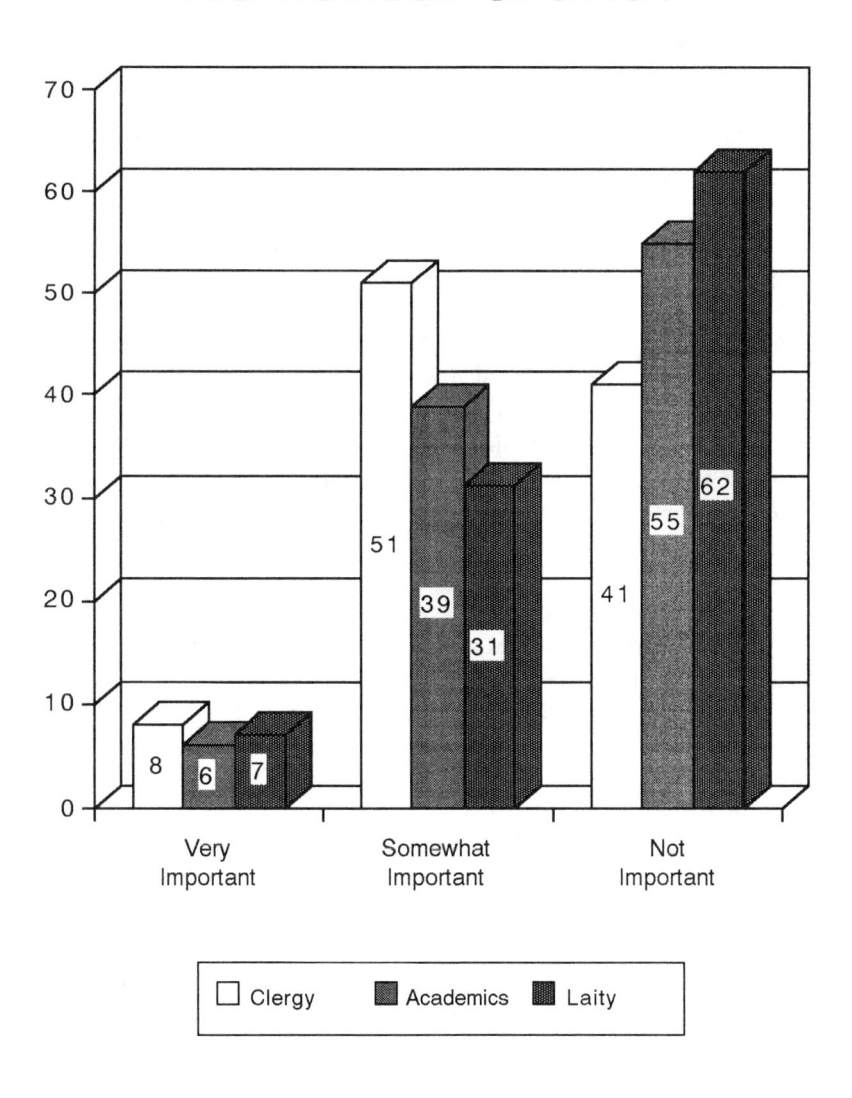

	Very Important	Somewhat Important	Not Important
Clergy	8	51	41
Academics	6	39	55
Laity	7	31	62

Graph shows percentage of respondents who marked each choice as their preference in church emphasis.

outreach is unimportant. Rather, they are saying that an emphasis on church growth (i.e. numerical growth) is not an effective strategy for growth.

At the same time, Christians place a strong emphasis on evangelism within the local community. Overall, 70% of Christians surveyed rated a "strong commitment to local evangelism" as a high priority in selecting a church to attend. This percentage was much higher among clergy than among lay members and academics. Nonetheless, the percentages express a concern for local evangelism on the part of all three.

The results suggest that Canadian Christians do not necessarily equate church growth strategies with evangelism. A female lay member from a Baptist church in Alberta noted that "a church may be highly effective in reaching its community outside the church walls, and these numbers may not appear in numerical growth statistics."

Commitment to world missions

The survey results reveal that Canadian Christians are more enthused about local outreach than global missions. Only half of those surveyed viewed world missions as a high priority compared to the 70% who viewed local evangelism as a high priority. Academics were more likely to view world missions as a high priority than clergy or lay members.

Concerns about matters of justice

Christians perceive a response to questions of social justice as an inherent part of the gospel. Three-quarters of Christians, particularly academics, felt that effective churches will address social problems like domestic violence, child abuse and racism from the pulpit. Those from both mainline and conservative churches held the same views on these particular justice concerns.

Another justice realm concerns the matter of gender equality. When asked about the importance of attending a church which provides equal status and leadership opportunities to men and women, 43% rated this "very important" while an additional 40% rated it "somewhat important." Gender equality was more likely to be viewed as "very important" among academics than among clergy or lay members. *(See Fig. 2.6)* Mainline Christians were more likely to view gender equality as "very important" than were conservatives. Interestingly, there were no differences between male and female respondents on this issue.

Understanding the main players: Pulpit, Podium and Pew

In the preceding pages we examined the priorities and preferences of Christians from our national sample of clergy, Christian academics, and active lay people. The discussion of those priorities and preferences touched upon the perceptions and differences between the three main players in the Christian church. What follows is a brief profile of pulpit, podium and pew perspectives.

Clergy

Among clergy, an emphasis is placed on the importance of "equipping the saints for the work of the ministry." Effective churches are viewed as ones which provide a practical expression of faith for lay members to take into the workplace. Clergy show a greater preference for worship that is expressive and uses non-traditional venues. Outreach is seen in terms of responding to the needs of the local community. Clergy place a greater emphasis on numerical growth and on cell group ministry than do academics or lay members.

Academics

Academics are characterized by a greater degree of tolerance for diversity in belief and practice than is exhibited among clergy or lay members. Academics place a high value on personal choice over prescribed rules of behavior. They are less likely than clergy or lay members to emphasize the emotional or family needs of members, and are more likely than others to express a need for the church to demonstrate an understanding of the culture. Outreach is seen in terms of tackling tough social issues as well as emphasizing the role of the church in world missions.

Lay members

Among lay members, a strong emphasis is placed on the community dimensions of involvement, belonging, family and personal needs. They are less likely than clergy or academics to emphasize the need to understand the culture. Lay members are more likely than other players to want clear rules for how to live and behave. For lay members, outreach is seen in terms of having one's own spiritual needs met in a way that lets them respond to the unchurched.

Effectiveness: Creating a Balance

Applying the notion of consumerism to committed Christians raises a host of questions. Have the Christians of today changed the churches of the past into places for spiritual shoppers? Does the re-ordering of priorities that puts concern for self ahead of concern for others signal a spiritual decline? Or are today's followers of Jesus simply more honest and realistic? Is there really anything wrong with wanting your spiritual hungers fed or with switching churches so that the needs of your family will be met?

The four dominant themes—orthodoxy, relevancy, community, and outreach—each suggest a set of needs which must be balanced against one another. The focus on orthodoxy suggests a need for transcendence, predictability, and stability. Relevancy suggests a need for flexibility, understanding and innovation. Community suggests a need for fulfillment, comfort and identity. Outreach suggests a need for responsiveness, challenge and compassion.

We can glimpse a resolution to these complex questions when we realize that effective churches strive for a healthy balance in the meeting of these various needs: between serving the desires of those already involved in the church and responding to the needs of those beyond the touch of the church, for example.

Identifying committed Christians as consumers also raises questions about the nature of the Christian community. Where is the balance between the needs of the individual consumer and the need for a cohesive Christian community? Individualism suggests that personal needs override collective needs. We live in an increasingly fragmented society and yet the Christian life is built on a model of a shared life with fellow believers.

One of the key "needs" expressed by committed Christians in our survey involves the need for community and belonging. Thus, an important part of what the committed Christian consumer seeks involves characteristics which inherently limit the consumer model. In essence, part of the committed Christian's set of needs involves the sense of belonging to a faith community and the sense of unswerving commitment to biblical standards. Rather than shopping for fragments, these Christians want a meaningful, integrated experience of faith.

Why People Leave Their Churches

Chapter Three

Before Margaret switched churches, she had been a loyal member of the same small fellowship for 12 years. Although she was not an accomplished organist, she was the only one they had. Over the years, her service to the church shifted from being something she enjoyed to a demanding duty.

"I finally reached a point," she recalls, "where I realized that all I was getting from that church was ulcers."

In the discussion group that evening, she surprised us when we asked her if that was the point at which she switched to the church she now attends.

"No," she replied, "I stayed for seven more years."

Margaret's spiritual and physical health suffered for a long time until she eventually told her pastor she "needed a break." The "break" provided her with an opportunity to go to another church and get some badly needed spiritual nourishment. The church she changed to had a style of worship that connected with her tired spirit. She also discovered other single Christians within her new church community. Today, she looks back at her own religious history and wonders why she stayed so long in a church that abused her.

Margaret is hardly the glib church consumer, shopping around for a church that will meet her selfish needs. She is more like a victim of a bad marriage.

Research tells us that what is often thought of as church growth is actually based on inter-church movement, "church switching." Research by Canadian sociologist Reginald Bibby concludes that, particularly among conservative churches, church growth really reflects a significant level of what he labels "the circulation of the saints."

From one perspective, evidence of church switching adds fuel to the "Christian consumer" argument. However, our findings indicate that terms like church-hopping or church-shopping convey a much more trivial image than what actually takes place.

Our research probed the reasons for why people switch churches. The answers are varied, but among committed Christians the motive is similar. With great frequency, people come to a point in their lives when they realize that their needs are not being met. They are not being spiritually nourished. They are not growing in their faith. And they begin to ask, "Where's a good church?"

For this reason, we acknowledge that "switching churches" is often prompted by negative church experiences. But we also contend that "switching churches" is frequently motivated by positive spiritual aspirations.

Our studies also demonstrate that church switching is a common part of the Canadian religious landscape. The majority of Christians in our sample have switched denominations at one time or another in their Christian experience. And a significant number have gone through periods of disassociation from the church before coming back with a renewed commitment.

A society of switchers

Church participation is only one manifestation of a larger societal trend in which permanence no longer plays a major role. Until recent decades, marriages and careers were marked by life-long commitment.

Divorce and re-marriage are now common and do not carry the social stigma that was associated with failed marriages 20 years ago.

Nor is the career the stable life-long choice it once was. Sports stars become screen stars; screen stars become politicians. Baseball and football players opt for free agency and sign on with whichever team offers the most money. The newscasters who report the changes follow the pattern and change networks themselves.

But the propensity to pursue new directions belongs not only to celebrities. It is a rare experience to find someone who has worked for the same company for 40 years, or even 30 years. We also see more and more people making career changes. People in their 30s and 40s attend university, find new careers, and experiment with options and alternatives.

In many realms, life-long patterns and commitments have been replaced by the inevitability of change. More and more, church participation and denominational affiliation is subject to the same phenomenon. As is the case with many other shifts, the impetus for change is often based on the necessity of having personal needs and goals met. This development raises another important "needs" issue. A Presbyterian minister responding to our survey wrote that, "Effectiveness is not as important to the church as faithfulness." It is difficult for a church to be effective if participation is conditional and temporary. Which should take precedence: the needs of individual or the needs of the institution?

Theodore Levitt's insights in *Innovation in Marketing*[1] were not intended as ecclesiastical recommendations, but nonetheless bear some important parallels. He urges his business readers to concentrate on the needs of the people, rather than on the needs of the institution. Applied to the church, it translates into a marketing issue in which the focus must change from the needs of the seller to the needs of the buyer.

Patterns of switching

It has become more common for Christians to switch denominations at some point than to remain with the same denomination for life. In our sample of active church attenders, more than half the respondents had switched denominations at least once in their life. Percentages were almost identical for lay members, Christian academics, and clergy. The switching pattern is no different for mainline Christians than it is for conservative Christians. Pentecostals and members of non-denominational independent churches display a higher incidence of switching.

While people remain strong in their personal commitments, their institutional commitments are open to change and transition. In his book, *It's a Different World*, Lyle Schaller notes that,

> Back in the 1950s many people saw uniting with a church as a destination in a religious pilgrimage. It was for life, unless one moved too far away to continue that relationship. It was the end of the journey. Today, for many adults, uniting with a congregation is a way station on a religious pilgrimage.[2]

The tables accompanying this section provide a comparison of current church affiliation with the affiliation of the respondents' religious upbringing. An examination of religious upbringing shows that most Christians end up close to their roots.

In the book, *Why Conservative Churches are Growing*,[3] Dean Kelley contends that people are switching from mainline to conservative churches, and that much of the growth of conservative churches is a result of this movement from the mainline churches. In fact, as pointed out by Bibby and Brinkerhoff (1992)[4], when considering absolute numbers, the traffic moves almost equally in both directions.

The data show that among active church members, the trade-off between mainline and conservative churches is roughly equivalent. About 20% of the conservative church sample is made up of people who have switched over from mainline churches. Almost the same percentage of mainline church attenders (18%) have switched over from conservative churches. These figures are made up of active church attenders; they do not include the high percentage of people who continue to identify themselves with mainline churches, but who are inactive and therefore do not participate on a regular basis.

In terms of "identification," or "affiliation," conservative Protestants make up 7 or 8% of the Canadian population while mainstream churches attract up to 35%. (An additional 50% or so are Roman Catholic). National data, such as that reported by Bibby and Brinkerhoff (1992)[5] show that almost one-third of conservatives have their religious roots in mainline churches, while only 4% of the total attending mainline churches have switched over from conservative camps.

Bibby and Brinkerhoff subsequently reason that although the affiliation percentages are unequal (4 to 1, mainline compared to conservative), the actual number of people switching back and forth between the mainline and conservative churches is roughly the same. If anything, the conservatives may come out ahead by a slight margin.

The relatively equal trade-off between conservative and mainline churches has different implications for each tradition. The mainline "switchers" to conservative churches account for much of the growth in conservative churches. The conservative Christians switching over to mainline churches help to bolster the percentage of mainline participants who are actively involved in their churches.

Mainline church switching *(See Fig. 3.1)*

Among lay members attending mainline churches, the majority had been raised in a mainline church tradition. This includes the total sample of mainline lay persons who had stayed in the same denomination since birth, as well as those who had switched denominations within the mainline tradition. Among current mainline attenders, nearly one in five had switched over to the mainline tradition from conservative churches.

Mainline clergy were much more likely to have grown up in the mainline tradition than were lay members. Among mainline clergy, most

Fig. 3.1
Switching Among Mainline Church Attenders

	Currently Attending Mainline Churches		
	Lay Members	Clergy	Academics
Denomination of Upbringing (in %)			
Mainline	71	84	65
Conservative	18	11	25
Catholic	6	2	5
None	5	3	5
Percent who have switched denominations within mainline tradition	21	37	20
Percent who have switched from conservative churches	18	11	25
Percent who have experienced prolonged inactive church attendance	54	38	30

had been raised in the mainline tradition. This includes those who had remained in the same denomination, as well as those who had switched from other mainline churches. Only one in ten had switched from conservative churches. A small number had switched from the Roman Catholic Church or had been raised in unchurched homes.

Christian academics attending mainline churches were much more likely than clergy or lay members to include switchers from the conservative camp. Among Christian academics, two-thirds had been raised in mainline churches. This includes those who had stayed in the same denomination, as well as who had switched from other mainline denominations. A full one-quarter of mainline Christian academics had switched over from conservative churches.

Conservative church switching *(See Fig. 3.2)*

Among conservative church attenders, almost two-thirds had grown up in the conservative church tradition, including Pentecostal and evangelical non-denominational churches. This includes those who had stayed in the same denomination since birth as well as those who had switched

Fig. 3.2
Switching Among Conservative Church Attenders

	Currently Attending Conservative Churches		
	Lay Members	Clergy	Academics
Denomination of Upbringing (in %)			
Conservative	63	65	87
Mainline	20	18	6
Catholic	10	7	3
None	6	8	3
Percent who have switched denominations within conservative tradition	22	20	35
Percent who have switched from mainline churches	20	18	6
Percent who have experienced prolonged inactive church attendance	34	29	16

denominations within the conservative tradition. One in five had switched from mainline churches.

Among conservative clergy, two-thirds had grown up in the conservative church, including those who had stayed in their denomination of birth and those who had crossed denominational lines within the conservative tradition. Nearly one in five conservative clergy had been raised in mainline churches and a small number had been raised as Roman Catholic or grew up in unchurched homes.

Among conservative academics, most grew up in conservative churches. This includes those who had stayed in the same denomination as well as those who had switched denominations within the conservative tradition. Only 6% reported mainline roots. Church switching among academics is much more likely to follow a conservative to mainline direction (25%) than mainline to conservative (6%).

Again, these data do not reflect the percentages of non-active affiliates who identify with but who do not actively participate in the life of the church.

A second qualification in interpreting the data is that over one-half of the Roman Catholics who switched to Protestant mainline or conservative churches did so in Quebec. In our national sample of 761 Protestant Christians, 8% of them grew up with Catholic backgrounds. Of the 60 people who grew up in Catholic homes but who now attend Protestant churches, 34 came from Quebec.

Our sample shows that 4% of current mainline attenders and 9% of current conservative attenders have switched over from the Catholic Church. In Quebec, one-third of those attending Protestant churches grew up in a Catholic tradition. If we were to exclude Quebec from the sample, the national total of Roman Catholic switchers would be less than 4% across the entire sample. Since the data were collected from active attenders in Protestant churches, and not Catholic churches, we do not have comparative measures of how many Protestants may have switched over to the Roman Catholic Church.

When Leaving is Justified

In our survey of active Christians, we asked them to indicate whether they felt certain reasons were justified or not justified for switching to another church. Granted, the nine pre-selected reasons included in the survey questionnaire could not cover all of the things that motivated people to switch churches. But they do represent general categories which were drawn from our focus-group sessions. *(See Fig. 3.3)*

Personal needs

The most common reason given for switching to another church is that the current church fails to meet personal or family needs. Overall, 86% felt that switching churches was either sometimes justified or almost always justified if the church one attends is not meeting one's personal or family needs. There was no difference between mainline and conservative churches on this question.

More than one-third of lay members view this as "almost always" justifying a search for a new church, while clergy and academics were less likely to agree.

One of the key conclusions of our research into effective churches is that Christians bring to church a set of spiritual and social needs which must be met. If those needs are not being met, they will find themselves asking "Where's a good church?"

For a high percentage of lay members in Canada's churches, the

Where's a Good Church?

Fig. 3.3
Perceptions of When Church Switching is Justified

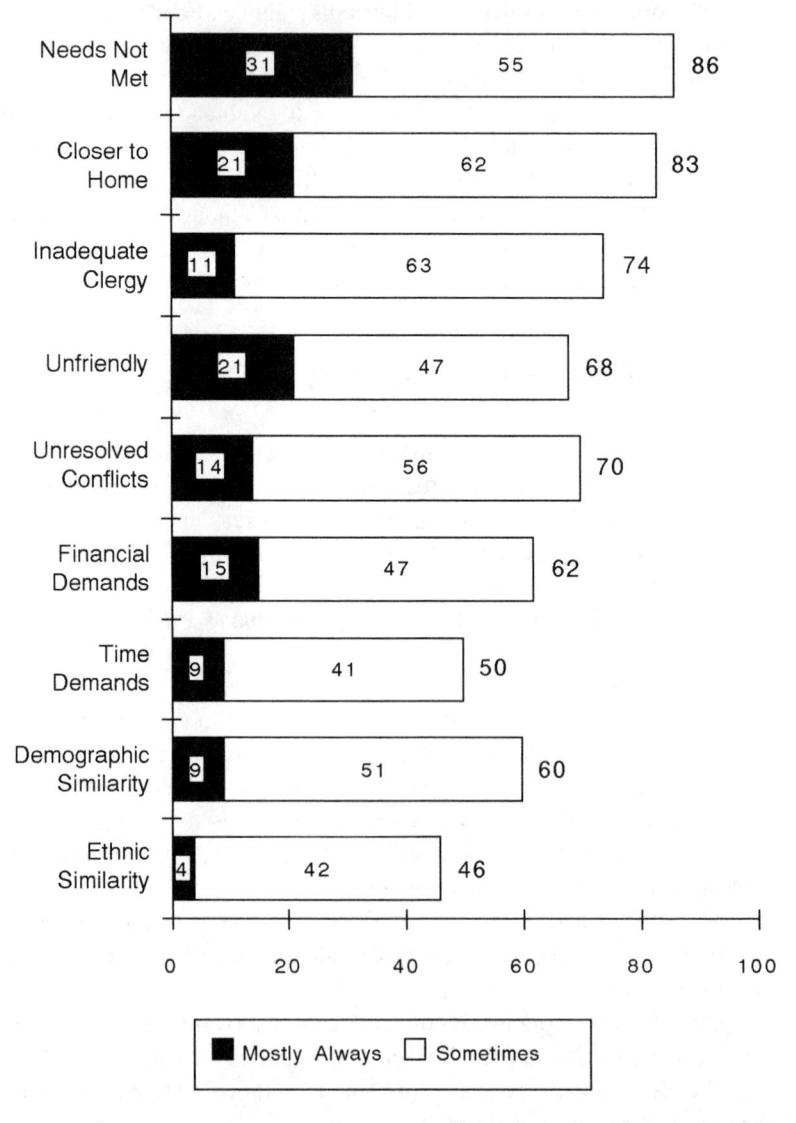

Reason	Mostly Always	Sometimes	Total
Needs Not Met	31	55	86
Closer to Home	21	62	83
Inadequate Clergy	11	63	74
Unfriendly	21	47	68
Unresolved Conflicts	14	56	70
Financial Demands	15	47	62
Time Demands	9	41	50
Demographic Similarity	9	51	60
Ethnic Similarity	4	42	46

■ Mostly Always   ☐ Sometimes

Graph shows percentage of respondents who viewed each reason for switching churches as "Mostly Always Justified" or "Sometimes Justified."

power of the family is unequalled. Because parents value their children so highly, they are often ready to sublimate their own preferences if the spiritual well-being of their children is at stake. To further exacerbate the situation, for many parents, today's world is a scary place in which to bring up children. The scenario becomes predictable. Especially for families with teenagers, when local churches do not provide healthy environments and they think their children will benefit, parents are prepared to change churches. It happens repeatedly. Parents have no real desire to leave their church, but because their adolescent children get connected to friends going to another church and the situation looks promising, the whole family makes the switch.

Though the decision-making dynamics aren't always explicitly understood, the power of the family is stronger than the leverage of the church.

Proximity to home

Of the survey sample, 83% felt that switching to a church closer to where you live is either sometimes or almost always justified, making it the second most common reason given. This view was more commonly held among conservative attenders than among mainline attenders.

The survey respondents' justification for finding a conveniently located church must be understood in the context of an increasingly mobile society. Particularly in urban areas where people often have to fight traffic all week long, they want a Sabbath break from spending unnecessary time in their cars. The high priority given to family involvement also means that close proximity allows children and youth to participate more often than just on Sunday. In defense of those charged with being "convenience Christians," it should be noted that closeness to home did not emerge as a high priority when we asked people what they would consider important if they were going to switch churches. Only 20% rated this as a high priority, when compared to issues such as involvement, relevance and outreach.

Clergy leadership

Leadership style ranked third highest among the reasons for which Christians feel that church switching is justified. If the clergy leadership style is inadequate, three-quarters of the respondents feel that switching churches is either sometimes justified or almost always justified. Lay members were much more likely than either clergy or Christian academics to state that switching is "almost always" justified if the clergy leadership style is inadequate.

Active Christians in mainline churches were more likely than those who attended conservative churches to say that switching is "almost always" justified in the case of inadequate clergy leadership.

The question of clergy leadership style is an important one in assessing the characteristics of effective churches. Chapter Nine is devoted entirely to issues related to clergy leadership.

Unfriendly churches and unresolved conflicts

A female lay member of a Lutheran church in Alberta responded to the survey and wrote, "I look on the church and its members as my family, and you don't switch families if trouble arises."

This respondent is in the minority. Overall, two-thirds of Christians felt that "If the church you attend is unfriendly, and you don't particularly like the people there," switching churches is either sometimes or almost always justified. Lay members are more likely to feel that leaving an unfriendly church is "almost always" justified than are academics or clergy. Christians who attend mainline churches are more likely to feel that leaving is "almost always" justified than are Christians who attend conservative churches.

Similarly, unresolved conflict among members is seen as a justification for switching churches among 70% of Christians surveyed. Lay members are more likely to feel that unresolved conflicts "almost always" justify church switching than are either clergy or academics. There is no difference between mainline and conservative churches in terms of whether switching churches is justified where there is "unresolved conflict among members."

These findings underline the value of supportive networks among church attenders. If community and common ground are lacking, Christians are more likely to seek a new church.

Financial and time pressures

While there is some feeling that unrealistic financial pressures and time demands which unduly impinge on the family "almost always" justify switching churches, these emerge as secondary priorities. The findings suggest that those who are involved in church life expect demands upon their time and pocketbook, and that switching churches is only justified when such demands become unreasonable or excessive.

Lay members are more likely than clergy or academics to feel that switching churches is justified in the face of unrealistic financial or time demands. Among lay members, nearly one in five feel that unrealistic financial demands justify switching, twice as many as either clergy or academics. Similarly, more lay members than clergy or academics say that if the demands of the church leave them with little time to spend with family, it "almost always" justifies switching to another church.

The findings suggest a need for balance and signal a word of caution. There is a tendency in organizational life to over-use the more talented and willing members. The effective church is one which identifies the appropriate gifts and talents of its members, but which can anticipate possible burn-out before it happens. George Barna notes that effective churches often encourage persons who have been serving for an extended period of time to take a break and recapture their energy. By identifying gifts and strengths, the possibility of burn-out and disenchantment is minimized.[6]

In the area of financial stress, stories abound of small churches that have over-extended themselves attempting visionary program ventures and overwhelming building projects. If the vision of the clergy leader and the lay decision makers is misaligned with sound economics or congregational support, the result can be disastrous.

The operative word in regard to time and financial demands is "reasonable." Christians in our survey did not object to demands being placed on them. In fact, the opportunity for involvement is a strong priority when it comes to choosing a church to attend. The question of whether the demands placed upon individuals within a congregation are excessive or not requires sensitivity, judgement and wisdom. Both an openness to listen and an acceptance of lay members' concerns are needed to determine whether or not expectations are excessive. A more painful way is to notice when lay people no longer fill the pews.

Community does not mean sameness

When asked whether switching churches was justified in cases of "wanting a church where there are more people like yourself, in areas such as age, family composition, education and income," 60% of the sample felt that switching was sometimes or almost always justified. Lay members were slightly more likely to justify switching on demographic grounds than were clergy or academics. There was no difference between mainline and conservative Christians in terms of the relatively low emphasis on demographic similarity.

Wanting a church where there are more people like yourself in terms of ethnic background was the least popular reason for switching churches. Very few respondents (4%)—lay members, clergy and academics alike—

rated this as an "almostly always" justified reason for switching to another church. Another 42% of the survey respondents felt that switching to an ethnic church was "sometimes" justified. Among lay members, mainline attenders were slightly more likely to support ethnic-based switching than were conservative attenders.

The Canadian church's openness to ethnic diversity stands in contrast to the homogeneity models built into much of the American church growth literature. Canadians have a proud tradition of accepting the subcultural and ethno-cultural differences among them. Living with the diversity of multiculturalism is becoming more and more a part of what it means to be Canadian.

Interpreting the results

How do we interpret the above findings? Do the findings show that church switching is a reflection of one church's inability or unwillingness to respond to consumer demands? Or do they indicate that church switching is motivated by positive spiritual aspiration?

We propose that much of the church switching among active Christians is related to the dimensions of orthodoxy, relevance, outreach and community in church life. When one or more of these cornerstones is missing or imbalanced in a person's current religious setting, the consequences contribute to switching. This is not to argue that any particular church is "doing it wrong." Switching goes both ways—some people leave, new arrivals replace them. Each church has to assess for itself whether it is winning or losing numbers as the "saints circulate."

Effective churches recognize that they do not have the resources or flexibility to be all things to all people. In his assessment of "user friendly churches," George Barna notes that,

> In speaking with pastors of declining churches, a common thread was their desire to do something for everybody... Despite the urge to be all things to all people, the successful churches resisted the impulse to be the answer to everyone's every problem by focusing on their vision for ministry, by reaffirming their commitment to quality, and by recognizing their limitations.[7]

In our discussions with clergy, it was not uncommon for them to acknowledge that, for some people, "this wasn't the church for them." In these cases, the clergy had no difficulty with recommending a more suitable church home. This helps ease the guilt that sometimes accompanies switching and hopefully saves the lay member the sense of disloyalty that is frequently associated with "looking for a good church."

Priorities for Choosing a New Church

Our survey included a list of nine characteristics often possessed by churches. Respondents were asked to rank these characteristics in terms of the role each would play in attracting them, if they were planning to switch churches.

The top four priorities for choosing a new church were consistent with the demand among Christians for orthodoxy, relevance, community and outreach. *(See Fig. 3.4)*

Excellent preaching

Overall, three-quarters of the respondents listed "excellent preaching" as a top priority in terms of selecting a new church to attend. There was no difference between mainline and conservative churches in terms of the emphasis they place on this aspect of church life. Lay members and clergy were similar in their emphasis on preaching, while academics were slightly less inclined to view preaching as a top priority.

Commitment to evangelism in a local community

"Evangelism," or the importance of witness and service to the local community, was viewed as a top priority among 70% of those surveyed. This percentage was much higher among conservatives than among mainline churches. This difference may be largely due to the choice of the word "evangelism" rather than "outreach" which represents a more inclusive term. Local "evangelism" was much more of a priority among clergy, especially conservatives, than it was among lay members or academics.

A strong commitment to world missions was less likely to be viewed as a top priority. Overall, one-half of respondents viewed this as a top priority. Academics, followed by clergy, were a little more likely than lay members to consider an emphasis on world missions as a priority concern when selecting a church to attend.

In touch with the times

Relevance was viewed as a top priority among two-thirds of survey

Where's a Good Church?

Fig. 3.4
Priorities for Selecting a Church

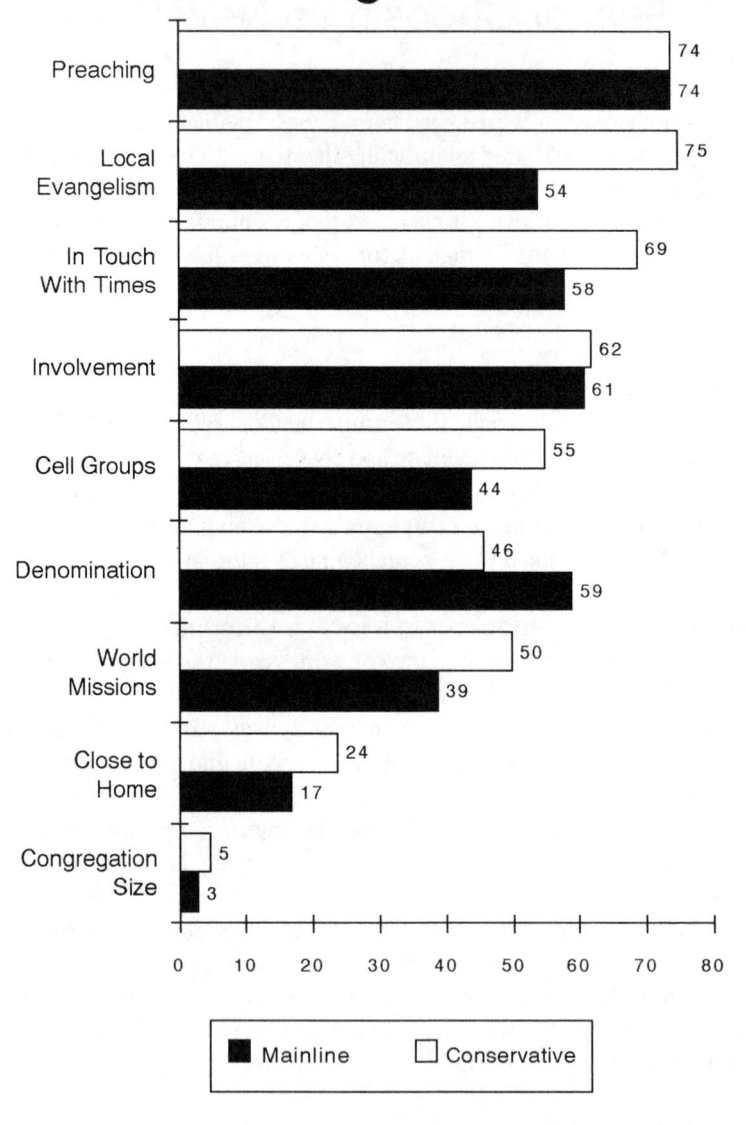

Factor	Conservative	Mainline
Preaching	74	74
Local Evangelism	75	54
In Touch With Times	69	58
Involvement	62	61
Cell Groups	55	44
Denomination	46	59
World Missions	50	39
Close to Home	24	17
Congregation Size	5	3

■ Mainline   □ Conservative

Graph shows percentage of respondents who place "Top Priority" on each factor in terms of selecting a new church.

respondents. Clergy were much more likely to rank this as a top priority than were lay members or academics. Despite the fact that many lay members perceive clergy as being out of touch with the times, the desire for a relevant expression of faith emerged as a priority for clergy, lay members and academics alike when choosing a new church.

Opportunity to be involved

Community was a top priority among almost two-thirds of those surveyed, with no difference between mainline and conservative churches. Involvement was, understandably, more critical to clergy, but remained a strong priority among academics and lay members.

A related dimension involved the opportunity to join small cell groups, such as home Bible study groups, neighborhood prayer groups or small groups organized around common interests that meet together for prayer and fellowship. This was more of a priority among conservative Christians than among mainline Christians. Clergy in both mainline and conservative churches were much more likely than either lay members or academics to view the opportunity of joining small cell groups as a top priority when selecting a new church to attend.

Denomination—a second level priority

Only one-half of those surveyed indicated that the selection of a particular denomination was a high priority in their decision of what church to attend. Leith Anderson notes that today's Christians are "choosing churches, not denominations."[8] The evidence does not support a rejection of denominationalism, but it does suggest that denominational association is a secondary consideration for many Christians, and that it is not as important as preaching, community, relevance and outreach.

Mainline Christians were more likely to stress the priority of denomination than were those who attend conservative churches. This was evident in the different patterns of intra-tradition switching. For mainline Christians, flexibility is built into the denominations themselves. Mainline denominations tend to offer a wider range in terms of style and function within the same denomination.

Conservatives have a much wider range of denominations from which to choose. Among conservatives, much of the denominational distinctiveness is based on style and form of religious expression, with less intra-denominational latitude. Conservatives seeking a more expressive type of worship involving choruses, experimental venues and contemporary musical styles, for example, will likely have to cross denominational lines. Among mainline Christians, the flexibility within the denomination itself precludes the necessity of switching denominations in order to find a different style of worship.

Lower priorities

Closeness to home was ranked as a top priority for selecting a new church by only 20% of those surveyed. The same percentage ranked proximity as a "low priority." The balance viewed it as a medium priority. Proximity was more important to conservatives than mainline Christians. Interestingly, closeness to home was ranked as a high priority for one-third of academics, much higher than for lay members or clergy.

Congregation size was least likely to be ranked as a high priority characteristic. Half of those surveyed viewed congregation size as a low priority when selecting a church to attend. Mainline Christians were slightly more likely to view congregation size as a low priority than were conservative Christians. Overall, lay members were more likely to view church size as a low priority than were clergy or academics. Those attending either smaller churches (under 125) or larger churches (over 500) were more likely to state that congregation size was a low priority while those attending mid-sized churches were less likely to give size a low priority.

The Dynamics of Switching

In assessing the patterns of church switching among Canadian Christians, we must not be confused between something that happens **commonly** and something that happens **easily**. An examination of patterns of cross-denominational switching, in terms of aggregate percentages, produces some insight into the structural process involved in church switching. However, it ignores the social psychological element of the decision to switch churches and paints a picture of church selection as a rational, passionless choice. This is not the case. Research into various factors and characteristics one evaluates in choosing a new church or in deciding whether church switching is "justified" provides some insight into these social psychological dynamics. However, it was in our discussion groups with people who had switched churches that we found that the decision to switch churches is not an easy or automatic one.

To help appreciate the social psychological dynamics of the process of switching, we have outlined a number of the common elements which prevailed in our discussion sessions with church switchers. The methodology was fairly straightforward. We contacted growing churches and asked to speak with a group of new attenders who had come to the church within the past year. Margaret, whose story introduced this chapter, was among them.

Her story was typical. All of the group participants had an extensive religious history. Most were raised in the Protestant tradition. The first lesson we learned was that people do not change churches the way they trade in a used automobile for a new one. Switching to another church was most often a difficult, soul searching experience accompanied by feelings of guilt. Like Margaret, the "switchers" weren't out "Sunday shopping" for something to do; they were spiritually hungry.

While the situation is not the same for everyone, it appears that six common factors operate in the decision to switch churches.

Dissatisfaction

A common experience involves the sense that one's spiritual and social needs are not being met. Others experience a sense of "burn-out" due to excessive involvement in demanding programs without a nurturing balance. The switchers typically do not "bail out" at the first sign of trouble, but quite often endure a rather lengthy period of dissatisfaction and spiritual drought.

During the focus group discussions, strong dissatisfaction was expressed regarding how women are being viewed in some churches. In one instance, a mother said that her family switched churches because, "I did not want my daughter growing up in a church where she would feel like a second-class citizen." She went on to explain that, "Because of my family's history in the church, I had been ready to accept the restrictions placed on women in ministry and worship, but my daughter is growing up in another age and it's not spiritually healthy or necessary for her to have to deal with those issues."

In another case, a professional woman candidly said that, "There were several reasons why my previous church was a disappointing place to attend, but it was after the minister promoted men over women and no one in leadership did anything about it that we decided to leave." In both instances, it was dissatisfaction regarding the lack of gender equality that became the reason for families deciding to switch churches.

A triggering event

Triggering events refer to either a "final straw" experience or an "escape hatch" reason to leave. For the discussion participants, the final straw events were as varied as those who were present. For one respondent who felt that the sermons were not biblically connected, a series of sermons on financial planning was a final straw. For another, an excessive preoccupation with numerical growth created a "final straw" response when overt gimmickry was introduced to bolster Sunday school attendance. In another instance, the spouse of the minister criticized a couple for being absent from an important church event; the couple consequently made a permanent departure.

"Escape hatches" varied as well, and included events such as a change of pastor, marriage to a partner who attended a different church, relocation to a different part of the city, relocation and loss of friends within the church community, and, in one case, the death of the participant's mother whom he had faithfully brought for years to a church he disliked.

Significant others

Much of the switching was based on the presence of family or friends in another church situation. Marriages, birth of children, divorces, deaths and other changes in one's pattern of social relationships provided the impetus and in some cases the direction for change.

Attractive alternatives

In some, but not all cases, an attractive alternative was available in a church where personal or family spiritual needs could be met. For parents of teenagers, if the choice is between their own preferences and a church where they believe their teens will be spiritually well-served, there is no contest. Parents will often subordinate their own desires to benefit the interests of their children. Typically, people become aware of alternative churches through friends or relatives.

For church switchers, the alternative provided the direction for change, dissatisfaction and spiritual hunger provided the impetus, and triggering events provided the opportunity.

Tough decision and spiritual renewal

Two other common characteristics were observed. These relate to the process of switching itself.

First, the decision to switch was a "tough decision." It involved soul-searching and guilt. Typically, those in the discussion group relived the pain of the experience as they shared their stories with us.

A second characteristic of the switching process was that it prompted some type of spiritual renewal or reawakening. Although we would not want to overstate the observation, no one thought that changing churches was a spiritual step backwards.

Overall, the social psychological process of switching churches looks very much like the process involved in religious conversion as described in sociological literature; the religious seeker takes and uses the elements of the social world around her and actively constructs a more satisfying religious life experience.[9]

Conversion and Other Types of Identity Transformation

To this point, we have restricted our focus to people's movement between churches or their circulation within the Protestant church. What about people who come into the life of the church from outside the Protestant church tradition? Unfortunately, there are very few to mention. In the total sample of 761 people, only 7% of current church attenders were raised in unchurched homes. The findings are especially intriguing because there is very little difference between mainline and conservative churches when it comes to the number of people being "converted out of the world." Almost the same percentage of active Christians in either tradition have come from non-religious backgrounds.

In Canadian society, conversions from outside the Christian tradition are rare. Part of this stems from a demographic reality; there are very few Canadians who do not initially align themselves with a Christian denomination or tradition.

Just as there are distinctive religious traditions, mainline and conservative categories of church structure, and a range of styles within denominations, there are also various views with regard to how religious conversion takes place. In fact, each individual Christian has his or her own "story" of how the transforming work of Christ was operative in his or her own life. We would argue that there are two dominant views that frame theological thought and shape church practice.

Process-oriented conversionists envision the Christian life as a journey with God. People grow into the faith. Disciples are learners.

Children and youth study the teachings of the faith and are invited to appropriate them as truth for their personal lives. The faithful are expected to mature in the ways of God and live "in Christ." Along the journey, people are encouraged to worship and live as converts of the faith and in the end enjoy God forever.

Decision-centered conversionists focus on a moment in time when those who believe become "new creations in Christ." The invitation is extended to be "born again" and in response to the decision to believe, sinners are forgiven and welcomed into the family of God. The emphasis is placed on the change of status that transpires before God. Prior to conversion people are spiritually lost; after conversion people are "saved." After conversion they are expected to change their ways and pursue the path to eternal life.

In orthodox Christian thought, the underlying motivation that propels both decision-centered and process-oriented conversionists is to unite the human creation with the Divine Creator. It is to connect people with the redemptive purpose that motivated God to send Jesus to earth, to endure the cross and triumph in his resurrection.

People will continue to hold differing views of how best to appropriate the life that God desires to give to all creation. Unfortunately, there is often judgment, ridicule and antagonism expressed toward those who hold contrary views. Greater empathy will result when we look beyond the differences in theological assumptions and methods that divide the church and move on to an understanding of the shared commitments that all God's people hold in common. Whether differences exist around baptism, decision-centered or process-oriented conversion, church polity or theories of atonement, when the intent is to encourage people to affirm their faith in the God of creation and the Christ of redemption, at the very least, all God's people should be given the benefit of the doubt.

A number of sociological researchers in the area of religious conversion prefer to use the term "alternation" rather than "conversion" when discussing some types of religious transformations (see for example, Pilarzyk, 1978[10] and Richardson, 1985[11]). In most cases, the use of the term "alternation" recognizes that some religious changes in people's lives are significant, but they are not full-blown conversions. Rather, they involve the integration of a series of elements that result in less disruptive life changes than defined by conversion. In fact, a general conclusion from the social psychological literature is that the nature of personal transformation is rarely radical enough, or sudden enough, in our society to qualify as a conversion.

The term "alternation" was originally suggested by Peter Berger to refer to the possibility that "an individual may alternate back and forth between logically contradictory meaning systems."[12] Berger preferred the term alternation to the more religiously-charged term "conversion." Richard Travisano, however, has suggested that conversion and alternation be used to refer to two quite different types of transformation.[13] He defines conversion as the negation of a former identity. Conversion is a radical and fundamental shift in identity that results in clear changes in values, ethics, morals and lifestyle behaviors. Alternation, on the other hand, implies some linkage and continuity between the past and the present. The ensuing identity and lifestyle grows naturally out of its predecessor.

This distinction between alternation and conversion helps us to appreciate that some changes in life are less dramatic and more easily accomplished than others. In alternation, a supportive framework and an ideological framework is already present. In conversion, a whole new world is entered; the past no longer has a direct bearing on the present. Conversion is non-cumulative. Alternation is cumulative. And analysis suggests that most of the instances reported in "church growth" charts are alternations rather than conversions.

An additional difficulty with much of the literature on church growth is that it confuses conversion with recruitment. Since most "new members" come from within the same tradition, rather than from outside the church, very few people are actually being converted.

The above discussion is based on a sociological definition of conversion, rather than a theological one. But often a problem for the church arises when there is a lack of conceptual clarity between the two. In asking people to "become converted" what are they being asked to do? How does the person raised in the church describe a cumulative, possibly gradual identity change when the language available for describing "how I became a Christian" involves some sort of affirmation that a sudden non-cumulative change has occurred? Our conversion models often do not match our people's experiences. We will do well to re-think the metaphors and symbols used to describe conversion.

Religious transformations can involve a range of structural shifts and personal changes. The spiritual implications may be relatively minor or radically disruptive. Subjectively, the changes and transformations that we describe below will undoubtedly mean different things to people from different denominations and religious traditions. Still, they are offered to clarify the terminology being used in this discussion.

Switching:
- switching churches within the same denomination
- switching denominations within the same tradition(conservative/mainline)
- switching across traditions

Alternation:
- returning after a period of non-belonging to one's original denomination
- returning after a period of non-belonging to a different denomination within one's original tradition
- returning after a period of non-belonging to a different tradition

Conversion:
- converting from an unchurched or non-religious background
- converting from a different world religion or from a firmly held ideological stance that is antithetical to the Christian faith in some important respect

The list is undoubtedly incomplete. Still, it recognizes that the further afield one goes, the more difficult or more rare transformation by conversion really is in Canadian churches. Meredith McGuire, for example, discusses identity changes which involve the consolidation of elements of previous identities or the reaffirmation of elements of one's past.[14]

Richard Travisano argues that ours is a day of alternation and not conversion. Whatever subjective growth and transformation is happening in the lives of people in Canadian churches, the reality is that they did not usually have to travel very far to get there.

Accepting imperfection

The survey of active Christians shows that 43% had gone through a prolonged period of religious inactivity in their lives. Surprisingly, almost half of the respondents did not attend church at all for an average period of 10 years. Then, for various reasons, they moved from being inactive to becoming highly involved. The percentage of inactivity was higher among mainline Christians than among conservatives. Periods of non-participation were also higher among lay members than among clergy or academics.

While the survey did not collect data from respondents on why they opted for a period of absence, and what prompted the return to active participation, we can speculate that much of the impetus for a return to active faith was based on similar factors seen for denominational switching. Further research could examine levels of pre-return dissatisfaction, factors which prompted a felt need for spiritual renewal, and interpersonal patterns between friends, relatives, spouses and children which act as catalysts for a return to the church.

Often people are prevented from finding a good church by their own expectation that they find a perfect one. William Willimon notes that when we ask where the "real" church or the "true" church is, we are feeling embarrassed about the present church. The present church, he notes, "never fully meets our expectations of what the church ought to be. We keep looking for more."[15] The distinction between the real and the ideal was reconciled in the Middle Ages with the dualistic notion of the church as both the visible collection of believers and the invisible church as God intends it to be. Dietrich Bonhoeffer warned against the tendency to idealize the church and to then hold the ideal up to the real. In *Life Together* he writes,

> Every human wish-dream that is injected into the Christian community is a hindrance to genuine community and must be banished if genuine community is to survive. He who loves his dream of a community more than the community itself becomes a destroyer.[16]

Willimon's statement that "What appears to be a failing, decrepit, declining society of the religiously inclined is, in truth, none other than the very body of Christ" recognizes that the visible church will never match up to the invisible church.

It is easier to criticize the church from outside, but if love for the "invisible" church is driving you away from the "visible" church, there is little chance you can make a contribution to either.

> The Church is not reformed by idealists and romantics. It is formed by realists who know that commitment to Christ must be realistically, visibly embodied if it is to be faithful to the way of Christ himself.[17]

David Read has suggested that today's new hypocrites may not be the smug Pharisee in Jesus' story, but rather the publicans outside the church who pray, "God, I may not be the best person in the world, but at least I am better than all those religious hypocrites in the Church."[18]

Where switching churches reflects a genuine desire to find a satisfactory level of community, orthodoxy, relevance and outreach, it can be a sign of spiritual growth and renewal. When dissatisfaction with one's present church drives one outside of active involvement in the church, it is a statement of spiritual protest which benefits no one.

Why Denominational Walls Are Tumbling Down

Chapter Four

After a spiritually dormant period lasting several years, Linda, a middle-aged accomplished professional, returned to active involvement in a church. In the evening discussion group, she was particularly candid: "Denominations do not matter any more. If our present pastor were to leave and a dud were to replace him, a bunch of us in the church would go looking elsewhere. And we could end up at a Lutheran church just as easily as a Baptist church."

Many church officials disagree and contend that Linda's perspective is the exception rather than the norm. However, if it hasn't already happened, in the future Linda's attitude toward the sanctity of denominational structures will become more normal than unusual. Denominational walls are tumbling down.

Walls are Tumbling Down

Our choice of the metaphor of "walls" is a deliberate attempt to convey two messages. First, denominational distinctions are, in the main, a human construction. Second, the metaphor of "walls" is useful in understanding the "building blocks" that have gone into their past construction as well as their current erosion.

Christian thinkers have long recognized that while denominational structures have been erected with godly intent, they are the product of human enterprise. The classic work dealing with denominationalism as a social structural invention is Richard Niebuhr's *The Social Sources of Denominationalism*.[1] Niebuhr proposes that denominationalism is simply a product of cultural, social structural, political and organizational differences. Regrettably, he ignores the historic importance of the doctrinal differences which have differentiated major traditions and denominations. On the other hand, Niebuhr counters those who tend to reduce denominationalism to doctrinal differences and to ignore the significance of other social realities.

Denominations, as organized structures, are meant to serve the body of Christ. They are a "means," not an "end" in themselves. Denominations enhance our human ability to handle diversity and to incorporate the multifaceted nature of the universal church. Still, as individuals, we implicitly recognize that God relates to each of us, not as Baptists, Presbyterians or Pentecostals, but as people in an extended family of faith.

This is not to say that denominations serve no purpose. Rather, their role is changing. Some aspects of denominationalism are outmoded and will not serve the church in the future.

The notion that denominationalism was never intended to last forever is implicit in our theological thinking. For example, no one really expects denominationalism to survive Christ's second coming. God's people simply do not see themselves congregating in denominational groupings in heaven! The point is that the denominations have a limited purpose.

The danger of any social construction is that we forget that we constructed it. We start to think of it as an object independent of our participation in it. Once we have "objectified" denominationalism, it begins to control and direct our lives. When a tool becomes the master of the tool maker, we no longer have control over what we have fashioned and designed. Instead, our tool controls us. Behind the liberation movements which began in the 1960s has been a recognition that we need not be governed by our own social structures. Rather than being the passive recipients of our own social structures, we have the ability to transform our social world into one that serves us more capably.

The same is true of our denominational world. Here, too, we have the ability to bring about transformation.

Over the last two decades, we have seen the weakening of denominational structures. Church consultant Lyle Schaller lists 20 factors that have contributed to the erosion of denominational loyalty in the United States. The factors listed by Schaller show that denominational walls are not predominantly doctrinal. Rather, they are influenced by cultural, social structural and organizational differences as well. Some of the reasons he lists, such as the rise of large nondenominational megachurches, are more appropriate to the American religious scene. However, in our judgment, several factors pertain to Canada. These include:

- Increases in interdenominational and interfaith marriages
- Upward social and economic mobility, resulting in the termination of old loyalties and the establishment of new ties (many denominations had a particular foothold within a certain socio-economic strata)
- Pronouncements by national and international denominational leaders which alienate members of their denominations
- The rise of nondenominational parachurch organizations
- The Charismatic Renewal Movement of the 1960s which crossed denominational lines
- Emergence of home Bible study and community-based church movements
- Ministers trained in seminaries of denominations other than the one in which they now serve
- An emerging youth generation with weak denominational loyalty
- Reluctance of denominational churches to advertise their affiliation
- Decline in subscriptions to denominational magazines
- Rising anti-centralization, anti-headquarters, anti-institution sentiment[2]

Any of these factors will produce post-denominational pressures.

Pressures on Denominations

Several aspects of the data which we dealt with in the preceding chapters verify the notion that denominational walls are tumbling down.

Denominational switching

This subject has been profiled in detail in the previous chapter. We mention it again only to underscore the reality that 55% of the people in the survey switched denominations at least once in their lifetime.

Switching becomes one of the significant indicators that helps define the emergence of the "post-denominational age." The fact that Christians switch so readily across denominations, and even across traditions, becomes a pressure point for those seeking to build up denominational structures. Congregational life becomes unpredictable when individuals attach little value to the denominational label of the church they attend.

There is no evidence to conclude that the "saints" of today will stop "circulating" in the future. Switching will continue to contribute to the crumbling of denominational walls. As we mentioned, the traffic between mainline and conservative denominations moves with relatively equal fluidity in both directions, as far as regular church attendance is concerned.

Denominational demotion

While almost three-quarters of the survey respondents identified preaching as a priority in choosing a church and two-thirds said finding a church that is in touch with the times is crucial, only half gave equal importance to the denomination of choice. This means that "denomination" is relatively important to only about half of those who regularly attend Canadian churches. Other factors relating to orthodoxy, relevance, community and outreach are more important, and are not necessarily linked to denomination.

Our research shows that effectiveness is a nondenominational phenomenon. Factors which determine effectiveness for churches are very much the same across denominational structures. In Chapters Two and Three, we noted that Christians are looking for a balance of orthodoxy and relevance, of community and outreach, and that these preferences, for the most part, transcend denominational differences.

There are two dominant reasons for this conclusion. First, the perceptions of effectiveness and the preferences of Christians in terms of what they look for in a church experience did not differ much along denominational lines. Second, people are quite willing to cross denominational lines to find a good church.

Consequently, finding a good church is more important to active attenders than denominational loyalty. The focus of loyalty is the local church, not the denomination. People are looking for effective churches, not effective denominations.

Institutional disillusionment

Canadian public opinion polls consistently document a lack of confidence in our bureaucratic institutions. As a nation, we no longer believe they can solve our problems or adequately represent our collective interests.

The church has not escaped this erosion of faith in bureaucratic and centralized organizational structures. Neither has the collective reputation of the clergy served to lift the level of confidence in their leadership. Across the land, denominations are perceived as institutional structures. The erosion of denominational loyalty reflects a gradual shift in thinking; institutions may no longer serve the best interests of people.

An increasing level of institutional disillusionment in the culture at large is another reason for the declining influence of the institutional church on Canadian life.

Passing of Christendom

Entrenched denominationalism was one of the luxuries of Christendom. The strength of denominations lay in their ability to carve out a "niche" and to be a major player within the culture. Stanley Hauerwas and William Willimon note that today, "all sorts of Christians are waking up and realizing that it is no longer 'our world'—if it ever was."[3]

Today, religion has been both the marginalized and privatized. This has effectively reduced the power of denominations as a major force in society. To make itself more vocal and more influential in society, some denominations have established multidenominational task forces. These working groups can present a unified and stronger voice to government. Ecumenical and evangelical church alliances have established consortia to make more effective in-roads to government policy makers. The voice of a single denomination carries little weight. By acting together under an association, the various Christian groups implicitly admit that their denominational distinctives are less important than the need to lobby effectively.

This is not a criticism. It simply recognizes that most individual denominations do not carry the institutional weight necessary to influence government. Part of the trade-off involves setting aside denominational differences.

A "return" to intense denominational seclusion and competitiveness would probably be counter-productive. Robert Bellah, in *The Broken Covenant*, suggests that while a return to exclusive identities seems attractive in the face of cultural chaos and confusion, it is unhealthy, both for the group and for the society. Structure provides a certain amount of security. It gives people a clearer definition of who they are. At the same time, a retreat back to denominationalism may be based on fear, and may well result in the intolerance and ethnocentrism that have characterized denominationalism in the past. Bellah notes:

It is questionable whether a "return" to inherited ethnic and religious identities...would be particularly healthy. A return to primordial loyalties in the face of cultural and social breakdown can be defensive, more based on fear than joyous reaffirmation.[4]

Arrival of post-modernism

For most of the 20th century, the influence of the Enlightenment shaped our perceptions and expectations. Accordingly, the modern world, or modernism, placed a high value on rationalism and the potential of human reasoning. This orientation set the stage for the reign of science and the pursuit of technology. At the same time, the pull of the culture was toward increasing secularization and the entrenchment of pluralism.

In more recent years, without abandoning the rational and the cognitive, the human spirit has been on a quest to experience the emotional and affective realms of life. Instead of logic and rationality always being in charge, the intuitive side of life has emerged as a legitimate force.

One of the defining patterns of post-modernism has been a willingness to express feelings and a willingness to experiment with personal experience. If one of the tests for human behavior in the past was, "Does it make sense?" the equivalent in the present is, "Was it a good experience?"

Writing on the shifts in the theology of missions, David Bosch from the University of South Africa observes that, "New paradigms do not establish themselves overnight. They take decades, sometimes even centuries, to develop distinctive contours." Referring to the emergence of post-modernism, Bosch asserts that, "The new paradigm is therefore still emerging and it is, as yet, not clear which shape it will eventually adopt."[5]

But clearly, beyond the enormous ramifications of escalating secularism in Canadian society, post-modernism is ushering in a less rationally controlled world. Bosch goes on to say that reason, as championed by the Enlightenment, "has been found to be an inadequate cornerstone on which to build one's life." Rationality has not been abandoned, but has been "expanded to include experience."[6]

In his discussion of the role of religion in the post-modern world, Robert Bellah argues that, "Perhaps the revitalization of our religious traditions will come from new efforts to live them as experienced realities, rather than objects of thought, by those who find them meaningful, whatever their own origins may be."[7]

Part of the impact of post-modernism on contemporary life is that the subjective is invading the objective; the affective or feeling side of life is impacting the cognitive or thinking realm of life. One expression of this trend, in the culture at large, is an increasing desire to experience the mystical. New Age spiritualists place their confidence in the power of crystals and pursue the supernatural through channelling. Reason alone can no longer determine what is real. The craving of the spirit for expanded realms of reality and experience has gained recognition and respectability.

In Christian circles, the renewed interest in expressive worship, the hunger of the heart for inner healing, and the increasing appeal of contemplative spirituality are also linked to the emergence of post-modernism. Underneath these surging interests lies the unspoken desire to augment former forms of spirituality, which were often cold and cognitive, with expressions of spirituality that are warm and experiential.

What are the implications for denominations?

Elmer Towns points out that, "Formerly a doctrinal statement represented the reason for a denomination's existence. Even churches that lacked an official doctrinal statement were at least connected by a similar hermeneutic."[8] Yet doctrinal distinctiveness continues to give denominations their identity. Doctrines are derived from ideas. They are constructed out of ideological convictions, mainly rooted in the scriptures.

The difficulty for denominations that choose to depend on the assumptions of the past is that ideas of any kind have lost a lot of their former power. Because the power of objective ideas has been weakened by a subjective desire for experience, the ideological foundations of denominationalism have been undermined.

Throughout the centuries, various religious traditions and denominations have developed their doctrines into belief systems. Millions of books have been written to articulate these doctrinal premises. Catechism curricula have been transmitted from generation to generation. People have been invited to believe sets of ideas and to link their particular beliefs to specific denominational distinctives.

While orthodoxy remains critical, doctrinal hair-splitting has lost its appeal to the masses. Said another way, orthodoxy creates stability; "hair-splitting" creates instability. On a fundamental level, denominations are still important. But the primary identity of denominations is no longer differentiated on doctrinal lines so much as organizational, social and style differences. Leith Anderson concludes that "the church of the

21st century may be less divided over baptism than race, money, abortion, homosexuality and gender roles."[9] Denominations that carve out their identities around the new rules will gain. Denominations that depend excessively on their doctrinal distinctiveness will wane.

New denominational patterns

The pressures exerted on today's denominational structures are already producing some new or post-denominational patterns. Some of the patterns exhibit themselves inside the church; others surface when the people of God encounter each other outside their church buildings.

Increasing importance of shared faith

In the everyday work world, most church attenders consider it a blessing to discover another confessing Christian of any stripe. Finding another person of faith, a believer in the midst of a world of unbelievers, is a welcome surprise. When this happens, shared faith overrides doctrinal and denominational differences.

When the church was a dominant force in the culture, denominations were the natural places for like-minded people to gather. Obviously, people will continue to frame their faith and find places to belong inside denominational structures. But increasingly, denominational identification is viewed as irrelevant in social interaction. Christians in workplace settings, professional associations, and support groups meet together to encourage one another in their common faith. In the future, we shouldn't be surprised when increasing numbers of God's people gather on neutral ground, to relate across denominational lines and to pursue their shared spiritual concerns.

Local church loyalty

One of the most significant challenges facing denominational structures lies in the shifting locus of loyalty among Christians. Will they or will they not commit support to a functional denominational identity as well as belong to and participate in a local church?

Historically, loyalty within the Christian church has involved three parameters:
1. Commitment to Christ
2. Identification with denomination
3. Belonging to local church

Today's church has seen the separation of identification from belonging in two areas. First, the "cultural Christians," discussed in Chapter One, separate belonging from identification. They identify themselves with a particular denomination, but then restrict their active involvement to minimal observances. Second, an increasing number of "conditional participants" belong to and participate in a local church, but do so without any real attachment to the associated denomination. In some large churches, we have even noted a locus of loyalty at a smaller "cell group" level. In these cases, a member's loyalty can be **two** steps removed from a denomination.

The paradox is that the "denominational" tag often identifies people who do not attend church with any regularity. For others, who do participate on a regular basis, the power of the local church is stronger than that of the denomination. Consequently, when circumstances prompt a decision to switch churches, people base their decision on factors related to orthodoxy, relevance, community and outreach as opposed to denomination.

These factors, we have argued, are general patterns not necessarily linked to any particular denomination.

George Barna observes some of the same tendencies in that many Christians reject the constraints imposed by identifying themselves with a particular Protestant denomination, and choose, instead, to call themselves simply "Christian" or religious.[10] Again, the prevailing tendencies come at the expense of denominational structures.

Existential commitment

Another post-denominational pattern in the modern world is existential commitment. Increasing numbers of today's church attenders remain involved only as long as they stay satisfied. If dissatisfaction builds, they start wondering where they can find a good church.

Leith Anderson reads the scene in the following way and recommends a pro-active prescription:

Most won't just "show up" at a Sunday church service to hear the Gospel. They will be attracted by modern nursery facilities, excellent pre-schools, and attractive youth programs for their children. Baby boomers appear to be opening up to the message of Jesus Christ during the transition times of their lives, such as divorce, remarriage, the birth of a child, unemployment, or the death of a parent. Churches, then, need to rely less on the Sunday morning sermon and more on divorce recovery workshops, unemployment support groups, or workshops on grief, ministries to offer boomers Christian community in their hour of need.[11]

In the present environment, effective and growing local churches will be made up of a core of "committed participants" alongside increasing numbers of "conditional participants" who will attend as long as they and their families are having positive church experiences. Unfortunately, this situation works against the building up of denominational loyalties.

Demand for customized programs

This new denominational context increases the demand for customized programs. Rather than just offering standard worship fare and the religious basics, present circumstances are pressing both denominations and local churches to diversify and specialize.

Peter Berger, in *The Sacred Canopy,*[12] notes that whenever religious institutions occupy a monopoly position in society, they have the power to determine their content according to the perceptions of the religious leadership. A monopoly position in society means, according to Berger, that the church does not have to "listen" to the people.

As the power of the institution declines, however, its survival depends on its ability to meet the needs of its members. Where needs are not being met, in all likelihood, membership will decline and people will switch over to "competing" organizations or resources.

According to Berger,

> The crucial sociological and social psychological characteristic of the pluralistic situation is that religion can no longer be imposed but must be marketed.
>
> It is impossible to market a commodity to a population of uncoerced consumers without taking their wishes concerning the commodity into consideration. To be sure, there still is strong "product loyalty" among certain groups of "old customers." Furthermore, the religious groups can to a certain extent restrain disaffection among the same groups by means of their own promotional activities.[13]

Observers of this marketing trend have raised a number of important questions relating to the integrity of the gospel. In our orientation to consumers, how do we make the gospel attractive, while at the same time remain true to biblical standards? This is especially so for the less attractive demands for commitment, morality, sacrifice and repentance. How do we bridge the gap between culture and orthodoxy? Can we make the Bible relevant to today's religious consumers without sacrificing its sacred message? These questions are obviously not new. What is new is the audience. In the past, in many cases, the search for a relevant expression of faith was motivated by a desire to communicate the gospel in a way which would bring the unchurched into the fold. Although many will deny it, attempts to make the gospel attractive in today's churches are often aimed at retaining market share among those who already call themselves Christians. Despite the fact that the majority of Canadians continue to think of themselves as Christians, churches still face the challenge of developing programs and "products" which will bring consumers in, and at the same time keep the essential message intact. Our analysis of effective churches shows that this issue is a fundamental one to any church which attempts to relate the gospel to contemporary Canadians. It is also clear that effective churches will find the direction for resolution in synthesis rather than compromise.

Post-Denominational Challenges

Inclusive or exclusive?

These days, national leaders and local church decision makers face the challenge of deciding whether to be inclusive or exclusive. On the one hand, we need to assert every organization's right and responsibility to self-define. On the other hand, every denomination needs to be guided by its overall purpose to be redemptive.

In his book *The Future of the Church,* United Church theologian Douglas John Hall says that,

> The Christian message is not just what anyone decides one morning that it should be! We are the inheritors of a tradition. But the danger that "the message" will be whatever this or that individual, generation, or human grouping determines that it should be is a danger that has been present in the church from the beginning, and it is not lessened today but, if anything, more potent.[14]

Another way to express the tension of being inclusive or exclusive is to distinguish between accommodation and differentiation. The alternatives are to bend and bow to the trends of the times, or to draw straight lines and be distinctive in the midst of the mood of the day.

The future will usher in a myriad of issues with moral and ethical ramifications. Whether they are related to lifestyle and sexual alternatives, family structures, birth technologies, justice concerns or changes in universal medical care, church decision makers will have to decide whether they will embrace or reject what emerges. If the decisions were just related to theoretical ideas, they would be relatively easy to resolve. But people are involved: people who can be positively and adversely affected. In the end, church decision makers will be pressed to pass judgment on ideas and issues that will lead to the acceptance of some people, and the rejection of others.

Cooperation or competition?

Church leaders may think that what happens to other denominations does not affect them. But when one part of God's family is scandalized or disgraced, perceptions of the whole church suffer. Whether it is institutional abuse in parochial schools or the moral downfall of a prominent evangelist, the reputation of the church suffers and its credibility falls in the eyes of those outside its walls.

One implication of the switching phenomenon, the tendency for Christians to select churches on the basis of personal needs, is that it places the churches in a competitive context. On the issue of whether or not churches should "buy in" to this competitive context, a lay leader in a British Columbia Nazarene church wrote,

> If the church, the whole body of Christ, is going to be effective in today's world, we have got to grasp the concept of Romans 12:4–5. Christ is not divided, and the world will not see him, if we, the Body of Christ, are divided.

Expressing a similar spirit, a female clergy leader in an independent Alberta church stressed the importance of "working alongside other churches in the city. There is only one Church," she writes. "Christ is coming back for his bride, not a harem."

Articulating a more academic perspective, Peter Berger, in *The Sacred Canopy*, suggests that the collaborative efforts of Christian denominations have created religious "cartels."

> Cartelization in competitive market situations has two facets: the number of competing units is reduced through

mergers; and the remaining units organize the market by means of mutual agreements. Ecumenicity in the contemporary situation is, of course, characterized by both of these facets. At any rate within Protestantism, churches have merged at an increasing rate and negotiations looking forward to further mergers are continuing apace. Both within and beyond Protestantism, there has been increasing consultation and collaboration between the large bodies "surviving" the merger process.[15]

One of the greatest challenges facing religion is that it cannot coexist with other religions without some significant change to its structure and content. Writing from his Catholic perspective, University of McGill's Gregory Baum points out that religious pluralism inevitably leads to the decline of religion.

If there are several religions, all of which are regarded as valid, it is possible to choose between them and adopt the one that seems best suited to one's life; in this way religion becomes a private affair, a spiritual hobby as it were, and loses its nature as the ultimate ground of reality.[16]

One by one, denominations will continue to decide whether to compete with each other or whether to cooperate with each other. What incredible progress for faith it would be if churches across denominations and traditions would at least cheer for each other.

Instead of the present denominational competition, consider the possibilities offered by the example of athletes at the Special Olympics. This unusual athletic event features mentally and physically disabled athletes from around the world. One image, in particular, stands out. During a foot race among persons with Down's Syndrome, the runners were close together as they came around the track toward the finish line. One of them stumbled and fell. The rest of the contestants stopped, helped the fallen runner to stand, and then resumed the race. Their success was wonderful, and it wasn't in the achievement of being better than others.[17]

In the midst of the pressures and challenges that are cracking and crushing our denominational walls, it will take a miracle for God's people to live like the Special Olympics athletes. But don't God's people say they believe in miracles?

Conclusion

The image of the symphony orchestra provides another analogy for the church universal. The church, so imagined, is comprised of many people in various denominations and groups, using an assortment of instruments to play many different kinds of music.

If it were possible to gather the breadth of the church into a mammoth concert hall so that everyone could play together, the music on the program would range from the standard classics to the most modern scores. Sometimes the music would be loud and boisterous: at other moments, quiet and mellow. Each section of the orchestra would have a part in the musical score written just for them. There would be no guest artist.

If Jesus were on earth again, would we let him call his church together so that we could play God's music? Would we let Jesus be the conductor?[18]

Jesus **is** on earth. He resides in the people who make up his church. May we let him conduct us.

Section II

Mapping the Canadian Context

Cultural Shifts

Chapter Five

Until the mid-1960s, the pieces of the Canadian puzzle were pretty much put together. That doesn't mean life was everything it should have been, but it was predictable. A family was defined as a man and a woman living in a dwelling with one or more children. A single income was most often adequate to raise a family. In the main, women got married and stayed at home to raise their children. Sexual decision making was linked to moral choices. Sexual intercourse was morally right when it was expressed within the covenant of marriage. Outside of that framework it was morally wrong.

Gender roles were clear. Men got an education and acquired the skills to be "the providers." Women supported them emotionally and sometimes added a little income for the "extras" to make life a little more pleasurable.

In the religious realm, two out of three people went to church with some regularity. There was even a touch of psychological and social stigma projected in the direction of those who didn't make the effort to show up for worship.

Times have changed. The pieces of the Canadian puzzle have been pulled apart and turned upside down. We have experienced the sweeping social changes of the 1960s. Canada has seen a massive increase in its cultural and ethnic diversity. Technological changes have moved more quickly than our ability to develop an ethical and moral framework to handle the choices technology affords.

For those pining for the old ways, cultural disarray prevails. Pluralism, despite its benefits, has "pulled the rug out from under us." We put quotation marks around the terms "right" and "wrong." The language of choice and subjectivism prevails. Canadians today face a bewildering array of possibilities with little basis upon which to make decisions.

Family structures have diversified. Divorce and remarriage is ordinary, blended families are a reality, single parent families are bonafide entities, and politicians and the courts are deciding whether or not same sex unions qualify as full-status family forms.

Sexual liberalization is a fact of life. For the majority, sexual intercourse is no longer a moral matter. The content of relationships determines the decision. When love is the mutual feeling, for nine out of ten Canadians, sex is assumed to be part of the relationship. Same sex intimacy has become the norm for many.

Increasingly, people expect equality between men and women to be the norm. In the main, men understand the rationale for equality and know in their inner spirits it ought to be that way. But, for many, the reality of losing cultural power is another matter. Some men are still a little dazed. Many women still struggle with what Karl Marx called "false consciousness," unsure whether or not they want liberation.

Positive social change is not without pain. Our yearning for the "good old days" is mixed with ambivalence. Archie and Edith Bunker, caricatures of the old order, sang a duet through the 1970s and '80s: "When girls were girls and men were men." But the '70s and '80s are gone and we are headed for the year 2000. Both men and women wonder what is going on around them and what will happen next.

The church does not exist in a vacuum. Throughout its 2000-year history, the church has both critiqued and reflected the various cultures in which it has found itself. This characteristic of the church—its ability to both critique and reflect culture—is no less evident today than it has ever been. What **has** changed for the church is the pace and degree of cultural change with which it must cope. Change now happens so fast that the church seems to have little time to discern which aspects of the surrounding culture it should critique or reject, and which aspects it should reflect or integrate into its own life.

Today, although the Canadian landscape is still dotted with the brick and mortar of church buildings, the lineups for the promise of the good life form at the lottery ticket kiosks. Those who attend worship are the unusual ones. Social stigma has shifted from "those who don't" to "those who do." With increasing cultural force, "those who do" feel somewhat overwhelmed by "those who don't."

Now **we** are the outsiders.

Social shifts on the Canadian landscape

When the pieces of the social puzzle are interlocked with coherence and design, life is simpler. Life makes sense. Decisions come ready-made. When there is cultural consensus and common agreement about the big issues in life, it takes less energy to work through the months of a year. When you have been the majority in the society and have been used to having life go your way, it is especially disruptive when the puzzle pieces are disconnected and flipped upside-down. And it is particularly disconcerting when disconnectedness is the preferred way of life. Consequently, the 1990s are a trying time for many Canadians who identify themselves as serious Christians.

There are social forces weaving their way through the days and nights of Canadian life that are both perplexing and upsetting to many Christians across the country. These forces are formidable. They are macro in size and they impact everybody's micro worlds.

Consider what cannot be escaped.

From mainly white to multicultural

Canada is a country of immigrants. Aboriginal peoples are the only ones who can make a case for not being relatively recent arrivals. Marking the beginning of the nation at 1867 puts a limit on the number of generations any family can claim when it comes to "being Canadian." Certainly, there was some diversity in the beginning. Historians can confidently claim that Canada began with two "founding nations." But almost exclusively, French and English were both "white."

Modern Canada has shifted from a mainly white culture to a multicultural society. In new ways, we are experiencing the coloring of Canada—especially in our major cities.

In Toronto, 38% of the population qualify as immigrants. On the west coast, 30% of the population who call Vancouver their home were born outside Canada. The pace of change combined with the sheer numbers of new arrivals feed the potential for multi-ethnic tensions.

The percentage of Canadians who were not born in Canada but were granted the right to live here permanently has remained almost exactly the same, at 16%, since the Second World War. That's a ratio of one in seven. What **has** changed is the origin of the immigrants.

In 1961, 90% of immigrants came from European countries. Be-

Fig. 5.1
Immigrants Who Came to Canada Between 1981 and 1991

Hong Kong	96,540
Poland	77,455
China	75,841
India	73,105
United Kingdom	71,365
Vietnam	69,520
Philippines	64,290
United States	55,415
Portugal	35,440
Lebanon	34,065
Total	1,238,455

Source: Statistics Canada

tween 1981 and 1991, this figure plunged to 25%. The immigration increases in the past decade have come from Asian destinations. Shifting from 14% of the whole in 1981 to 25% in 1991, Asian-born people comprised the largest single sector of all the immigrants who came to Canada during that ten-year period. The federal government's 1971 formal policy of multiculturalism is no longer just theory—it is a Canadian reality. *(See Fig. 5.1)*

Ellen Gee, a sociologist at British Columbia's Simon Fraser University, reasons that "the changes have taken place so rapidly that the result is a recipe for social unease."[1] The complications extend far beyond the smell of strange foods and the sights and sounds of foreign festivals and unusual folk dancing.

The complications for the church are equally real. On the one hand, the church may wish to speak out against expressions of racism, for example. At the same time, it may discover that it too feels uncomfortable with the increasing number of "strangers" in its midst.

Research conducted by the Angus Reid Group for the federal government's public consultations on 1991–1995 immigration levels revealed a divided public. The desire of some people to be humanitarian

and accepting conflicted with an underlying sense of threat over the impact of increased immigration levels by others.[2] While a good many Canadians recognize the benefits of increased immigration levels and welcome newcomers with open arms, pockets of resistance remain. Three manifestations of threat were observed:
1. Economic threat—manifested in the belief that immigrants would take jobs away from Canadians or fill the limited number of graduate spaces at local universities.
2. Social threat—the belief that increased immigration would contribute to problems of urban crowding, crime, and depletion of social services resources.
3. Cultural threat—an uneasiness about how the presence of newcomers would affect Canadian culture. This expression of threat was particularly predominant in Quebec, where French language issues and the Francophone proportion of the population would be affected by increased numbers of immigrants to that province.

The public opinion research did not conclude that threat and racism were prevailing attitudes of the majority. Those attitudes were, however, representative of a significant proportion of Canadians, a fact which cannot be ignored. Across the country, we have already seen numerous instances where swirling social change has proven to be a recipe for racism, at least in some segments of the population.

Coloring of congregations

Canadians who are a part of effective churches, however, are not attitudinally resistant to the coloring of their congregations. When asked to state their personal preference on whether they would like their church to be "a congregation that is comprised of a multi-ethnic mix" or one that is "comprised of people who share the same ethnic background," only 8% said they would "very much" or "somewhat" prefer sameness. A majority of 58% favor a diverse ethnic mix in their congregations and an additional 34% took an in-between and somewhat ambivalent stance.

A comparison of gender, regions of the country, clergy, laity and academics, as well as mainline Protestants with conservative Protestants reveals little variance in the pattern of response. Those from small churches with fewer than 75 in attendance are less enthusiastic about embracing an ethnic mix while those between the ages of 25–34 were most open to ethnic diversity in their congregational life.

A message affirming diversity was also communicated in response

Fig. 5.2
Preferential Ministry Focus

Target Group	More inclined toward Broad Spectrum
Quebec	Atlantic
Males	Females
Older	Younger
Conservative	Mainline
Clergy	Laity

to the question: "Effective churches are more likely to focus on a particular ministry or target group, rather than on reaching a broad spectrum of people." Approximately one-third of the respondents favor a monolithic strategy while two-thirds opt for serving a broad spectrum of people. On this issue, however, segments of the sample hold somewhat different views. *(See Fig. 5.2)*

Religious diversification

Sometimes Canadians assume that the visible minorities who come to Canada from other countries also embrace the tenets of a world religion other than Christianity. Certainly, there is no question that the shifting immigration patterns also feed the phenomena of religious diversification. However, those who simply assume that a different skin color equals another faith perspective are both misreading the scene and forgetting the impact of over 100 years of missionary activity. Many newcomers are arriving from countries where the percentages of church attenders is higher than in Canada.

Specifically, 26% of visible minority youth who came to Canada as first generation immigrants identify themselves as "Christians." When visible minority youth who are born in Canada are asked to state their religious identity, 44% say they are either Catholic or Protestant.[3]

Not only are a significant number of the new arrivals in Canada increasing the multicultural mix already Christian, the embrace of Christianity in the generations that follow is escalating. Obviously, one of the reasons for the increasing embrace of Christianity by Canada's visible minorities is the vibrancy of the faith expressed by people in their own ethnic communities.

From coast to coast, but particularly in our major cities, local churches from every denomination share their buildings with ethnic-based congregations. Church signs in multiple languages are a common sight across the country. In fact, if it were not for the growth and multiplication of Chinese, Korean, Vietnamese, Portuguese and other ethnic churches, denominational increases would be fewer and the declines would be much more severe than the present pattern.

Still, the shift from mainly white to a more multicultural society is a complicating factor for the church. Visible minorities, particularly in the first generation, feel more comfortable alongside people in congregations who share the same language, customs and worship styles as themselves. As a consequence, they tend to create a sub-culture and isolate themselves from the broader Christian community. In the second generation, children want to be more Canadian and less locked into their ethnic heritages. Conflicts inevitably result.

The established churches with history in a local community also face struggles. Long-standing members who have built and paid for their facilities—now shared—want to be magnanimous, but can end up being patriarchal. Changing neighborhoods and the integration of visible minorities into established congregations disrupts social patterns and challenges power structures. Young people start dating across ethnic lines and parents get nervous.

Just understanding the complexities of another culture is difficult. Accommodating and integrating new cultures into the life of an established church is often traumatic.

Effective churches accept the reality of the changing Canadian context and, whether the implications are straightforward or complex, resolve to make progress.

From male domination toward gender equality

It's a matter of historical record that women have been subordinate to men in Canadian life. Women were not allowed to vote until the early 1920s. Native women were kept out of the voting booths for another 40 years. Generally, women were discouraged from higher education until the 1960s and restricted from entering the male-controlled professions until the 1970s.

In 1970, the federal government's Royal Commission on the Status of Women both concluded and chided, "The equality of opportunity for Canadian men and women is possible, desirable, and ethically necessary." Still today, although a woman is the head of one of the opposition parties in parliament, when the Prime Minister and the ten Premiers gather around conference tables, the only women in the room are ministerial assistants.

In the workforce, women still perform most of the support roles. But that too is changing. Increasing numbers of women serve as middle managers and make decisions in the country's boardrooms. In late 1992, The Church of England voted to allow women priests, and California elected two women senators. In Canada, there is a ground swell of awareness and concern that women be given their full right of access to opportunity and equality.

A recent newspaper headline symbolizes the times: "Not just for the boys: Scouts Canada finally goes co-ed." The sarcastic lead in to the article articulates what is and what will be: "Boy scouts be prepared: Little girls are joining the ranks."[4]

We are not there yet, but in today's world, the social shift is apparent. We are beginning the long trek toward gender equality.

In the church, the role of women has been a debated and often divisive issue. Of the 80 religious denominations tracked by Statistics Canada, just 29 ordain women, 31 said they did not, and 20 said they either had no clear policy or did not have a formal designation for clergy.[5]

Like the culture, the church has been patriarchal, only more so. In church life, women have been the primary "doers of the work." Men have been the board members and the primary "decision makers for the work." Women have been allowed to run the programs of the church and assume informal leadership, but they have often done so without being given the formal titles. In churches where the ordination of women is practised, it is often a hollow victory. The church often relegates women who have gained formal stature to the pulpits of small and marginal churches. Too often, women have been treated as second-class citizens in a realm that proclaims that all human creation is created in the image of God.

Fig. 5.3
Gender Equality
Percentage indicating "very important"

Mainline	Conservative	Academics	Clergy	Laity	Male	Female
49	41	57	44	39	42	41

Fig. 5.4
Gender Equality
Percentage agreeing with the statements

	Mainline	Conservative	Roman Catholic
Women have too little power	60	45	54
Unequal treatment of women is a "very serious concern"	43	30	41

Source: Project Teen Canada '92

In the responses from those participating in effective churches, 4 out of 10 people said it was "very important" for their church to give equal status and leadership opportunities to men and women. Some of the variations of response are expected, others are surprising. Mainline attenders give a higher priority to gender equality than conservative participants, academics exceed both clergy and laity, but male and female responses are essentially the same. Of all the respondents, young academics registered the highest level at 75%. *(See Fig. 5.3)*

Using an even broader survey group, one which included Roman Catholic perspectives, Project Teen Canada's findings regarding gender equality were compatible with the effective-church findings. *(See Fig. 5.4)*

Every organization has both the right and responsibility to self define. The breadth of the Christian church will always leave room for diversity and the issue of women in leadership will forever be subject to some debate. It would be tragic, however, for churches to simply ignore what is happening in the culture regarding gender issues.

Good churches deal with relevant issues. They do not respond to every faddish idea or temporary trend, but they are ready to re-examine entrenched positions when the concerns are substantive. On issues of gender equality, they will face up to tough-minded questions like:
1. Have we subscribed to a patriarchal model for church life? If gender equality is what God desires, what would a genuine partnership model look like?
2. Have some of our theological views on the issue of women in

ministry been framed within cultural biases rather than within an enduring biblical hermeneutic?
3. What effect should the primacy of the gospel's redemptive purpose have on the opportunities given to women for ministry?

Recently a colleague had a spiritually focused discussion with a young professional woman who stated her point of view clearly: "I want no part of a male chauvinist God." She speaks for an increasing number of women in Canadian society.

When women perceive the faith in ways that cause them to reject it, then it is time to revisit our theology and ecclesiology.

From absolutism to relativism

The movement from absolutism to relativism represents another social shift that has major implications for the church in Canada.

All across the country, conspicuously painted on various sizes of farm buildings and grain elevators, are the equivalent of Christian tracts. Using the privilege of their private property, Christians convert their buildings into sign boards which proclaim that "Jesus Saves" or that "Now is the time to repent."

In Southern Ontario along the 401 highway there is a large roofed barn with the message "Only Jesus Saves." The farmer, whether he knows it or not, is sounding a warning about syncretism. Accordingly, "There is one way and only one way to be saved." The farmer is implicitly announcing, "There won't be any relativism in my barnyard."

Historically, the church believed in absolutes. Assuming that truth exists and that it can be known, the church positioned itself to defend the idea that some things are categorically right and other things categorically wrong. Out of this bias, the church has often had a strong role in shaping the moral conscience of the culture.

In contemporary Canada, the majority of Canadians have concluded that what is right and wrong is a matter of personal opinion. Just over 50% of adults and 67% of young people believe that they have the prerogative to cast the final vote on what is morally right or ethically wrong. The shift away from absolute assumptions to relativistic premises is profound. A popular board game entitled *Scruples* illustrates the point. A player is given a hypothetical situation which involves a moral or ethical choice. The other players try to guess what choice that player will make. Fifty years ago, a game like this would have been comparable to asking each other arithmetic questions. The answers would have been clear and they would have been the same for everyone. Today, moral and ethical questions do not have a correct answer. Answers are problematic, individual, and negotiable.

In practice, relativism means that in the realm of beliefs, morals, ethics, values and lifestyle alternatives, personal opinion is in charge. Instead of searching for truth and God's mind for direction, relativism encourages self-direction. Rather than looking externally for convictions about how to live, many people seek internal conclusions. The objective bows to the subjective. When fully operationalized, relativism reduces truth to a matter of personal opinion. As sociologist Harold Fallding has observed, the current attitude states that "What was right for another time and place is not necessarily right for now. What is right for another person is not necessarily right for me. What was right for me last time is not necessarily right for me this time. It all depends."[6]

Reducing truth to a matter of personal opinion does not mean that people who do so are bereft of principles to guide their decision making. Personal opinions can also be made out of strong substance. Christian presuppositions are not the only building materials for erecting value systems and establishing moral convictions. Adherents of other world religions and thoughtful people who make no religious claims have numerous options for making sense out of their lives too.

Still, when relativism rules as the prevailing mood in the culture, rather than speaking truthfully, the best one can do is speak tentatively. Without truth as a shared assumption, when there is debate about what's right or wrong, what's good, better or best, life is lowered to "You have your view, I have my view. You have a right to think as you think. I have the same right. You do your thing and I'll do my thing."

Although many may disagree, it is the conviction of the authors that because relativism denies the existence of truth as an objective reality which we can seek to understand and live by, it is an enemy of the faith.

In 1947, C.S. Lewis reasoned convincingly in support of the "doctrine of objective value." Lewis defended "the belief that certain attitudes are really true and others really false."[7]

Effective churches and their leaders will resist the spirit of the age. Without endorsing a simplistic approach to the complexities of modern life, they will seek the mind of Christ on matters pertaining to both life and death. Rather than being guided by the latest opinion poll, they will link the wisdom from the past with the ambiguities of the present. While neither pompously pronouncing that their truth is the full and final revelation of God's truth, nor apologizing about their faith, effective churches will possess a confidence that resides in their inner spirit.

The Reverend Canon Herbert O'Driscoll's counsel is a wise word for the day: "This then is not a time for endless qualifications about the mysterion of the Christian faith. It is a time for affirmations of faith to be made with all the simplicity and directness of the early church's statement 'Jesus Christ is Lord.'"[8]

From the institutional to the individual

To have healthy social life, we always have to deal with both individual and collective concerns. Whether the organization is the family, school, government, workplace or church, life runs better when there is a balance of power between the person and the group—between the individual and the institution. In today's world, the pull is away from the institutional and toward the individual.

Few would argue that increasing institutional disillusionment is a Canadian fact of life. Both politicians and religious leaders have made major contributions to the prevailing mood. The graffiti that was painted on the wall of a downtown building is an example of the pessimism hurled in the direction of politicians: "Don't vote, it only encourages them."

The long parade of sexual and physical abuse in too many of our religious institutions has not only instilled deep skepticism about the church, it has damaged the credibility of the gospel. Clearly, one of the reasons for movement toward individualism in the culture is simply the loss of confidence in our institutions and those who are responsible for leading them.

There are always reasons for social changes. Pay equity was introduced as a way of recognizing that the work women do is of equal value to the work men perform. Affirmative action was introduced to help women gain access to career opportunities that had long been denied them. These initiatives appear on the social agenda as correctives. They are meant to make right what has gone wrong.

Perhaps we are simply balancing the imbalances of the past. But for a variety of reasons, in the 1990s, "We are stressing individual rights over social rules and hiring legal technicians as our referees. Our team spirit—our social spirit—is frequently non-existent."[9]

A glance back over one's historical shoulder will readily reveal that those in charge of organized religious structures frequently lived with an authoritarian mentality. Too often, the posture was "Don't question—just believe." In other words, leaders were conscious of their power and they flaunted it: "God has spoken. The church is the conduit of what God has said. I am speaking for the church; now do as you are told to do."

When the pendulum leaves one extreme it seldom stops before swinging to another excess. But just as there has been institutional abuse of power in the past, the present pull of life can lead to individual excess and therefore individual abuse. Becoming consumers of institutional services without any sense of responsibility to give something back becomes exploitive. Individual rejection of group authority leads to "law-unto-yourself" decision making. Excessive individualism inevitably leads to living outside the checks and balances of community—and that is dangerous. Expressing caution about living without community, American sociologist, Robert Bellah, rightly reasons that "It is a powerful cultural fiction that we not only can, but must make up our deepest beliefs in the isolation of our private selves."[10]

The temperament of the times means these will be hard times for churches who depend on institutional appeal to bring people into their buildings. The population is not looking for institutional answers. Instead of formally joining organizations, people today put their lives together around informal alliances with their friends and colleagues.

The future will be brighter for churches who retain their commitment to the institution while at the same time affirm the ministry of individuals both to serve in the world and to attract others to attend church with them.

From words to deeds

Too often, people say one thing and do another. Promises turn out to be deliberate deceit. Verbal disclaimers prove to be cover-ups for dark deeds. The past 25 years of high-profile scandals have resulted in a distrust of what people say. Word power has diminished and another social shift has transpired.

A sign posted on the glass door of a bankrupt book store tells the story: "Words Failed Us."

No one made an announcement, but intuitively people know that the past power of words has shifted to the power of deeds. Left on their own, words are weak. And when the good news of Jesus Christ is reduced to words alone, it too is weak.

An incident between a father and his adult daughter makes the point. The father was raised as a Protestant in a time and place in Canada when it was simply assumed that it was impossible to be both a Catholic and a Christian. In his later years, about the time the father had a severe heart attack, he and his wife moved next door to Catholic neighbors. Because the father was physically disabled, he was unable do much manual labor. The Catholic neighbors were not only aware of his predicament, they frequently shoveled snow, cut the grass, shopped for groceries, and helped out whenever a need was evident.

The point of the story was graphically portrayed the day the father made this comment to his daughter: "Our Catholic neighbors sure know how to care for people. I think they must be Christians."

Words are still the vehicles we use to describe the theory of the faith, but it is the practice of faith that creates credibility.

The President of Poland, Lech Walensa, rightly assessed the situation when he recently said: "There is a declining market for words." Good churches will understand that words alone are inadequate. They will deliberately and creatively do the deeds of truth to authenticate the theory of truth.

Religious shifts on the Canadian landscape

Just as the seasons of the year affect the activity patterns of our weeks and months, the social shifts in society at large affect what happens inside our churches. Social shifts have triggered a series of religious shifts.

A couple of Christmas seasons ago, my neighbor, Bruce, synthesized what happened to church attendance in Canada. As I was shoveling the snow off my driveway, Bruce drove by in his mini-van and stopped to talk. After a few pleasantries, he launched into his revelation.

"Don, you will be interested in what happened between my son and me last week. We were in the car together and I was singing along with a Christmas carol that was playing on the radio. Without asking permission, my son reached over and switched the station to his favorite rock music.

"I turned to Jeff and said, 'I was singing. Why did you change the station?' His reply was somewhat understandable. 'I changed it **because** you were singing.'

"We moved into a conversation about music and guess what I discovered?

"My son doesn't even know the words to *Away In a Manger.* He is illiterate about the Christmas carols I know by memory.

"I've thought about the differences. Do you know what happened? When I was young, my parents sent us to Sunday school. They didn't go to church themselves but they made sure we showed up. And let me tell you, we went faithfully until we were about ten years old, and then we quit. What I'm now understanding is that we learned some important things during those early years.

"But the difference between my parents and my generation is that they sent their kids to church and we didn't send ours. You know, I think our kids lost something when we didn't send them."

Bruce and I talked about the implications.

If we could step back one earlier generation and catch a glimpse of Bruce's parents, we would discover that in the majority of families, the grandparents of today's young people both went to church and took their children with them.

Here's what happened in the generational sequence for the majority of Canadians:

Until the 1960s, the majority of parents both attended church and took their children with them.

When the children who were taken to church became parents, they sent their children to Sunday school, but did not attend church themselves.

In the sequence that led to decline for the church, when those who were just sent to Sunday school became parents, they neither sent their children nor attended themselves.

The shift away from regular involvement in church life over the past three generations is the primary reason why Sunday school is no longer a means of outreach into the community and why it only provides Christian education for the children of families who attend on a regular basis.

There are still other religious shifts that have had profound implications for the life of the church in Canadian society.

From the power of the pulpit to the influence of television

I remember the first time I saw Elvis Presley sing and shake on television. It was on *The Ed Sullivan Show* on a Sunday night. For someone like myself, growing up in a conservative religious home in Southern Alberta, that created two problems. In my family, television was off limits on Sunday. We were expected to go to the Sunday evening service. Without spelling out the details and contrary to my parent's preferences, I remember watching Elvis live up to his reputation.

During the 1950s and 1960s, *The Ed Sullivan Show* did more than just lower Sunday night church attendance. The launch of television served as a notice that the competition for people's time would intensify. And although some preachers decried the evils of "the box," no one articulated the shift from the power of the pulpit to the cultural influence of television.

Today, if we were to equate the intake of television to alcohol, most Canadians would be candidates for "tele-holics anonymous." The pervasiveness of television is dramatized by both the immediate access Canadians have to the medium and the amount of time they spend watching it.

In 1982, 85% of Canadian homes had one color television and 12% had two. By 1992, 98% of Canadian homes had one color set while 43% had at least two.[11] When it comes to viewing, Statistics Canada reports that, in 1990, Canadians watched an average of 23 hours per week.[12] Although younger people watched less than older people, the proportion of young people who watch television is on the increase. One conclusion seems clear. Watching television has become the national pastime.

The debate about television often centers around whether or not it reflects culture, or more importantly, shapes culture. Surely, given the enormous intake of television in Canada, it does both.

Television writers, producers and directors are tuned in to the prevailing cultural frequencies and know how to connect with what exists. The creators of popular programs are also often on the leading edge of creativity and innovation. They nudge life beyond the present tense.

There is no feasible way to firmly document the total impact of television on Canadian culture. Whether you focus on the general public's perceptions of current social problems or on the increasing levels of violence in society, whether you assess people's unrelenting desire for material prosperity or listen to what people talk about during coffee break—there is a correlation between what television transmits and what people embrace.

In other ways, television often acts as a social tranquillizer. The medium appeals to the glamorous and unreal and in so doing dulls the intellect. When the minds of the viewing public are only half awake, the onslaught of visual images and the repetition of both implicit and explicit messages eventually creates a fictional reality.

In the fall of 1992, an 11-year-old Quebec girl made national headlines when she personally delivered a petition with over two million signatures to Prime Minister Brian Mulroney. The petition protested violence on television. While researchers are still not completely convinced that watching violence on television breeds violent behavior, an 11-year-old girl reminds us that life, in its immediacy, should not always wait for conclusive data.

The preceding comments sound judgmental and negative. But rest assured, as authors, we also watch television and would argue that, just as books are not evil, neither is television evil. The point is that television is profoundly influential, potent and culturally powerful.

Journalist Peter Trueman recently took a shot at Canadian churches by contrasting them with the virtues of the programming on Vision TV. Asking the question, "Where do young people learn about morality in ordinary human relationships these days?" Trueman said, "Churches, which once put young and old alike through spiritual calisthenics that were both personal and rigorous, now seem more concerned with the application of religious principles to politics and economics." By contrast, he contended that on programs like Callwood's *National Treasures*, Vision deals with "ethics, values, and spirituality in a way that makes its programming both refreshing and vital."[13]

Effective churches will compute the implications of the power of television. Worship leaders will perceive that people who watch carefully choreographed sketches during the week will have similar expectations when they worship on Sunday. Preachers will excel at painting visual pictures by telling stories. Unless worship styles in a particular church contravene the norm, there will be a time consciousness that will link the length of sermons to a half-hour sitcom with time out for commercials.

From declining participation to occasional consumption

The displacement of the pulpit by the pervasiveness of television reminds us that life is dynamic. Life implies movement. Dead things are static and stationary. Society itself is an elaborate interaction of many living things. As a living entity, the Christian church in Canada has been profoundly impacted by the multidimensional facets of societal life around it. In particular, there have been three departures away from the church that have left it feeling frail.

Departure one

In the 1940s and 1950s and into the 1960s, the majority of parents both went to church and took their children with them. These families not only identified themselves as either Protestant or Catholic, but also went to worship on a regular basis. During that time the gravitational

Fig. 5.5
Religious Affiliation, Experience and Expectation
Percentage agreeing with statements

	Adults	Youth 1984	1992
Identity with a group	90	85	79
View self as committed	26	39	24
Receive high level enjoyment	32	24	15
Religion will gain influence	19	19	16

Source: Project Can90 and Project Teen Canada 1992

pull of the culture was toward the church. In many senses, Canada was a churched culture.

But along the way, disenchantment with the importance of the church began to surface. And just as a stone thrown into a pool of water causes ripples to move outwards, although people still said they were "Protestants" or "Catholics," they started distancing themselves from the church by attending less. Increasing disenchantment with the church triggered the first departure:

From affiliation with majority participation
to
Affiliation with declining participation
(See Fig. 5.5)

Departure two

As people began to think and feel that life would go on without regular involvement in formal religious life, attendance levels tumbled. In other words, disenchantment led to disengagement. Many parents, who had gone to church with their own parents, still sent their children to Sunday school, though they themselves no longer attended. Although the trend in society was to attend less, that in no way equalled a complete severing of ties with church structures.

Even today, approximately 85% of Canadian adults continue to hold on to their religious identities. They identify denominational affiliations on Statistics Canada forms, they plan to seek out the church during the sacred moments of life: birth, marriage and death. But regard-

Fig. 5.6
Attendance Frequency
In percent

	1985	1986	1987	1988	1990	1991
At least once a week	27	27	27	26	24	23
At least once a month	15	15	14	12	12	11

Source: Statistics Canada

less, the step from disenchantment to disengagement signalled a second momentous departure:

From affiliation with declining participation
to
Declining participation with occasional consumption
(See Fig. 5.6)

Although today's teenagers are beginning to surrender their religious identification, presently at 79%, most young people still intend to use the services of the church selectively. When asked if they anticipate turning to religious groups for ceremonies relating to birth, 80% say "yes." In the case of weddings, the number increases to 85%, and when future planning relates to funerals, the increase steps to 90%.[14]

Consistent with the adult pattern, Canadian young people plan to ask the church to turn "hatching, matching and dispatching" into moments of sacredness. It will take at least until the next generation before the pattern will drop off drastically.

Reginald Bibby's thesis in *Fragmented Gods* still stands—at least for those who have previously been referred to in this book as cultural Christians:

Canadians give little indication of abandoning their ties with the established groups. Nonetheless, things have changed. As the century draws to a close, people in greater and greater numbers are drawing upon religion as consumers... Canadians appear to be moving away from Christianity or other

Fig. 5.7
Canadians Reporting No Religion
In percent

1985	1986	1988	1989	1990	1991
10	10	11	13	12	16

Source: Statistics Canada, General Social Service Survey

religions as meaning systems addressing all of life. They are opting for Judeo-Christian fragments... Canadians are into "religion a la carte"... The gods of old have been neither abandoned nor replaced. Rather, they have been broken into pieces and offered to religious consumers in piecemeal form.[15]

When the majority in a culture retain their religious identity while only a minority attend places of worship with any regularity, religious institutions and the clergy get trapped.

On the one hand, if they deny the religious consumer's request for the rites of passage, they slam the church door in the faces of the very people they would like to involve. On the other hand, if they respond to the request and offer the same ceremony that is extended to those who participate regularly and demonstrate genuine faith commitment, they risk compromising the service and trivializing the sacred.

Because cultural/religious identities are particularly high and attendance levels are especially low for both Catholics and mainline Protestants, the dilemmas are often burdensome for those faith communities. In the case of birth-related ceremonies and marriage requests, many churches require formal preparatory sessions to reinforce the spiritual significance of the ceremony. These required sessions can lead to recurring contact and decisions of spiritual reaffirmation.

Departure three

Declining attendance and occasional consumption may not be the biggest problem facing the present-day church. The greying of congregations along with the escalating absenteeism of young people is a more consequential long-term concern. According to a 1992 Gallup survey, as many as 48% of Canadians 65 years of age and older "attended a church, synagogue or other place of worship in the past week."[16] Project Teen

Fig. 5.8
Attendance Frequency by Age
In percent

	1985	1986	1987	1988	1990
15–24	19	19	20	18	15
25–44	22	20	21	20	18
45–64	36	36	36	34	32
65 and older	44	45	44	40	42

Source: Statistics Canada

Canada's results show that once young people reach their senior teens and early 20s, only 13% actively involve themselves in organized religion. Any organization that is replacing an exit level of 48% with an intake of 13% is facing an unavoidable crisis.

The greying of the older generation and the abdication of the younger generation combine to usher in the third departure:

From sustained church participation of the older generation
to
The abdication of the church by the younger generation.
(See Fig. 5.8)

Effective churches will neither be caught off guard by what is happening around them nor be surprised by the impact of the broader picture. They will decide how they want to respond to the cultural demand for the sacred services linked to the "rites of passage." They will honestly assess how much of their resources are being invested in ministry to young people. Rather than simply waiting for youth to drop out of church in their teens and then return when they have children of their own, they will give priority to helping young people personalize their faith with God and to keeping them linked with the church.

From the majority to a minority

In Canada, there are no traffic jams on Sunday morning. Consequently, for those who still venture out to worship on a regular basis, there is a feeling of being shoved to the sidelines of society. There is an increasing awareness that although religious traffic used to travel on the Trans-Canada highway, it has been pushed back to the secondary roads.

It didn't used to be that way. Church leaders knew what it was to possess cultural power. They held center stage. In communities from coast to coast, ministers were esteemed. They were the best-educated and acknowledged authorities on matters of both life and death. Politicians knew they had to take the clergy seriously, and did.

Today, confidence in the clergy has declined. For many Canadians, the church as an institution is like an illuminated tombstone. No one made a formal announcement, but in the minds of many the church has outlived its usefulness. The majority of Canadians sense that religion is out of date and that the institutional church is out of touch. Organized religion has become a sunset industry.

A Catholic research report endorsed by the Assembly of Quebec Bishops went so far as to link church participation with "fear in relating to the outside" world. "The majority of Catholics feel helpless when meeting people who have drifted away from the church, members of other religions or sects, or unbelievers. They dare not express their faith."[17] What Catholics feel, Protestants also feel. Increasingly, a sense of cultural and psychological intimidation goes hand-in-hand with overtly claiming a Christian identity.

A middle-aged mother of three articulated what many people often feel: "It's hard to hang on to your faith. In a world like ours it's easy to let go."

Still, memories of former glory remain. There is a nostalgia for what used to be. Beyond sentiment, there is regret that the Lord's Prayer is no longer recited in the country's public schools, that religion has been all but pushed out of the school curriculum, and that indifference toward the faith is so natural for so many. It is difficult being a member of the minority when you are used to carrying the majority. Missiologist Lesslie Newbigin is insightful yet empathetic when observing, "Nostalgia for Christendom is very understandable, but it is futile."[18]

Acknowledging the decline in attendance, the aging of its members, the absence of young people, the decrease in the number of priests, the reduced public influence and its shortage of money, the Quebec Catholic conclusions are sobering, but they are also hopeful: "Many members are conscious of the urgency to do something drastic. They now realize clearly that by continuing on their current course, communities are simply heading for gradual extinction. Therefore, they are prepared to try something new and to take risks. This consciousness is an asset to be emphasized."[19]

Good churches will recognize the opportunities inherent in the challenging circumstances of the present. Rather than lamenting a lost past, they will deal with how to live as members of a minority group when the dominant culture lives in other ways. They will bravely and fearfully take risks and try what has not been attempted before. Instead of striving to reclaim what used to be, they will give expression to the creativity of God and work to translate what is into what can be.

From Christian consensus to secular pluralism

When the majority in a society shift from a point of previous consensus, they do not shift from something to nothing. Rather, they shift from something to something else. Eventually a new majority emerges to establish a consensus affirming a different point of view. In the Canadian context, the shift has been from a Christian consensus to a consensus around the tenets of secular pluralism.

Secular pluralism rests on two separate assumptions. Secularism proposes a view of life without need for God. In Canada, that doesn't mean that when asked, Canadians deny that God exists. Rather, it means that the majority of Canadians construct their daily lives without any awareness of God's existence. They see no need for God's active role in their lives. In practice, rather than being active atheists, most Canadians are passive theists. The result is a functional secularism.

Pluralism is different from secularism. In speeches and print, Canada is frequently labelled as a "pluralistic society." Simply stated, pluralism is based on the premise that there must be room for many views of life. Canada's social structures have been built to accommodate a diversity of creeds and cultures. In the realm of beliefs, pluralism demands a multiplicity of belief ultimates--one as valid as the other. Life cannot be reduced to one set of truths. Instead, diversity is beautiful. Accordingly, many ways of thinking, believing and behaving are given equal status. Tolerance parades as the golden rule. The only view that is intolerable is the view that states there is only "one way."

Making the cultural shift from a Christian consensus to secular pluralism continues to be stressful for many committed Christians. When the church was center stage in the culture, life was easier for the faithful. In an article which appeared in the *Catholic New Times*, Albert Beaudry stated, "It is difficult to leave the cocoon of Christendom to become an effective minority in a pluralistic milieu."[20]

Accepting increasing diversity has been confusing for many of God's people. Seeing the decline of the influence of the church has been disappointing. Realizing that Christ's ways have lost their unique status and are now just one alternative among many other alternatives has been disconcerting. And establishing the new rules and regulations for how a healthy pluralism should work in our society has been elusive.

Addressing a Jewish-Christian-Muslim consultation in the United States, George Gallup Jr. identified an assumption that many people hold as they attempt to deal with the increasing diversity around them. Mistaken or not, many people "believe that a pluralistic society requires us to be silent about our own religious convictions."[21] This tendency toward silence is accentuated in Canada because of our preference to privatize our faith convictions.

As Christians in Canada, we will make progress as we give permission to people to believe as they choose to believe while at the same time taking permission to believe what we believe. Canadians will step toward maturity as we find greater measures of freedom to be open with each other and to discuss what and why our beliefs and practices are important to us.

A lay leader from an Anglican church in Ontario offers a healthy and balanced perspective: "A church needs a stance with which it is comfortable and of which it is convinced, without being defensive, closed, dogmatic."

In a complimentary manner, a lay participant in a United church from British Columbia states: "Very important to me is a strong, basic doctrine that does not deny the validity of other faiths and the opportunity to discuss faith and belief systems openly."

"Permission giving" and open discussion will move us forward, but they will not be a panacea. Because designing life without God is a contradiction for the people of God, effective churches will perceive the unrelenting secularization of Canadian life as an enemy of the faith. Secularism cannot be blessed in the church or in the culture.

On the matter of pluralism, however, churches in touch with the times will encourage a different attitude. Because pluralism makes room for the people of God to live alongside those who hold other views, it is a friend of the faith. Good churches will help their people figure out how to live with the increasing diversity in society without losing their integrity and without hiding their faith.

From Christian concrete to cultural gravel

Canada of the past was poured into Judeo-Christian concrete. In the realm of values, morals, ethics, and assumptions about a wide range of beliefs, the tenets of Christianity established the norms. Those norms were applicable to both those who lived with a religious commitment and to others in the culture who had arrived at different conclusions about life.

Consequently, the cultural gravitational pull was toward the church and God's ways. Belief in God's existence and the divinity of Jesus were weighty matters. Honesty was an uncontested virtue. Forgiveness was deemed a desirable practice and generosity was a quality to be applauded.

Obviously, people who comprise the Canada of today have not abandoned all the belief and value assumptions of the past. But a closer examination reveals that some of the values that served society so well in the past are being eroded. Specifically, the cherished values of honesty, forgiveness and generosity are in decline. In particular, research data clearly concludes that those who worship regularly in Canada's churches are retaining the values of honesty, forgiveness and generosity at a higher level than those who do not attend.[22]

What does this trend say about our future? What are the implications for those who affirm religious faith and how they view those who do not?

Jesus' parable about the wise and foolish builders (Matthew 7:24–27) gives direction. At the end of the Sermon on the Mount Jesus reminds his hearers that people who put his words into practice are wise, while those who do not are foolish. In the analogy, the wise build their houses on rock and the foolish build their houses on sand.

Interpreting the parable, preachers and Sunday school teachers have repeatedly informed their listeners that wise people build their lives on the rock of Christ and the truth of his teachings. Foolish people however, build their lives on the sand of the world's ways of thinking and living.

The rock and sand images are powerful. They are meant to convey the conclusion that building one's life on Christ makes a positive difference. But the images may also distort how followers of Jesus view those who do not follow Christ. Is it not the case that committed Christians often see themselves as stronger and more virtuous than those who believe other things? Comparing sand to rock is like comparing mass produced costume jewelry to individually designed 24-carat creations.

Obviously, one does not have to go to church or be Christian to live virtuously. People who have little or no regard for God are not totally bad any more than people who are deeply committed to Christ and his ways are totally good. But sand is not rock and taking Jesus and his teachings seriously does make a difference.

However, applying the sand imagery to people in Canada who have little or no regard for Christ and his teachings is derogatory. Passing Jesus' parable through a Canadian cultural grid can provide a more accurate image for describing people outside of God's family. Is it not so that people who figure what to believe and how to behave without reference to God usually construct their lives out of cultural gravel? In the main, they piece their lives together using many of the fragments of our Judeo-Christian heritage. Our religious legacy is still so pervasive that even people who live with distance between themselves and God are using broken rock to make sense of who they are and how they live.

While having a wholesome understanding of those who construct their lives out of cultural gravel in Canadian society, people in effective churches will also have a clear sense of who they are in Christ. Clinging to the grace of God in their lives, and fully aware of the pieces of rock they still have to cement together, they will know they have something precious to offer to today's broken world.

A Christian nation?

In the late 1980s, the rumor mill generated a report that the United Nations had taken Canada off the list of Christian countries. A little detective work produced two clear conclusions. The United Nations is not in the business of making religious decrees. And evangelists' newsletters should be scrutinized for accuracy. The rumor was traced to a national newsletter from a prominent Canadian evangelist.

Still, the question remains: Should Canada be described as a Christian nation? A national referendum would probably evoke a "yes" vote, but very little would change. In theory, the majority of Canadians do identify themselves as either Catholic or Protestant. But in practice, only a minority of Canadians attend church regularly or apply "their faith" to their daily living.

Some would contend that if the test for determining whether or not Canada is a Christian nation depends on the degree to which people live their faith, then the situation today is what it has always been: "Canada has never really been a Christian nation." They would argue that "just going to church" doesn't make anyone genuinely Christian. That could well be the case, but there is another side to the story.

When the majority of a society goes to church, the consequences for the whole culture are enormous. The gravitational pull of the culture is toward what God had in mind for the shape of creation. A lot of right ways of thinking and behaving find their way into the flow of life.

It follows that when only a small minority come under the influence of God's ways, the pull of the culture is away from what God had in mind for creation. With the waning of a churched culture, more and more rock is being broken into gravel and more and more gravel is disintegrating into sand. In contemporary Canada, effective churches will help their people be like cement.

Canadian Religion Is Not American

Chapter Six

All the players knelt at center court. The previous day Magic Johnson had gone public with the shocking revelation that he was HIV positive. Pat Riley, coach of the New York Knicks, led the athletes and the throng of basketball fans in praying the Lord's Prayer for their friend and idol. In true American style, a national sports hero was held up to the God of the nation before the night's game at Madison Square Gardens.

It was an American moment.

Is a comparative Canadian scenario possible? Would hockey players drop to their knees to pray for a teammate at center ice prior to a game at Maple Leaf Gardens? Could any circumstances prompt the fans in the Montreal Forum to be led in prayer for a Canadian sports star? Can we imagine Canadians uttering the name of "Jesus Christ" as anything other than an expletive? Can we imagine fans looking out at the blue line using his name reverently in prayer in the Calgary Saddle Dome or the Vancouver Pacific Coliseum?

Canadians and Americans can be united on many issues. But when it comes to religion, what makes for effective churches in either country is often as different as each nation's position on universal health care.

Especially in the realm of religion, Canadians are private people. We don't wear our religiosity on our sleeves. From the point of view of the majority, only religious zealots put bumper stickers on their cars to draw attention to their spiritual commitments.

Let us be clear. The intent of this chapter is not to generate anti-American sentiment. Many Americans are more than just good neighbors, they are members of God's extended family. The flow of people across the border means that there are many Canadians serving in the United States, and significant numbers of Americans ministering in Canada.

Just as it would be ludicrous to resist embracing the benefits of a medical technological breakthrough first discovered in the United States, so it would be absurd to deny the benefits of adapting ministry effectiveness from the United States that would benefit the church in Canada. Still, the reality remains that, in the religious realm, Canada is not the United States. We must pursue the "Canadian way" of doing the work of God—a way that best connects with our culture.

Religion and political influence in the United States

Pat Robertson, for example, is an American original who has no counterpart in Canada. He's a national political force with fundamentalist Christian roots. He and his troops, carrying the stars and stripes in one hand and a Bible in the other, paraded with prominence at the 1992 Republican convention. They will try again in 1996. According to Robertson, he wants to see "a working majority of the Republican Party in the hands of pro-family Christians by 1996."[1]

Pat Robertson may not represent mainstream America, but he can take center stage at mainstream political events. And while there are many merits to a pro-family agenda, Robertson defines his vision of the family more narrowly than many Americans and the majority of Canadians. In September 1992, he outlined his views against the Equal Rights Amendment in the United States. About the ERA and feminism in general, he wrote, "It is a socialist, anti-family political movement that encourages women to leave their husbands, kill their children, practice witchcraft, destroy capitalism and become lesbians."[2]

The tone of the letter speaks for itself. In unique American-fundamentalist fashion, infanticide and witchcraft are heaped in with the horrors of anti-capitalism. Such unabashed mud-slinging on an issue of national debate by a leading member of the clergy (and one with clearly defined political aspirations) makes Pat Robertson an American original.

Religion and political influence in Canada

Canada also has people as dogmatic about their faith as Pat Robertson. They have often added to our national debate and participated in politics. But seldom has such overt fundamentalism captured center stage.

In Canada's history, J.S. Woodsworth, with his Methodist message of social reform, was a key figure among our nation's Christian opinion leaders. When Woodsworth stood with the workers in the 1919 Winnipeg general strike, he signaled that God was not necessarily on the side of the wealthy and influential. Woodsworth guided future generations of social activists with his mixture of evangelicalism and compassionate social outreach.

William Aberhart of the Social Credit party in Alberta, and Tommy Douglas of the Cooperative Commonwealth Federation, were also politicians of Christian conviction. They drew inspiration for their separate political views from the social gospel movement espoused by the likes of Woodsworth earlier in the century.

While personally identifying with the Christian faith, William Aberhart's protege, Ernest Manning, the Premier of Alberta for decades, and his son Preston, the current leader of the national Reform Party, have not made their Christian faith a central plank in their political platforms. Their faith may be a motivating principle behind their actions, but to call for a distinctly Christian coalition to take over Parliament Hill would leave them on the fringes of Canadian politics.

Brian Stiller, head of the Evangelical Fellowship of Canada, represents a large coalition of evangelical Protestants in Canada. He takes the concerns of his constituency to politicians of all three major political parties and has earned entrance to the offices across Parliament Hill. Stiller wryly observes, "A political party with a narrow theological base just won't work here. One religion can no longer build a social convention."[3]

Different social conventions

Building that social convention is what separates most Canadians and Americans on the issues surrounding faith communities and their effectiveness in our two countries. Like the differences between each nation's stand on social programs and universal medicare, effective churches reflect their country's cultural realities.

Canadian churches have, by and large, been more ecumenically minded. Canadian geography and demographics played a significant role in this development. James Sauer explains:

> Most pastors in any major denomination in the United States will find at least one other pastor of the same denomination within a few miles. Ecumenism is an option. In Canada, ecumenism is often a necessity. Especially in the north and west, the only other pastors within 100 miles or more may well belong to different denominations.[4]

More significantly perhaps, Canadians have been more tolerant of religious pluralism primarily because we have always been a religiously

pluralistic nation. Mark A. Noll sums up this difference in *A History of Christianity in the United States and Canada*:
> Compared to Christianity in the States, Christianity in Canada was less fragmented, more culturally conservative, more closely tied to Europe, more respectful of tradition, more ecumenical, and less prone to separate evangelical theology from social outreach. But the greatest difference remains the first difference: Canada was not so much a Christian nation as two Christian nations, Catholic and Protestant.[5]

Church/state alliances in Canada

North America, as settled by Europeans, has a robust Christian heritage that impacts both Canada and the United States to this day. Priests and bishops broke bush and guided colonists, fur traders and adventurers through the wilderness in what was to become Quebec. Puritans established settlements along the Atlantic seaboard and guided Protestant pilgrims to a new land and a new society. During the 17th and 18th century, "Roman Catholic Quebec and Puritan Massachusetts were the most visible regions on the Christian map in North America..."[6]

The inhabitants of Quebec City were loyal to the Catholic Church and brought the established church to the new world as their cultural centerpiece. After the British and French skirmished on the Plains of Abraham and England secured the territories of New France, the victorious English did not want to create a vacuum by removing that Catholic centerpiece. Consequently, the Quebec Act of 1774 established the authority of the Roman Catholic Church in French Canada. For some time, French Canadian Catholics enjoyed the unique distinction of being the only Catholic officials allowed in the administration of the entire British Empire.

Although Catholic Canada was well established by the time American patriots took on the mighty British empire in the War of Independence in the 1770s, it wasn't until after the American Revolution that Canadian Protestant settlement really took form.[7] The War of Independence in the United States was fought in the churches as well as in the countryside. Some churches preached revolution, some preached loyalty. The conflict drove a wedge between patriots committed to American independence and congregations loyal to King George.

Many of these "Loyalists" fled to Canada as the Revolution swept throughout the American colonies. Those who came helped ensure that Canadian Protestantism would remain closer to European patterns. The

Church of England developed the faith of most English-speaking worshipers in the British colonies that eventually would be united in Canadian Confederation.

Throughout Canada the church did more than just mediate between God and the new settlers. Both the Roman Catholic Church and the Church of England received overt government support, and in turn gave strong support to the established political and social order. By the time of Confederation in 1867, the Anglicans shared their influence with the Presbyterian and Methodist Churches. These established churches consolidated national unity in Canada as much as any social force of the day.[8]

The Canadian religious ethos was based on a church-state relationship that would legitimize the sovereignty of the state and the privileges of the church. "Both the Church of England and the Roman Catholic Church, in return for government support, endorsed the established political and social orders up to the post-World War II era."[9]

As a counter-revolutionary society, Canadians took security in a relatively established church. Both linguistic groups sought to preserve values and cultures by reacting against liberal revolutions and supporting a strong role for both the church and the state. As author Margaret Atwood has said, "Canada must be the only country in the world where a policeman [the Mountie] is used as a national symbol."[10]

The image of the Mountie symbolizes a society that endows national institutions with the power to bestow privilege, dispense justice, and administer "peace, order and good government." Consistent with this institutional orientation, Canadians trusted kings and queens and bishops for direction and guidance. We envisioned life less competitively and more in terms of community. Mark Noll states that, after the Revolution, British Loyalists created a uniquely Canadian faith which balanced "…an American openness to innovation, optimism and personal liberty with a British commitment to stability and tradition."[11]

American separation of church and state

In contrast to their northern neighbors, Americans did not trust the power of the state. National institutions protected the rights of the individual so that he or she could enjoy, "life, liberty and the pursuit of happiness." Kings, queens and bishops stood in the way of individual freedom, so they were not institutionalized.

The Baptist insistence on congregational autonomy is a religious institutional expression of the American way. It is an anathema for someone steeped in Baptist polity to consider submitting to an ecclesiastical hierarchy which collectively dictates the spiritual life of the faith community. Each Baptist congregation will defend and define what is right for its members, and each individual member will have the right to vote on matters which impact the spiritual lives of those who have voluntarily joined a faith community.

This suspicion and avoidance of central or hierarchical authority begins with the pilgrims landing on Plymouth Rock. The pilgrims came seeking religious freedom. They rejected the church structures of Europe. American puritanism developed from a small persecuted sect which underscored self-reliance and the responsibility of the individual. They came to North America to create a new promised land under God, not to settle a wilderness for the crown.

From the beginning of American history, personal faith wasn't the business of the state, but a sacred matter between the individual American and God. In 1791 the relatively new United States Congress institutionalized the separation of church and state by passing the First Amendment with its provision that, "Congress shall make no law respecting the establishment of religion, or prohibit the free exercise thereof."[12]

From today's perspective, the First Amendment may seem a bit antiquated; religion is very much a political tool in the United States. But for a religiously motivated public celebrating the rights of the individual in the post-Revolutionary United States, the pursuit of truth was an individual's prerogative, guaranteed by the state. God and the average American could build a new society with all the freedom and entrepreneurial spirit the American frontier afforded them. The distinctive indigenous religions that sprang up from this frontier—Mormonism, Christian Science, Seventh Day Adventists, Jehovah's Witnesses—testify to the American goal of freedom of religion.

Summary differences

Harry H. Hiller summarizes the difference of religion in the founding of the two North American nations in this way:

> While the American continent has been a breeding ground for religious experimentation and innovation, the Canadian frontier was less so than the American frontier because of the presence of institutional controls in which alliances between state and established religious institutions were deliberately sought to discourage religious experimentation.[13]

This heritage has had an impact upon the day-to-day life of both nations.

Today's religious landscape

While the basic cultural terrain upon which faith communities are built north and south of the 49th Parallel remains, today, the religious landscape has changed in both countries.

The differences between church attendance in Canada and the United States state the story. In Canada, including Protestants and Catholics, approximately 25% participate regularly in organized church life. In the United States, the level is close to 40%. Particularly alarming for the institutional church is that far more young people are involved in the United States than in Canada. In the case of our southern neighbors, approximately 40% of those in their late teens and early 20s are regularly involved in formal church life. In Canada, the level is only about 15%. We are not the same.

Canadian secular society

In Canada, as individuals have become more and more urban and modern, religion and faith have become fragments of life rather than cornerstones of existence. While Canadians continue to profess a belief in God and continue to refer to themselves as Catholics, Anglicans, Presbyterians or whatever, the majority in society only use the services of religious institutions for the rites of passage: baptism, marriage, and burial.

For Canadians, there is no moralistic universal drive imbedded in our national identity to move us through the next century. Canada has no unifying "civil religion." The dominant strain of "Canadianism" may evoke some echoes of our faithful forefathers in terms of tolerance, compassion and that much trumpeted, if elusive, Canadian virtue of compromise. But on the whole, Canada is a much more secular society than the United States. Simply stated, God is not central to our national social and political dialogue. And, perhaps consequently, neither is God a major part of our personal dialogue.

Even when going to church was expected and respected in Canada, faith was more institutional and probably less personal than for our American neighbors. In the main, you were part of a diocese or a parish. You may have been a good Catholic or a bad Catholic, a good Anglican or a bad Anglican, but you looked to the institutions and formalized religious systems to help define and guide your faith.

Canadian church attendance patterns

That is not to say Canadian Christians were religiously indifferent or inactive. Donald Bloesch refers to the evangelical renaissance when he describes the religious boom which occurred throughout North America between 1952 and 1965. During this period, evangelical groups increased their membership by 500–700%; mainline Protestants and Roman Catholics increased by 75–90%.[14]

Although the pace of the numerical growth slowed down through the 1980s, groups like the Alliance Church, Pentecostals, and Fellowship Baptists showed impressive gains. However, by the end of the decade, these gains had leveled off too. During the same period of time, mainline Protestant denominations (Anglican, Lutheran, Presbyterian and United) encountered harder times in both countries and have not kept up with national population growth.

Currently, while mainline denominations have been experiencing both membership and attendance declines, most conservative Protestant denominations have either been growing modestly or at least maintaining past levels of participation. According to Statistics Canada and others,[15] approximately 30% of Canadians identify with mainline Protestant denominations, while only 7 or 8% identify with conservative Protestant denominations. However, in terms of Sunday participation, the combined attendance at conservative-evangelical churches exceeds the attendance at Canada's mainline churches:

| Mainline | 810,000 |
| Conservative | 1,016,000[16] |

Although conservative church growth and attendance statistics may seem impressive, sociologist Reginald Bibby counsels caution in response to denominations claiming impressive gains in today's secular culture. Bibby's studies suggest that 70% of new congregants are church circulators who have decided to move from one evangelical community to another.[17] *(See Fig. 6.1 and Fig. 6.2)*

The 761 respondents in our sample support the conclusions of Bibby's study. They, too, attest to high instances of "switching." When only 6% of those surveyed indicate that they were not active in church life during their childhood years, it becomes apparent that religious conversions out of the world and into the church are limited to a few.

As we have noted, the historical imperative of the church in Canada has diminished as the cultural consensus to attend church has eroded. People no longer have the social or the cultural need to leave their homes and attend church on Sunday morning.

Mapping the Canadian Context

Fig. 6.1
Membership in Thousands, 1931–1985

	1931	1941	1951	1961	1971	1981	1985
Total	1778	1886	2408	2966	2791	2458	2417
United Church	671	717	834	1037	1017	900	881
Anglican	794	861	1096	1358	1109	922	856
Baptist	132	134	135	138	132	128	130
Pentecostal	*	*	45	60	150	125	179
Lutheran	*	*	121	172	200	218	208
Presbyterian	181	174	177	201	183	165	163

* Not available
Source: Reginald Bibby, *Fragmented Gods*, used by permission.

Fig. 6.2
Membership as Percentages of Total Population 1931–1985

	1931	1941	1951	1961	1971	1981	1985
Total	17.2	16.4	17.3	16.3	12.9	10.1	9.5
United Church	6.5	6.2	6.0	5.7	4.7	3.7	3.5
Anglican	7.7	7.5	7.8	7.5	5.1	3.8	3.4
Baptist	1.3	1.2	1.0	0.8	0.6	0.5	0.5
Pentecostal	*	*	0.3	0.3	0.7	0.5	0.7
Lutheran	*	*	0.9	0.9	0.9	0.9	0.8
Presbyterian	1.7	1.5	1.3	1.1	0.9	0.7	0.6

* Not available
Source: Reginald Bibby, *Fragmented Gods*, used by permission.

Comparing apples to oranges

Still, many Canadian pastors and church leaders, particularly those in the more conservative-evangelical community, continue to look south for support, publishing facilities, speakers and large congregations which provide inspiring models of ministry.[18] Take a walk through your local Christian book store. It is cross-border shopping without having to cross the border. Almost all the books, tapes and videos are published or produced in the United States. They are written by Americans about American churches.

This creates a problem for Canadian churches because Americans have a different church mentality. Take the emphasis on numerical growth. The book, *10 of Today's Most Innovative Churches* promises to help apply their ideas to your congregation. But the average worship attendance size of these ten innovative churches is over 6000! In Canada, there is not one Protestant church in the entire country that actively involves even half that number of people. How can principles derived from enormous American churches apply to this county's congregations? Two-thirds of all Canadian churches have 125 or less people in attendance on Sunday morning. And of these churches, over half have fewer than 75 people in attendance. Reading books about American mega-churches may provide some inspiration, but the innovations they speak of are based on congregational models that simply do not exist in Canada. It's a bit like comparing apples to oranges.

If you are a religious pedestrian in the United States, you may very well attend one of these mega-churches. Although the Roman Catholic Church, benefiting in part by a growing Hispanic population, has become the largest denomination in this once almost exclusively Protestant nation, Protestantism still attracts a significant percentage of the church traffic in the United States. Specifically, 38% of Americans hold a literal fundamentalist view of the Bible and 22% can be grouped as evangelicals. The Baptist churches attract most of the Protestant pedestrians, as one-fifth of all Americans adhere to a Baptist church.[19] The combination of the more evangelical heritage in the United States and the current strength of American evangelicals gives Americans a more universally acceptable national religious creed. *(See Fig. 6.3)*

The Puritan vision of a free Christian nation that grew into the religious rights enshrined in the Constitution of the United States is a binding factor for Americans. Civil religion recognizes and responds to this heritage. Americans—Catholic or Protestant—feel that they have a moral fiber built into their nationhood that draws much of its strength from their Puritan ancestors.

Mapping the Canadian Context

Fig. 6.3
United States Denominational Size, 1940–1988
(All denominational figures given in thousands)

	1940	1960	1980	1988	% change 1940-1988	% change 1980-1988
U.S. Population (in millions)	132	178	227	246	+86	+8
Roman Catholics and Southern Baptists						
Roman Catholics	21284	42105	50450	54919	+158	+9
Southern Baptists	4949	9732	13600	14812	+199	+9
Newer Denominations (Fundamentalist, Pentecostal, "Sectarian")						
Assemblies of God*	199	509	1064	2147	+978	+102
Christian & Missionary Alliance*	23	60	190	260	+712	+37
Church of God (TN)	63	170	435	582	+824	+34
Mormons	724	1487	2811	4000	+452	+42
Seventh-Day Adventists	176	318	571	687	+290	+20
Jehovah's Witnesses	n.a.	250	565	805	–	+42
Church of the Nazarene	166	308	484	552	+233	+14
Presbyterian Church in America	–	–	150	217	–	+45
Salvation Army	238	318	417	433	+82	+4
Older "Ethnic" Churches						
Lutheran Church–Missouri Synod	1277	2391	2625	2604	+104	0
Christian Reformed Church	122	236	212	226	+85	+7
Mennonite Church	51	73	100	93	+82	-7
Evangelical Lutherans⁺	3118	5296	5276	5251	+68	0
Wisconsin Evangelical Lutherans	257	348	407	419	+63	+3
Baptist General Conference	n.a.	72	133	135	–	+2
Older "American" Denominations						
Reformed Church in America	255	355	346	334	+31	-3
Episcopal Church	1996	3269	2786	2455	+23	-12
United Methodist	8043	10641	9519	9055	+13	-5
Presbyterian Church in U.S.**	2691	4162	3362	2930	+9	-13
United Church (Cong.)	1708	2241	1736	1645	-4	-5
Disciples of Christ	1659	1802	1178	1073	-35	-9

* Growth rates for the Assemblies of God and the Christian and Missionary Alliance are exaggerated by a change in enumeration that took place in the 1980s, from tallying only duly processed members to counting church constituencies, including children and attending nonmembers (from *Yearbook of American and Canadian Churches: 1990*, ed. C. H. Jacquet, Jr. (Nashville: Abingdon, 1990) and information provided by Robert Patterson, National Association of Evangelicals).

+ Evangelical Lutherans equals the Evangelical Lutheran Church in American, which was formed by the union of the American Lutheran Church and the Lutheran Church in America.

** Presbyterian Church in the U.S. equals northern and southern Presbyterians.

Source: Mark A. Noll, *A History of Christianity in the United States and Canada* (Grand Rapids: Eerdmans, 1992) p. 465, used by permission.

In a manner different from Canada, civil religion pervades American society. Religion has imbedded itself as part of the character of American culture. Consequently, religion is one of the general themes in American life.

Yet the content of civil religion is non-specific. In other words, civil religion is religion with very little theology. It is an orientation to God without specific content that may even serve as folklore for the culture. Still, civil religion in American life remains as a powerful force that rests in the soul of the nation.

It is this civil religion that feeds into the expectation that all American presidents will have a clear-cut Christian commitment. It is a civil religion that launched the awesomely televised Desert Storm against an evil Christian-mocking tyrant. To fight this conflict, the United States draped a religious blanket over the whole nation and asked God to help them defeat the wicked enemy. As CNN began reports of smart bombs blitzing the streets of Baghdad, geopolitical intricacies were secondary to American moralism, used to justify the carnage. One insight suggests,

> Americans are utopian moralists who press hard to institutionalize virtue, to destroy evil people, and to eliminate wicked institutions and practices... The United States is seen as the new Israel. "Europe is Egypt; America is the promised land. God has led his people to establish a new sort of social order that shall be light unto all nations."[20]

American civil religion is not specific to any particular creed. It is inclusive, and based on a moral and religious order that is essentially Christian. The American patriot and the Union or Confederate soldiers are testament to an individualistic, evangelical emphasis in the religious culture—a culture pointing to a personal relationship with God. There is a link between the pioneers, soldiers, gunslingers, sheriffs and cowboy heroes and the image of the solo disciple crying out in the wilderness.

Church growth and American evangelical culture

In the United States, the convergence of a pervasive American civil religion with church attendance patterns weighted heavily toward conservative Protestant churches has created an aggressively evangelistic culture.

If you have God on your side and you have a vision for the way things ought to be, why not go out and shout it from the mountain tops? Better yet, convince your neighbor to believe as you believe—whether that neighbor resides on your home street, half way around the world, or in the Presidential Palace in Panama City.

The intriguing equation is that the national ethos that relies on a "moral imperative" to justify the invasion of foreign countries by American troops has a trickle-down effect at the personal level. If the President of the United States can justify taking over a country by citing a "moral imperative" to do so, the average American can justify an aggressive evangelistic outreach with a similar moral imperative.

When American troops invaded Panama to oust and capture General Noriega and imprison him on American soil, not even the Papal Representative could give the former Panamanian leader permanent sanctuary. In the final triumph of the American way, on October 24, 1992, Manual Noriega was led from his prison cell and voluntarily baptized by six Southern Baptist representatives in a fiberglass baptistry transported into a Miami courtroom.[21]

Whether it be Billy Graham leading in prayer at President Clinton's inauguration, or church leaders uniting to back President Bush's leadership in the Gulf War, American churches participate in public life to such an extent that the separation of church and state, which the First Amendment guarantees, has largely disappeared. In contrast, Canadian churches, once very much connected to state activities, while not being exactly separated from the modern state, are isolated in a sea of secularism that dissolves our historic national connection between the state and our religious institutions.

Southern Baptists and American distinctives

A look at the United States' most strident Protestant denomination in terms of growth and evangelism will help clarify our national differences. The Convention of Southern Baptists, whose representatives baptized General Noriega and whose missionaries have come to Canada in recent years, is the largest American Protestant denomination, with over 14 million members.

The overwhelming size of the Southern Baptist Convention among the American church community and their general evangelical position lead many to categorize all American Baptists under this convention. While such a generalization is too broad, it remains true that talking about Baptists in the States most often means talking about those in the Southern Baptist Convention. In sheer numbers alone, Baptists are a vital force in American society.[22]

Again, a look at history is helpful. When the Northern states won the

Civil War, the Confederate troops, made up in a large part by Southern Baptist soldiers, were humiliated. Confederate soldiers had marched into battle believing that God was their ally. While both sides used the Bible to justify their cause, the faithful in the South believed that God was on their side, helping them to trample down the materialistic, industrial, ungodly, northern armies.

When defeat came for the South, the Southern Baptists experienced a severe shock.[23] How could God have abandoned them? God does not treat a chosen people that way! There must be another battlefield where God intended to give them victory. Bill J. Leonard, a contemporary authority on Southern Baptist church history, sums it up this way:

> The denomination of the defeated, itself born of schism and racism, had become God's "last" and "only hope" for evangelizing the world according to New Testament principles. Its numerical, financial, and spiritual growth, as well as its evangelistic zeal, was evidence of God's blessing on its ministry, its mission, and its method.[24]

Southern Baptists came to believe that God would ultimately vindicate their denomination. The Southern Baptist spirit of triumphalism and spiritual and numerical success is linked to the surrender of the South after a brutal civil war. Furthermore, to remain committed to their cause,

> A vehement nostalgia was combined with the rejection of subsequent history, so that nearly every new idea of the last third of the nineteenth century came to be rejected by the Southern Baptists, with the unhappy consequence that no other American denomination entered the twentieth century with so pervasive an investment in anti-intellectualism.[25]

The combination of historic triumphalism and the tendency toward anti-intellectualism of much of Southern Baptist thinking combined to produce a current of fundamentalism that is a major theme throughout much of this denomination. Although there is a more moderate Southern Baptist segment, for the most part the Southern Baptist Convention is made up of a very conservative tradition which is unique to the United States and a result of that republic's history.[26]

Future denominational influences

The Southern Baptists have become such a dominant force in American religious life that, while the future of other denominational influences is difficult to foretell, Southern Baptists will remain a dominant expression of American religious life. This is so even though the American traditions of freedom of religion and the rights of the individual, not to mention their entrepreneurial enthusiasm for protecting these freedoms, has created a diverse population of faiths under the banner of their civil religion. With regard to the religious diversity in the United States Harold Bloom notes that

> ...the United States will not yield readily to any predictions (however informed) as to its denominational future. Our vastly increasing Hispanic population, now divided between a waning Roman Catholicism and a ferociously vigorous Pentecostalism, doubtless will become more diverse in spiritual orientation as it gains economic and political power. Our crucial Asian-American communities...are all but impossible to foretell, in the area of religious concern.

Then on the Southern Baptists, Bloom concludes,
> What seems certain, to me, is that...the Southern Baptists ...will be at the center of what is to come, since...they are imbued with the ambivalent vitalism of our national faith.[27]

Canadian Baptists and Canadian distinctives

Because of that vitalism, one cannot help but wonder whether or not the nature of Canada's historical religion is, at least in some measure, being Americanized. Just as two-thirds of the television programming we watch comes from the United States, so too an increasing level of American-flavored religion is moving in from south of the border.

There are limits to what the Canadian church will absorb, however. In the 1980s, during the heady days of the American Moral Majority, attempts were made by some to use similar forms of social and political persuasion in Canada. Except for a little support from a few people, those initiatives floundered and failed. Canadians have never responded positively to aggressive religious approaches. The attempt to legislate morality, or to live with the mindset that "my way is the only right way," is untenable for Canadians. Canadians are too committed to living cooperatively with each other to widely endorse such approaches.

Baptists in Canada, for example, are not closely related to those in the United States. As Harry Hiller states,

> The right combination of socio-political and socio-religious factors which made the Baptist faith so congruent with Ameri-

can democracy and individualism was to a degree absent in Canada so that formality and tradition have shaped the church more than in the United States... Baptists in Canada have historically been considered part of the British tradition alongside Methodism and Presbyterianism...[28]

Although some groups of Canadian Baptists have continental links, on the whole they are very much an indigenous Canadian denomination. Why haven't Southern Baptists, such a force in the U.S., become a force in Canada, particularly in the past few decades when Canadians who are seeking a faith experience have shown themselves to be open to an evangelical message?

In a very real sense, Southern Baptist belief and church organization is as uniquely American as Mormonism or Seventh Day Adventistism. But it has little in common with the European church tradition which so many Canadian Christians draw upon. Furthermore, Canadians don't share the black-white racial controversy that is so much a part of American Baptist history. And no Canadian Protestant denomination has suffered the ignoble defeat which Baptists in the Confederacy had to deal with.

Consequently, the triumphalism and justification by numbers and growth that characterizes Southern Baptists is not a main fixture in Canadian evangelicalism or any of this country's mainline churches. Furthermore, Canadian denominations have not had to seek a revisionist history in order to work around the catastrophe of belonging to what they believed was God's side in a lost and devastating civil war.

Just as Pat Robertson's brand of politicking from a platform of faith does not translate in Canadian political arenas, the dominant evangelical denomination in the United States is so much a part of the religious culture of that nation that it is an American original and not translatable into Canadian terms. Further, the differences between American Southern Baptists and Canadian Baptists speak to the differences between religion in the United States and religion in Canada as a whole. American religious patterns as a whole cannot just be transplanted into the Canadian context.

Joining and belonging

There is perhaps one other important difference between American and Canadian styles of religious practice and affiliation that can shed light on overall church attendance and growth patterns in Canada and the United States.

James Sauer explains:
> In the United States, people join [churches] in order to belong. When they go to a new church, they do so with the intention of joining.
> In Canada...people rarely join until they have a sense of belonging.
> The most immediate implication lies in the areas of church growth and evangelism. In the U.S., the priorities are evangelism and rapid growth. Canadian congregations should place a high priority on issues of belonging and assimilation, and accept that church growth will be slower than in the United States.[29]

This point has been born out by our research. As we have seen, "community" has been identified as one of the four cornerstones of effective churches in Canada; belonging is an integral part of any experience of community. A sense of belonging was rated as "very important" by 83% of our survey respondents. Significantly, these findings were consistent across all denominations.

We are not American

The center-court prayer for Magic Johnson was an expression of America's civil religion. Such a phenomenon is not easily copied in Canadian sports arenas or other public venues.

The national day of prayer which George Bush proclaimed after surveying the ruins left by the Los Angeles riots was a similar expression of American civil religion. Is it conceivable that Prime Minister Mulroney would do the same if there was devastation in the streets of Montreal, Toronto or Vancouver?

The faith experience of contemporary Canadians comes out of our history which is counter-revolutionary and Europe-focused. Although Southern Baptists, for example, have sent missionaries to Canada, the dominant Protestant denomination in the United States does not duplicate itself well on Canadian soil. Today, Southern Baptists have approximately 15 million members in the United States. In Canada their membership numbers less than 6,000.

In the realm of religion, Canada is not the United States. The equations of religious life in the United States will not easily translate into the arena of Canadian life. We must pay the price of contextualization. And ambiguity will remain. Because we share so much in common, and because the "American way" is so internationally influential, some endeavors will produce positive results. Other attempts will fail.

Some aspects are clear. In politics, American politicians will tout a faith byline that is consistent with the precepts of civil religion. Canadian politicians will respect the faith of others and tenaciously avoid revealing their personal religious views.

If modern nations are built on historical foundations, we must recognize that the God of creation and redemption has chosen to work differently in each nation.

The God of creation is not a national God. And neither are Canadians culturally predisposed to consume American religion. We are not American. While there is much we can learn from our neighbors to the south, Canadian churches have their own unique heritage and their distinctive future to pursue.

The effectiveness of Canadian churches will be directly linked with the ability of clergy, academics and decision-making laity to respond to the expectations, wants, and needs of **Canadians**. Only in this way can the Canadian church become truly Canadian.

Contextualizing The Message

Chapter Seven

Visiting the city of Montreal is a pleasure. Besides being a fascinating, cosmopolitan city, it is one of Canada's best urban landscapes for people watching. The movement starts early every morning, as thousands of commuters travel from the surrounding suburbs to work in the downtown core. The pulsating action continues well into the night.

An urban landscape

Taking the commute from the perimeter of the city into the inner core awakens echoes from Canada's national history and arouses sounds of our modern ways. The resplendent sanctuary of Notre Dame Cathedral stands as a reminder of how life used to be, while the cavernous excesses of Olympic Stadium say more about the focus of life in the present.

Imagine you are part of the commuting parade on Monday morning. Walking down the street to catch the bus in the inner suburb of Chomedey, you step through a remarkable cosmopolitan neighborhood. When the Director General of the local school board wants to communicate with parents he sends home the communiques in three languages: French, English and Greek. As you walk down the street you offer morning salutations in several languages.

Before running the remaining few yards to climb aboard the bus, echoes of Canada's religious history might draw your attention to the local churches. Yesterday's voices bounce off the walls of the community Protestant church and rattle in the parking lot of the neighborhood Roman Catholic parish. The echo speaks of a time when the majority of Canadians went to church regularly. Thirty years ago, Sunday morning worshipers would have filled both churches with the sounds of singing and the words of the responsive readings and prayers. The local Protestant church once had a Sunday school that taught over 200 children. The Roman Catholic parish celebrated mass 45 times each week. Today, only 40 people gather on Sunday for the 11 o'clock service at the Protestant church. The Catholic church celebrates mass only eight times a week.

Any serious reflection on our religious history would be interrupted as you jockey for standing-room-only on the crowded bus which weaves and lurches through morning traffic. The commuters, snugly wrapped up in their own personal concerns, seem oblivious to the value systems offered by the various ecclesiastical structures that once dominated our nation's moral landscape.

After a short ride, the bus stops and the commuters spill out and down the steps into the Metro Station. They rush to catch the train that will take them to the heart of Montreal, the second largest French-speaking city in the world. Before the train reaches its downtown destination, however, it will pass through, or under, several different "Montreals."

The train will lose several of its occupants to one of the four universities that make up the Montreal of the student world. Others will exit onto the busy morning streets as the Metro passes through ethnic Montreal. A total of 80 different ethnic groups, 45 different languages, and over 650,000 people speak a language other French or English as their mother tongue. They remind you of the diversity of the city.

Unfortunately, the commute into the city also creates discomfort. Like any big city, Montreal has its population of the perpetually unemployed, the hurt, the sick, the lame. During the course of your journey you might rub shoulders with one of the city's AIDS victims; you might choose to ignore the request for spare change from one of the 15,000 street people; or you might easily mistake one of the several thousand teenage prostitutes for just another young person making his or her way through the demands of the day.

Over 750,000 people work in downtown Montreal. As the train reaches the downtown stops, most of its passengers get off and enter a world of glass and chrome skyscrapers, old churches, and marble shopping centers. They enter into the business work-week culture that they have created by their very presence.

Except for a few remaining passengers, some of whom may spend most of the day just riding the train, the train is virtually empty.

Concerned Christians might well ask, in the midst of this social mix, this awesome range of needs, what or where is the church; what has happened to the cultural cement which once formed the foundations of so many of the city's citizens and institutions?

A question of context

The cultural shifts that were underscored in Chapter Five are not just "cultural" phenomena for sociologists to study. Our data clearly indicates that Christians in Canada want the churches they attend to be in touch with the times as well as the truth.

The challenge is to faithfully and creatively frame the life of the church in response to the current cultural context. How can the biblical message be connected to the realities of the 21st century?

For Christians who live in rural Canada and who face population declines and the threat of foreclosure on their livelihoods, the church needs images that inspire hope. For an urban church, images which speak of "green pastures" miss the mark. For a church among Canadian native peoples, the success images of contemporary Christianity offer little help. Whether the context is rural, metropolitan, or native, we need to find images that depict the nature of the church and speak directly to our life experience.

Douglas Hall, United Church theologian from McGill University, has attempted to do this through the metaphor of the church as "the disciple community." Hall uses this metaphor to describe a community which exists as a cultural minority, "potentially, a significant minority— whose significance does not lie in quantitative considerations but in the quality of the alternative vision it represents."[1]

Hall explains the metaphor by describing disciples as people who are marked by discipline of thinking and living. "Christian disciples are persons who are seeking to discipline their minds, to wrestle in great earnestness with what their hearts and wills assent to, to comprehend that which has grasped them as 'ultimate concern.'"[2] For Hall, while the church no longer represents the majority in North America, the people of God are still significant, especially when they are a community of disciples.

Michael Griffiths, presently professor of missions at Regent College in Vancouver, adds to our understanding of the nature of the church when he states that,

> It is my conviction that a fresh understanding of the biblical doctrine of the church practically related to our daily, corporate activities as Christians, can and will give a new sense of

purpose and direction to our Christian lives. The church is not a third class waiting room where we twiddle our thumbs while we wait for first class accommodation in heaven. It is a dynamic new community, winsome and attractive, and with eternal significance in the purpose of God. The Bible makes it clear that the church is God's goal for mankind, for the new humanity in its new communities.[3]

Giffiths goes on to note the image of unharvested fields, used to depict God's sovereign initiative. He observes that the architectural image of "building-up" the church describes the human role in God's work.

> It is particularly interesting to notice the differing stress between the agricultural and architectural metaphors which Paul employs. In the picture of the unharvested fields all the emphasis is on God's sovereignty... In the architectural metaphor (building up the body of Christ), however, the stress moves in a very marked way from divine sovereignty to human responsibility...[4]

If the church is to be in touch situationally—if the church is to have relevancy—adequate effort must be made by those attending, running and ultimately building the church to understand both the larger societal shifts as well as the evolutions transpiring in the parish and the workplace. As John Frame stated, "We do not know what Scripture says until we know how it relates to our world."[5]

The challenge of contextualization

The word often used to describe the task of defining the existence and expression of the church within the circumstances of current culture is "contextualization." Although the word is relatively new in theological circles, the attempt to understand the biblical text and the nature of the church in a specific cultural context is an ancient one.[6]

The word "contextualization" literally means a "weaving together." In the setting of this chapter, it implies the interweaving of scriptural teaching with the gathering and discipling of God's people as the church in their human situation and particular circumstances.

The task of contextualization is the essence of theological reflection. The challenge of theological reflection is to remain faithful to the historic text of the scriptures while being mindful of the realities of the age. An interpretive bridge is built between the scriptures and the situation from which they sprang, to the concerns and circumstances of the local group of Christians who are doing the reflection. The first step of this hermeneutic or interpretive process involves establishing what the text meant at the time it was written, what the text meant "then." The second step involves the construction of the interpretive bridge which explores what the text can mean for people today, "now." The task is to determine the meaning and application of the teaching for those who will receive the message **in their particular circumstances**. The orientation is not just on the one communicating, or on the content of the communication, but also on the ultimate impact of the message on the audience.[7]

The process of theological reflection is not without its dangers or pitfalls. The first pitfall would be an approach to theology that sees the formation of doctrine as contextually neutral; that is, an approach that disregards the historical factors that influenced the formulation of the various doctrines in the first place. In this instance, the problem arises when theological emphases are indiscriminately **imported** from one context into another. For example, the construction of "liberation" and "feminist" and "urban" theologies have all been influenced by the circumstances that spawned their inception. Acknowledging the impact of these historical influences means that when particular theological emphases move into new contexts, they have to be interpreted again before they can be helpfully applied to local situations. Theological priorities for South America do not necessarily apply within Canada. Neither do Canadian theological concerns particularly relate to South Africa.

A second pitfall results from attempts to **export** theological formulations into foreign contexts and other cultures as if they were sacred scripture. Western missionaries have long and often been accused of exporting extraneous theology and the trappings of cultural Christianity to other parts of the world. Latin American theologian Samuel Esabor has stated that,

> When theological formulas are made sacred which are forged in other latitudes and with respect to other questions and there is a hesitance to read afresh the word of God itself, to search out its message, it is worth nothing to have correct theory about the authority of Scripture.[8]

Unless churches screen their theology through history and context, they will not only import and export extraneous theological emphases. They will arrest the church's pursuit of relevancy.

Doing contextualization

Over the past decade, various authors have attempted to develop a method to pursue the process of contextualizing theology in a given situation.[9]

Communities of faith who wish to map and contextualize their ministries will acknowledge that, although they desire to find fresh direction from God's word, they also come to the scriptures with a specific worldview already in place. After all, denominations are framed within a confessional background that is reinforced by their religious tradition. We do well to confess our biases and remember that, although our theology and our denominational traditions help us to read the scriptures, the content of our traditions and the content of the Bible are not always identical.

Another element in the process of contextualization involves acknowledging the contribution of past theological works. To do good theology in a modern neighborhood, the church must be informed about and enriched by how God has worked through the church in past centuries. For example, John Calvin wrote the *Institutes of the Christian Religion* while living in Geneva. To read this work without seeing the impact of Geneva, a free city in a turbulent century, on the writer, is to ignore something that Calvin himself freely admitted.[10] The clear message from the history of theology is, "Do what we did!" not just "Tell everyone what we thought!"[11]

Once we understand the scriptural teachings, learn what we can from the rich history of the church, and explore its relevance in our context, the shape of the church of the future will emerge.

God's concern for people has always included a commitment to the situation in which they live. Out of concern for Nineveh, God used Jonah to bring a specific message for that particular place. For Rome, Onesimus was the messenger. The same principle applies today. The Good News is not merely a general memo addressed in non-specific and impersonal terms. The task of the church is to respond specifically to different situations.

The interpretive process takes a step forward when local churches give specific attention to their particular setting. With the biblical text in hand, the effective church shaper asks, "What is God saying through the scriptures regarding the needs, the aspirations, and the concerns that exist in **our** community (the immediate context)?" As those in local churches understand the original context of the scriptures alongside the context in their surrounding communities, they will be in a position to implement contextualized ministries. Scripture illuminates life. And life illuminates scripture.

Harvey Conn raises the question to pursue:
How shall the child of God, as a member of the Body of Christ, respond with integrity to the scriptures in his or her context, in order to live a kingdom lifestyle in increasing obedience within the community of faith?[12]

The relative sameness of churches across the country indicates an absence of contextualization. Instead of contextualizing their ministry, most denominations come close to cloning. Across the country, churches look and feel as if they have been produced by photocopiers. This excessive sameness implies little contextual response to the specifics that exist in the various communities. Too many churches, in too many communities, are too much like each other.

The end result of contextualization should be churches that adapt to the realities inside their congregations and to the circumstances in their surrounding geographical communities. Almost without exception, churches will provide places for worship and teaching and the partaking of the sacraments. Not every church will be involved in compassionate outreach ministries. Some will give priority to youth programming; others will not. Some churches will respond to the needs of single parents, senior citizens, high-risk youth and special-needs children, while others will give themselves to day care and excellent Christian education programs.

From contextualization to communication

John Stott suggests that before the church can speak to the world, it must develop the discipline of double listening. It must listen first to the word of God, and then to the world. Stott calls for the
skills of cultural transposition so we can apply that word to ourselves in our own culture as we listen, and then to others in their cultures. Transposing the message of the gospel culturally does not change its message, just as transposing music does not change the melody and harmony and essence of a musical composition.[13]

John Stott's use of the musical image of "transposing" is an example of creative communication.

Particularly in today's world, communication can be enhanced with the use of images. Avery Dulles reminds us: "The Bible, when it seeks to illuminate the nature of the Church, speaks almost entirely through images."[14] Paul Minear isolates 96 images for the church in the New Testament.[15]

Paul's letter to the church in Philippi serves as a helpful illustration of contextualization. After a general introduction at the beginning of the epistle (Philippians 1:3–26), Paul launches into the substance of the letter with a "warning." Karl Barth observes, "There is no gradual introduction, no leading up to a theme, but rather an outburst." Paul provides clear teaching to the church about what Christ expects of them.[16] Rather dramatically, Paul declares, "Live your life as a citizen in a manner worthy of Christ." The injunction is to live with consistency. "Let your life exhibit the qualities that deserve to be associated with Christ. Live in your world as 'citizens' (politeuma)[17] of Christ's family should live" (paraphrase).

The idea of "citizenship" had special meaning for people who lived in Philippi. With its Roman infrastructure, and with people such as Lydia, who was involved in the silk trade,[18] the city of Phillippi was a "Rome in miniature."[19] Commentators have noted that the citizens of Philippi also enjoyed a unique legal position through their land rights and tax status. Local administration was exactly the same as if they were on Italian soil.[20]

In his assessment of the church in Philippi, Paul found no lingering counterfeit gospel as in Galatia, nor the deep moral problems of Corinth. Rather, Paul discerned conflict in the church. Simply put, the people in the church were not getting along with each other. There was rivalry in the community and self-centeredness in their midst. In response to the situation, Paul pleads for Christ-like citizenship. Paul presents the uniqueness of the Philippians' citizenship privileges, and the responsibility that implies, as a parallel to their status and responsibilities within the church.

In verses 1:27–2:11, Paul extends the use of the metaphor and pleads for a citizenship that pursues a unity of spirit, mind and intention. The imperative of this exemplary way of living is pursued through the call for encouragement, the consolation of love, a sharing in the Spirit and a compassion and sympathy that is found in Christ (2:1–4).

Seeking to communicate clearly and desiring a positive response to his message, Paul tunes in to the frequency of this audience, appeals to the commonly held metaphor of "citizenship" and then makes his plea.

A Community of Communities

If the metaphor of citizenship connected with the people in Philippi in the first century, what Canadian motifs or themes might be contextualized for the Canadian church of the 1990s?

Joe Clark once identified Canada as a "community of communities." Although Clark articulated the metaphor for political purposes, it has been widely discussed, if not accepted, as a description of the country and has been stretched by many people to explain a myriad of Canadian issues.

The description of Canada as a "community of communities" describes our national diversity, but it also describes denominational diversity. For this reason, it provides one possible working metaphor for the church. Obviously, there are many other metaphors that Canadian Christians can use to understand their context and envision their function in society. However, to gain an appreciation for the process of contextualization, let's take this metaphor and work through the process of applying it to Canadian churches.

When the metaphor of a "community of communities" is linked with the church's mandate to be a reconciling presence in the midst of increasing fragmentation, it gains even more power. The scriptural teaching about reconciliation in 2 Corinthians 5:16–6:1 pours content into the motif:

> [5:16]From now on, therefore, we regard no one from a human point of view; even though we once knew Christ from a human point of view, we know him no longer in that way. [17]So if anyone is in Christ, there is a new creation: everything old has passed away; see, everything has become new! [18]All this is from God, who reconciled us to himself through Christ, and has given us the ministry of reconciliation; [19]that is, in Christ God was reconciling the world to himself, not counting their trespasses against them, and entrusting the message of reconciliation to us. [20]So we are ambassadors for Christ, since God is making his appeal through us; we entreat you on behalf of Christ, be reconciled to God. [21]For our sake he made him to be sin who knew no sin, so that in him we

might become the righteousness of God. ⁶:¹As we work together with him, we urge you also not to accept the grace of God in vain. (NRSV)

The first step in the contextualization and interpretive process is to be clear about what the passage originally meant or said, and who it was for. The letter from which the above passage is taken was addressed to the Corinthian church. But more specifically, the people receiving the message are those who have been reconciled to God, through Christ.

Further, those who have been reconciled are given a "specific message." To them, God entrusts the message of reconciliation (verse 19). Along with this message comes a task. Those who receive the message are themselves entrusted by God to be ministers of reconciliation, ambassadors of reconciliation for Christ (verse 20).

Finally, ambassadors of reconciliation communicate their message in a "specific place." The appeal to be reconciled to God is to be expressed "in the world" (verse 20).

The final instruction from Paul in the passage is to "work together with God" in this multifaceted ministry of reconciliation (5:20, 6:1). The entire mission is portrayed as a divine-human partnership.

Taking the second step in contextualization process, Professor George Hunsberger builds an interpretive bridge from the experience of the first century Corinthians to our modern world. He does so by stating the biblical injunction for reconciliation in contemporary terms, and by placing it in an analogous modern setting:

> First, healing is needed for the internal fracturing each of us experiences. Second, healing is needed between us as Christians. And the third fracture line where healing is critical is between the church and the world.[21]

Internal fractures

Someone once observed that "Confession may be good for the soul but it is hard on one's reputation." Christians are sometimes pressed so hard to be healthy and whole that they deny their inner turmoil and brokenness. Those who deny their inner fractures will be the ones who cut themselves off from the healing that God desires to give.

Fractures between Christians

Although it is presumptuous to attempt the ministry of reconciliation in the world without first being reconciled to one another, Canadian

Christians continue to flail away at each other. Whether it is mainline and conservative Protestants lambasting each other in connection with the CRTC hearings on public broadcasting policy,[22] or preachers using the immunity of their pulpits to insult or denounce another Christian's point of view, the fracturing continues. Rather than working on behalf of each other, church communities work against each other.

As soon as Christian spokespeople realize that it is not necessary to announce that someone else is wrong in order to contend that one is right, the cause of reconciliation will move forward. Perhaps old-fashioned Christian repentance is the place to start.

Frankly stated, the extended family of God will have more integrity and become more vital when those who share differences learn lessons of mutual respect. If reconciliation is the motif for the modern church, when there is conflict between local churches, surely everything possible will be done to negotiate peace treaties. If Canadian churches truly represent a community of communities, then the various denominations and different traditions within the larger Christian community need to support one another. This same support should also operate between the Christian community and other faith communities which make up our pluralistic, multicultural nation.

The question is, "How can Christians who participate in different faith communities show how a community of communities can reconcile historic grievances and gross differences?"

Fractures between the church and the world

The church still has a highly visible presence in Canadian culture. The world also has expectations of the church. A recent headline blared, "Churches not fighting racism issue." The head of the Metropolitan Toronto Housing Authority charged that "Organized religion is not doing enough to fight racism."[23] Reverend Richard Choe responded by saying that "Inclusiveness is one of the biggest issues facing churches today." As pastor of a church with participants from 18 different cultural backgrounds, Reverend Choe stated, "Until that [inclusiveness] is made a priority, newcomers to Canada will be left with the message that 'this is the way we do it and either you do it our way or you don't come to church.'"[24]

Those who are reconciled to God and to each other will have the liberty to live as ambassadors for Christ in the world. The appeal, "Be reconciled to God" will have power when the invitation is bathed in the **experience** of reconciliation.

Reconciliation and the four cornerstones of effective churches

The motif and theme of reconciliation has direct application to the four cornerstones of effective churches.

Orthodoxy

Framing the faith as reconciliation provides a powerful message for today. Secular society does not have an intentional agenda for addressing the brokenness of the times. Each sector in society is preoccupied with its own vested interests. People are separated from God. People are alienated from each other. Understanding the gospel as a call to close the distance that separation and alienation produce is timely, truthful, meaningful and biblically orthodox.

Relevance

In these times, the message of reconciliation is profoundly relevant. As people struggle to link past ways of thinking and behaving with present assumptions and prerogatives, reconciliation is needed. When marriage partners undermine each other, when parents see their children make decisions that disappoint them, attitudes of reconciliation are crucial. Economic stresses tend to splinter society into specialized interest groups. In the face of entrenched regionalism and tensions around our multicultural differences, reconciliation is a relevant response.

Community

People cannot have community unless they are reconciled. The "two solitudes" that tended to segment Canada in the past are fracturing into "many solitudes." Our data indicates that unresolved conflict is one of the reasons why people leave their churches. Unless people inside local congregations can care for each other, churches are just places where individuals come to worship and seek God in pursuit of their own interests. As Christians discover how to live in reconciled communities in the church, they will be able to contribute to reconciliation in the world.

Outreach

The empathetic posture of reconciliation is the right emphasis for evangelistic concern today. Unchurched Canadians are wary of religious types who offer simple solutions to the complicated problems in their lives. Few people are "exhorted" into the kingdom of God. They are more likely to be "loved" into God's family. People need to be shown that the church is a safe place. The possibility of projecting a life where fractures can be healed and relationships can be restored is compelling.

The Canadian church is in a cultural position to make a desperately needed contribution to the current context. Can it be done? Will it be done? Is there a common will among Canada's Christians to pursue their divinely appointed ministry of reconciliation? We will have to wait to find out.

Demands of contextualization

As the final draft of this chapter was being written, I found myself on a plane sitting next to a symphony conductor and arts director from one of Canada's medium-sized cities. We started comparing the declining support of the general public for some sectors of the arts with what is happening to the church in Canada. In response to the new pressures for survival, the director explained all of the initiatives he was taking to keep his symphony solvent. At one point in the conversation he reached into his briefcase and pulled out a seminar outline entitled, "Cultural Survival in the Real World." His eyes lit up as he told me about the things he was now doing so that his love for music could be shared by others.

In the midst of the conversation, I suggested that one of the reasons symphonies struggle to retain past levels of interest is that the music format only appeals to one of our senses. People are ushered into their seats and required to listen to stationary musicians create their sounds. I suggested that people are now more accustomed to seeing visual images with lots of movement along with whatever music they may be listening to.

The conductor's eyes lit up again. He explained that last year his moment of triumph involved combining the art forms of music and film. He had spent several days at the National Film Board choosing film footage to complement the musical score that was played at the performance. His final word was, "When we finished playing, there was no applause. People sat in stunned silence. They were gripped by the power of what they had just seen and heard."

Performing symphony orchestra concerts the old way is easier. Taking days to look at films and make all the extra arrangements is time consuming and costly. But when the issue is survival, the extraordinary efforts not only bring hope for the future, they produce a product that is richer and more powerful.

Church leaders who pursue their vocations and commitments with the same passion can write stories of triumph too.

Section III

Charting New Directions

Striving for Balance

Chapter Eight

Following the benediction, we waited patiently to greet the minister. Attendance at the early service was sparse and we were among the last to leave the sanctuary, so there was no need to rush. I extended my hand to exchange a greeting and the minister paused and asked, "So what's new?"

Reaching for some common ground, I explained that I was working on a research project which probed the question, "What are the characteristics of effective churches?"

The minister's face lit up. Confidently, he responded, "I can answer that question. I was reading a book last week that concluded that there are three reasons why churches are effective. Actually, the answer is simple: 'Location, location, and location.'"

Before I could ask whether or not he had misunderstood the question, the minister went on to explain: "The book concluded that if a church is located in a neighborhood where there is a strong sense of community spirit and lots of activity, the church will be included in the activity of the community."

Rather than engage the minister in a discussion about the differences between real estate values and effective churches, I tried to explain that although "location" can be important, the results of the research stated other conclusions.

We didn't pursue the topic, but when we have the opportunity, we will discuss the significance of the four cornerstones of effective churches—the implications of seeking a balance in ministry between orthodoxy, community, relevance, and outreach.

Where's a Good Church?

Results of Survey

Orthodoxy—In touch with truth
Community—In touch with personal needs
Relevancy—In touch with the times
Outreach—In touch with the needs of others

The research reveals that these ministry commitments do not exist in isolation from each other. Rather, there is a dynamic interrelationship among the four cornerstones of effectiveness. Our survey of active Christians in Protestant churches across Canada concludes that church effectiveness depends on achieving a balance between these expressions of church life. When there is a harmonious ministry mix between the four components, they function in church life like a vocal quartet or an instrumental musical ensemble.

The models that follow in the chapter are designed to illustrate and explain the dynamics of the interrelationships between orthodoxy, community, relevance, and outreach. These four characteristics, identified by Christians as being crucial for church health and vitality, create the framework to help understand how churches have charted their way toward effectiveness.

Fig. 8.1
Cornerstones of Effective Churches

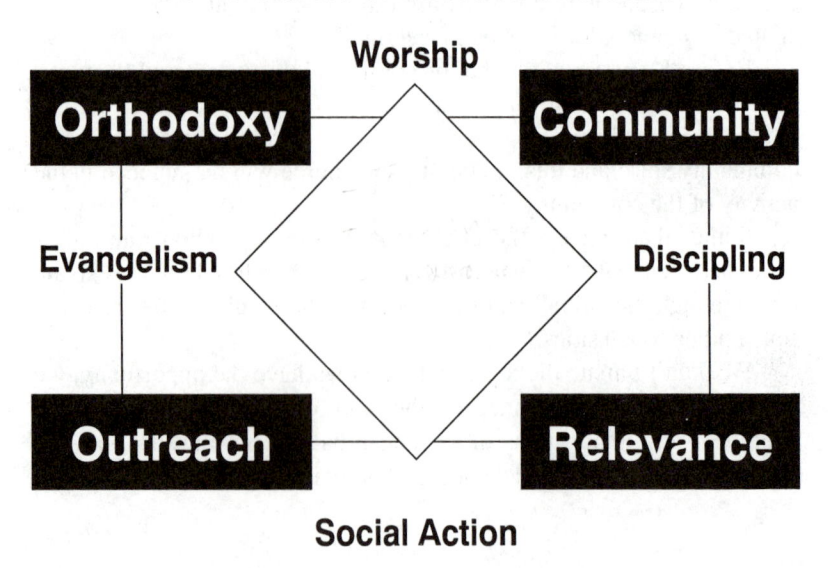

Worship

Orthodoxy — **Community**

Evangelism — Discipling

Outreach — **Relevance**

Social Action

152

Balance Issues

Using the four cornerstones as building blocks for the ministry model, *Figure 8.1* identifies horizontal and vertical parallels that suggest four "balance" issues. The horizontal and vertical lines connecting the four cornerstones create four links:
- orthodoxy and community
- community and relevance
- orthodoxy and outreach
- outreach and relevance.

When held in balance, the interplay between the dual ministry commitments act as a fulcrum or balancing mechanism so that both goals are accomplished simultaneously.

Balance Issue	Balancing Mechanism
Orthodoxy/Community	Worship
Community/Relevance	Discipling
Orthodoxy/Outreach	Evangelism
Outreach/Relevance	Social Action

The Orthodoxy/Community balance

The orthodoxy/community balance involves the need to be in touch with God as well as the need to be in touch with each other as members of a faith community. The balancing mechanism for accomplishing both of these goals simultaneously is found in worship—the shared experience of encountering God. The scriptures instruct God's people "not to neglect to meet together" (Hebrews 10:25, NRSV). Worship holds out the promise that wherever and whenever God's people gather, Christ is present with them (Matthew 18:20). Worship, then, is the means through which members of the family of God are brought closer to the God of creation and redemption, and closer to each other as a faith community.

People sometimes contend that they do not need church to "feel close to God." They can "pray at home" and practice religion privately. There is a one-sided truth to this argument. We certainly can and often do encounter God when we are alone or are in private prayer. However, the "go it alone" approach ignores the need to collectively affirm one's faith. It also leaves people without the input and influence that comes from being involved with a faith community.

In the words of a Christian and Missionary Alliance clergy respondent in Ontario, true worship creates "a blend of divine mystique and warm human caring." Worship is intended to express our collective faith, and to bring us in harmony with the truth as well as with each other. William Willimon writes that the ultimate proof of the Resurrection is not an empty tomb or the Shroud of Turin. "The ultimate evidence for the Resurrection is the existence of something so unlikely and inexplicable as the Church."[1]

The Community/Relevance balance

If "worship" is the fulcrum which meets the demands of both orthodoxy and community, then "discipling" is the ministry emphasis that simultaneously contributes to the community/relevance balance. In particular, discipling has an outward orientation that equips the saints for living between Sundays.

Our survey results show that 84% of Christians think that an effective church must provide practical guidance for living one's faith in the world during the week. Accordingly, the church must equip those who attend church to live coherently in the modern world as Christ's faithful followers. Discipling involves the task of providing Christians with the tools and resources and armor they need to live in the world. As a lay member of a United church in Alberta wrote, "My church helps me live with confidence in a world that is changing, complex, and traveling through uncharted waters."

The role of community in the life of the church involves both worship and discipling. Worship keeps the community in touch with God and with truth. Participation in a healthy Christian community will also include a style of discipling that is in touch with the times. The exchange of life in the community will provide opportunities for collectively responding to the culture. A lay leader attending an Associated Gospel church in Ontario reminds us to "develop ministries around people, rather than plugging people in to fit pre-existing programs." People-centered programming equips persons to live as Christ's followers in the moral mazes and the complexities of the times.

Discipling is an ongoing and changing enterprise. If the collective experience in the church community is out of touch with the world outside the church, people leave ill-prepared to live in the world. In some cases, they don't return to the church. As one respondent from Ontario noted, "Effective churches minister to the culture, and the culture is not static." A Lutheran clergy leader in British Columbia echoes this sentiment in the often cited comment that the "seven last words of a dying church are 'We have always done it this way.'" A Presbyterian minister in Ontario offers the opinion that "More people will leave a church because of lack of change than because of change."

The Orthodoxy/Outreach balance: outreach with conviction

Church attenders who are discipled will be equipped to contribute to the orthodoxy/outreach balance. With words and deeds, they will communicate Christ's message to those outside the faith community. The mechanism which simultaneously meets the demands of orthodoxy (being in touch with the truth) and the demands of outreach (being in touch with the needs of others) lies in recognizing the importance for others to know and respond to the truth of the good news of the gospel; the good news of the Christian faith; to be forgiven, to be welcomed into God's family and to be set free to live "in Christ."

While worship is an "inner circle" expression which brings believers collectively into a celebration of truth, evangelism is an external invitation for others to join the inner circle. We have chosen to stand in the long tradition of the Christian church and to continue to use the term "evangelism" as the best way to describe the church's mission to those who still stand outside the church and the Christian faith. But we would also like to introduce the idea of "**empathetic** evangelism" to define the tone that can best be used to invite people to consider Christ and his ways.

Although preaching and verbally explaining the gospel message has been the dominant method for evangelistic activities in this century, we do not want to restrict the expression of "empathetic evangelism" to just the proclamation of the gospel. As authors, our own convictions are that, in this age, deeds are more powerful than words and that "empathetic evangelism" will also involve compassionate ministries, community service, global sharing and, in general, an attitude that reveals sensitivity to the whole-person needs of others.

If that is the case, then any tendency to view outreach strictly in terms of "telling the good news" is inadequate. It fails to recognize that the same Jesus who mandated the Great Commission to go into all the world and make disciples also set the standard to minister to the needs of people who, for whatever reasons, are unable to care for themselves. A commitment to contextual social action allows the church to incarnate the presence of Christ and be a source of healing in a troubled world.

Still, "empathetic evangelism" also includes the practice of preaching and making the meaning of the gospel known to those who have not yet embraced it. The United Methodist pastor and leader William Willimon says this:

> If we or the world could be saved through human kindness or clear thinking, Jesus would have either formed a sensitivity group and urged us to share our feelings or would have founded a school and asked us to have discussions. Knowing the ways of God, the way of the world, and the persistence of human sin, He took up the cross, called disciples, gathered the church, and bade us follow Him down a different path to freedom.[2]

The Outreach/Relevance balance: outreach with compassion

The data have already established that church effectiveness involves being in touch with the needs of others (outreach) and being in touch with the times (relevance). A Presbyterian clergy leader in Ontario responded to the survey with the comment that "It is very difficult to relate the gospel to the world if you have severed all contact with it." A Pentecostal pastor from Nova Scotia states that the church often "talks about" outreach, but is "usually overly consumed with oiling the machinery of its existing programs."

The balancing mechanism which addresses both outreach and relevance involves the "compassion" side of outreach. It will prompt contextual social action.

Matthew 25:34–46 says that, at the time of judgment, Jesus will say to the righteous, "Come, you who are blessed by God; take your inheritance... For I was hungry and you gave me food, thirsty and you gave me drink, naked and you clothed me, a stranger and you welcomed me, in prison and you visited me..." (paraphrase)

When his listeners ask, "Lord, when did we see you hungry and give you drink...," Jesus says, "...whatever you did for one of the least of these, my brothers and sisters, you did for me." (paraphrase)

This scriptural teaching suggests that when the righteous see strangers needing food, clothing and shelter, they will take action. The "righteous" will feed people, set up clothing depots, and find housing for the homeless; others who are sick or unemployed and in need of care, or in prison and in need of solace, will receive the compassionate ministry of Christ's church.

Our intent is not to itemize the social problems that currently pervade Canadian society. It is, however, to contend that when Christ established his church, he expected his followers to care for those who have specific needs.

Outreach and Compassion and Conviction

Outreach, conceived as a response to the needs of others, affirms evangelistic ministry as both "word" and "deed." Our understanding of the term "empathetic evangelism" suggests that the tone of the "word" will focus on the specific recipients of the message, and that the expression of the "deed," the social concern, will focus on the specific needs of those receiving assistance. Consequently, outreach will have a dynamic or changing dimension, as well as a timeless message. The "message" will link to timeless truth, while the "method" and "specific response" will be a reflection of the social and cultural milieu in which it is presented. A Pentecostal minister from Manitoba notes that the church must be "continually re-inventing itself in order to apply the always relevant truths of the gospel to an ever changing culture."

The dynamic interplay of proclamation and social action is an important ingredient in church effectiveness. Outreach based entirely on "preaching" robs the church of its ethical thrust. Outreach based entirely on social action robs the church of its "soteriological edge,"[3] or perspective on salvation.

On the compassion side of outreach, we often find people who are so empathetic and inclusive that they have difficulty finding anything in the faith that qualifies as "the truth." Instead, they excel at tolerance and at handing out permission slips for almost everyone to believe and behave as they so desire. Although the overly compassionate person might never send out judgment signals that would offend anyone, seldom are they definitive enough in what they believe to inspire people outside the church to respond with faith and trust in Christ.

On the conviction side, a few moments of reflection will undoubtedly produce a short list of people in your mind who have an exceeding wealth of conviction. They function with clear truth categories and tend to view life as black or white. They know what they believe and are convinced that they are right. Although their intent is to be faithful to God, there is often a harsh edge to their judgments that pushes people away from even considering Christ's claims.

In our experience, both those who position themselves on the ultra-conservative side and those who stake out the ultra-liberal perspectives end up creating the same effect. Both are so convinced that they are right that they do not leave room for people who have come to faith convictions that are different from their own.

One of our respondents, a conservative Christian academic, articulated a warning about over-simplifying the mission of the church. He reasoned that "Prayer is important, but prayer alone is not enough to create constructive change." Some Christians tend to view outreach only in terms of preaching a message of salvation, of reducing the life of faith to a prayer and a momentary decision. That particular orientation to orthodoxy will be better balanced when it gives attention to the need for relevance.

Humanistic psychologists, following from Abraham Maslow, have contended that people cannot attend to their self-actualization needs when their stomachs are empty or their lives are in danger.[4] Those who view outreach as "compassion" have long recognized this—and often criticize those whose focus on conviction has allowed them to overlook the physical needs of others.

The fact that stomachs are empty or lives are in danger is reason enough to act. So too, the fact that souls are in danger is reason enough to proclaim the gospel. An effective approach to outreach and the work of the church will be one that balances concern for orthodoxy with sensitivity to the whole-person needs of others.

We recognize that many of the above comments are generalizations. Still, our reasoning illustrates the point that outreach involves both conviction and compassion. Conviction motivates evangelism to meet the demands of orthodoxy and outreach. Compassion motivates social action to meet the demands of outreach and relevance.

Sometimes, people feel that balance implies compromise. But in the case of the four categories cited above, **unless** churches balance the ministry equations, the gospel will be compromised.

In summary, the church can meet its demand for both orthodoxy and community through its worship. Discipling as a ministry links both community and relevance. Empathetic evangelism meets the need of both orthodoxy and outreach. And, both outreach and relevance are expressed through contextual social action.

Tension Issues

As we explore the interrelationships between the four cornerstones of effective churches, we need to make a distinction between "balance" issues and "tension" issues. In contrast to "balance" issues, in which a balancing mechanism serves to accomplish goals, "tension" issues are characterized by situations in which an overemphasis on one set of objectives can undermine a second set of objectives. For example, when community is overemphasized, it is at the expense of outreach. Instead of both priorities receiving their due attention, polarization results. *(See Fig. 8.2)*

First, consider the potential tension between orthodoxy and relevance. In the diagram below, this is depicted as a vertical tension. We have pictured it as a vertical tension because it involves the orientation of the church to either the sacred (up) or the secular (down). The second is the tension between community and outreach. This we have portrayed as a horizontal tension. We use the description "in/out" to describe the tension between responding to those outside the church, in contrast to ministering to those inside the church.

Fig. 8.2
Vertical and Horizontal Tensions

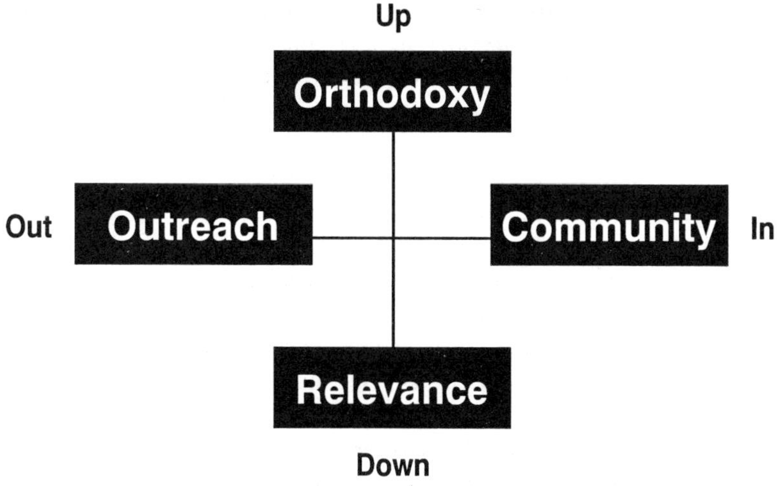

```
              Up
          Orthodoxy
              |
Out  Outreach —— Community  In
              |
           Relevance
             Down
```

The Orthodoxy/Relevance tension

The orthodoxy/relevance tension involves the issue of maintaining biblical and theological integrity while relating to the wider culture. The tension stems largely from a dualistic notion of being in the world but not of the world. According to the turn-of-the-century social thinker Emile Durkheim, religion is essentially the separation of the sacred and the profane.[5] The orthodoxy/relevance tension refers to the way in which we distinguish between the sacred and the secular, and to how we approach each domain. The large volume of academic literature on the topic suggests that there is no clear answer. As George Forell notes,

> The most persistent and disturbing problem confronting the Christian community since its birth in Palestine two thousand years ago to the very present has been and continues to be its relationship to the surrounding world... Christian thought had always to deal with the relationship of the Christian community and the individual Christian with the social and political environment.[6]

Views on the role of the church in the world range from accommodation (Christianity is no different from the wider culture), to separation from the world (Christianity is isolated and inaccessible to the wider culture).

The disciples of the early church were asked, "Why do you stand gazing up into heaven?" (Acts 1:11). Today, we could ask that same question of some other-worldly Christians. In an effort to remain orthodox, some Christian groups have taken world-rejection as a motif. They either live in a manner that prompts persecution from the world, or they view the world as a threat to their existence. Both lifestyles effectively preclude any meaningful outreach in the world.

George Forell's study on Christian social ethics notes that three dominant responses have operated in various ways throughout the history of the Christian church: separation, domination, and integration.[7]

The separation pattern reduces involvement with the non-Christian world to a bare minimum. Various cults and sects have attempted to effect such a separation through geographical or other forms of withdrawal. Despite the fact that isolation has been the most persistent pattern historically, the interdependence of church and culture makes such a response ineffective.

The domination pattern has emerged wherever the church has achieved a position of power. It attempts to use ecclesiastical power to outlaw any non-Christian manifestations of belief and behavior. From Constantine in Roman times to Jerry Falwell in contemporary American culture, attempts to impose a Christian social order have paid a price for excluding non-Christian minorities.

Gregory Baum talks about the danger of the church becoming its own idol:

> If idolatry be understood as the absolutizing of the finite and the elevating of a part to be the ultimate measure of the whole, then the Church's unmitigated claim to absolute truth and ultimate authority becomes problematic. From the Biblical point of view, the Church itself could become an idol... The Church is tempted by idolatry when it wants to multiply the absolutes and regard its teaching and its hierarchy as the ultimate norms for judging all forms of Christian life and faith.[8]

On the other hand, the pursuit of relevance has often resulted in a straying from orthodox truth. A Baptist clergy leader in Ontario writes that "The church today has lost its message and been absorbed into modern culture. It no longer speaks out against culture, culture has set the agenda for the church."

Rather than a dualistic approach that divides the secular and the sacred, the premise of this book is that the integration of faith with the realities of modern life is not only feasible but desirable. The integration pattern has sometimes been referred to as "dialogical."

This "pattern" attempts to articulate Christian convictions within the culture in which the church resides. Assisting God's people to integrate their faith into all areas of private and public life is the challenge for the church of our day. Indifference to the task of integrating faith into all of life will result in further marginalization of the church. An enduring commitment to the task will move the church toward a more viable future.

The Community/Outreach tension

Some of our survey respondents believe that the church exists for the purpose of reaching those who live in the world without regard for God. A Presbyterian clergy respondent in British Columbia, for example, argues that "The Church exists primarily for those who are not in it yet... This keeps us looking out to the community for outreach, not just inward as a club." Many others felt that the church must feed its own members first, before sending them out into the world.

In the "balance issues" section, we contend that healthy churches have both inner and outer functions. We believe that responding to "both ends" of the community/outreach equation is vital. The church is a community of believers and has an obligation to respond to inside needs. The church also exists for mission and has a responsibility for outreach. Worship and discipling essentially take place "within" the faith community. But worship and discipling also prepare members of the community to engage in the "outward" tasks of evangelism and social action.

William Willimon comments on the outward task:

> In its very existence, the church serves the world, not by running errands for the world, but by providing a light to the world, that is, by providing an imaginative alternative for society.[9]

In *Call to Conversion*, Jim Wallace offers a way of examining the inside/outside tension: "The community of faith incarnates a whole new order, offers a visible and concrete alternative, and issues a basic challenge to the world as it is."[10]

David Bosch states that

> The Church's offices, orders and institutions should be organized in such a manner that they serve society and do not separate the believer from the historical... Because of its integral relatedness to the world, the Church may never function as a fearful border guard, but always as one who brings good tidings.[11]

As we examine the tension between community and outreach, it helps to remember that while the faith community is the seed and the beginning of the Kingdom of God, it is not the full essence of the reign of God that is promised. We must, as Howard Snyder reminds us, live as "kingdom people" not as "church people."

> Kingdom people seek first the Kingdom of God and its justice; church people often put church work above concerns of justice, mercy and truth. Church people think about how to get people into the church; Kingdom people think about how to get the church into the world. Church people worry that the world might change the church; Kingdom people work to see the church change the world.[12]

An excerpt from the report of the World Council of Churches 1983 Vancouver Assembly issue group on "Taking Steps Towards Unity" expresses the church's mission in the world as dependent upon their being able to relate to the world while remaining unique in the world. The Church is called to be a prophetic "sign," a prophetic community through which and by which the transformation of the world can take place. It is only a church which goes out from its eucharistic centre, strengthened by word and by sacrament and thus strengthened in its own identity, that it can take the world on to its agenda. There will never be a time when the world, with all its political, social and economic issues, ceases to be the agenda of the Church. At the same time, the Church can go out from the edges of society, not fearful of being distorted or confused by the world's agenda, but confident and capable of recognizing that God is already there.[13]

Regardless of the difficulties to be overcome, people who go to church live most of their days and nights in the world. Effective churches will resolve the orthodoxy/relevance tensions and they will consciously wrestle with the community/outreach tensions.

Excess Issues

The diagram that follows takes the interaction with the four cornerstones of effective churches one step further. The commentary examines the consequences when any one of the cornerstone ministry commitments is excessively emphasized to the neglect of the others. When one facet of the faith dominates church life, an aberration of the faith inevitably results.

Figure 8.3 identifies four faith aberrations that result when imbalances and tensions within the orthodoxy, relevance, community, and outreach model orbit into unchecked excesses.

Unchecked orthodoxy produces self-righteous exclusivists

Self-righteous exclusivists are people and churches who live with a deep desire to be loyal to God.

At some point, however, they become so fixated on truth and doctrine that eventually they believe that "their thoughts are God's

Fig. 8.3
Implications of Unhealthy Excess

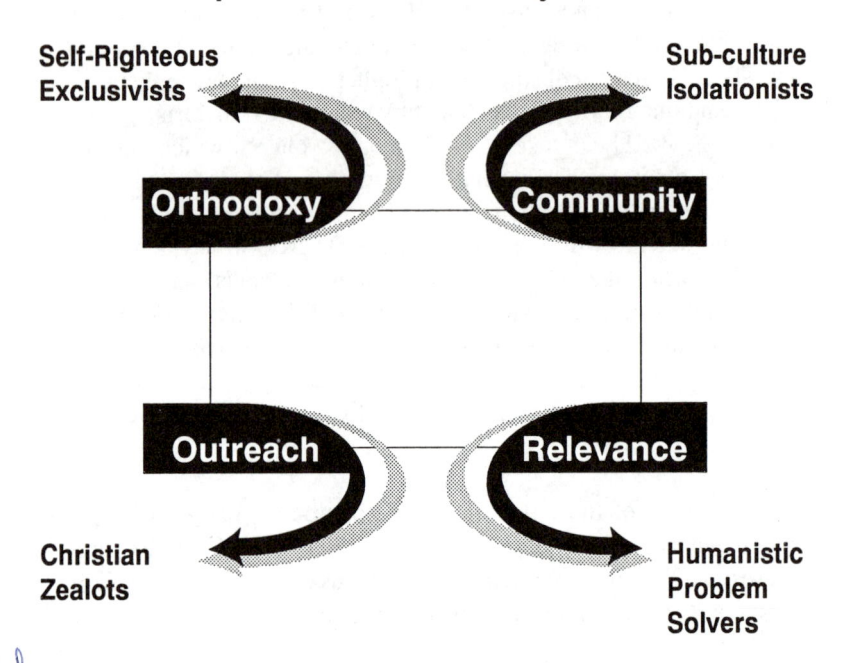

Self-Righteous Exclusivists — Orthodoxy

Sub-culture Isolationists — Community

Christian Zealots — Outreach

Humanistic Problem Solvers — Relevance

thoughts." From there, it is a small step to the conclusion that "their ways are God's ways." Unless you happen to agree with them on matters of faith, no dialogue is possible: they are right and you are wrong.

The church mentalities they construct leave very little room for God's extended family, for other churches and other denominations. These churches expect people who are born into their ranks, or who choose to join of their own volition, to embrace predetermined sets of dogma and lifestyle stipulations.

In this aberration, a person's or a church's desire to be godly propels them to attempt to transcend their humanity. They lose sight of their subjectivity and conclude that they have the corner on truth. The resulting imbalance causes these churches to reject the evils of secular society and to cocoon themselves against "contamination" from the world. Religious leaders in the exclusivist category call their people to lofty levels of personal holiness. Often without realizing it, they live in the midst of self-righteous pride.

Unchecked community produces sub-culture isolationists

Sub-culture isolationists primarily go to church for fellowship. They then proceed to build their lives totally within a Christian framework. Beyond worshiping with Christians, they belong to a small group, send their children to Christian schools, sleuth out Christian hair stylists, go on vacations with friends from the church, and consult the Christian yellow pages for guidance on where to shop.

Christian isolationists work in the world to get money for their personal needs and desires, as well as to support the costs of keeping church programs healthy and strong. They create a sub-culture within the main culture. Although all their behavior patterns may not be expressed at a conscious level, whenever possible, they insulate and isolate themselves from the world.

One thing is certain; they **will** make a contribution to their **own** Christian community.

Unchecked outreach produces Christian zealots

Christian zealots can never be accused of lacking spiritual conviction or boldness. Their single-mindedness generates a genuine passion for lost souls. They hand out tracts on the street, read plans of salvation out of booklets to people they have never met before, and are always ready to share the faith that resides vibrantly inside them.

Their "evangelistic" zeal is seldom accompanied by a complementary effort to relate to the world, or to meet the needs of those whom they are trying so hard to convert. Inside their own churches, little attempt is made to fuel and foster spiritual growth.

The primary purpose for being a Christian, from the zealot's point of view, is to win the world for Christ—whatever the cost. Many of God's people, and many of those who live in the world with little regard for God, find the spirituality of Christian zealots unattractive and often offensive.

Unchecked relevance produces humanistic problem solvers

Humanistic problem solvers usually start with a desire to serve the God of their faith. But in an effort to get close to the culture, they move away from orthodoxy and end up accommodating their ways to the ways of the world.

Unless the movement toward increased relevance is re-directed, this emphasis results in the substituting of secular alternatives for spiritual perspectives.

This aberration leaves little room for prayer or any other focus that represents specific spiritual substance. In the end, the church functions more like a community agency that offers social programs and self-help groups than a place that tries to provide spiritual help and to connect people with God. At this extreme, the church represents a group of humanistic problem solvers—totally anthropomorphic and introspective—who offer worldly wisdom as a solution to society's problems.

Too much attention to too few faith factors

One of the reasons the above spiritual aberrations emerge is that people in these churches give too much attention to too few factors of the faith. They become vulnerable to their particular excesses. Instead of being protected by a balanced ministry agenda, they become fixated on their special points of view.

To further complicate matters, groups that indulge in these excesses usually attract more of their own kind. Consequently, they expose themselves to another level of vulnerability. Instead of benefiting from the diverse perspectives usually found in a community of people, they sing the same songs and cheer the same slogans.

It would be naive to believe that the cornerstones of orthodoxy, community, relevance, and outreach can be mixed into church life in the same way that salad ingredients can be mixed and served for supper. We have too little control over too many things. We cannot control the cultural age in which we live. We cannot control the circumstances of people's lives. Life is simply too untidy to permit a balance of all the variables and all the tensions all of the time.

Still, if we possess a conscious awareness that healthy churches seek to balance the four ministry concerns represented by the cornerstones of orthodoxy, community, relevancy, outreach, many excesses can be avoided and corrected.

Convergence of Excesses

Figure 8.4 takes the cornerstone model a final step. It illustrates what will happen when the cornerstones converge and move toward a second-stage aberration. We have identified four types of "convergence outcomes" based on the tensions within the orthodoxy, relevance, community, outreach model.

The first two convergence outcomes involve excesses which lean in the direction of separation from the world.

Fig. 8.4
Additional Implications of Unhealthy Excesses

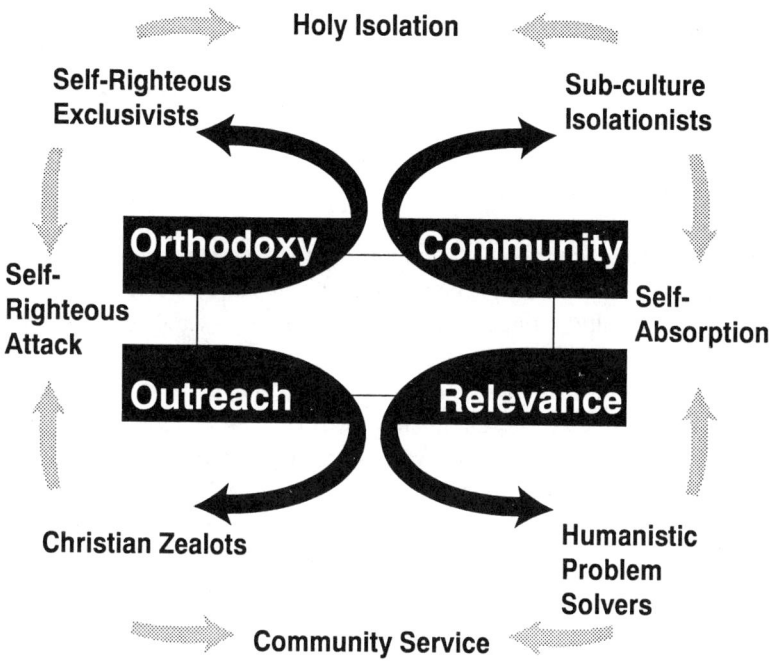

```
                    Holy Isolation
  Self-Righteous                        Sub-culture
  Exclusivists                          Isolationists

          ┌─ Orthodoxy ─── Community ─┐
  Self-                                    Self-
  Righteous                                Absorption
  Attack
          └─ Outreach  ─── Relevance ─┘

  Christian Zealots                     Humanistic
                                        Problem
                                        Solvers
                   Community Service
```

Holy isolation

Holy isolation involves an emphasis on doctrinal orthodoxy at the expense of relevance, combined with an emphasis on community at the expense of outreach. The resulting imbalance would lead to a church which rejects the world and cocoons itself against any "contamination" from the world.

The "holy island" is similar to Bryan Wilson's notion of the introversionist sect in which the world is seen as irredeemably evil. The only possible response is a full withdrawal from the world. This leads to the establishment of "a separated community preoccupied with its own holiness and its means of insulation from the wider society."[14]

Bosch points out that such an excess steps outside the boundaries of orthodox Christian faith.

> If the Church attempts to sever itself from any involvement in the world and if its structures are such that they thwart any

possibility of rendering a relevant service to the world, such structures must be recognized as heretical.[15]

Self-righteous attack

Self-righteous attack combines doctrinal orthodoxy at the expense of relevance, with an emphasis on outreach at the expense of community. In this instance, evangelism lacks empathy and takes the form of a diatribe against the world which only serves to confirm the group's sense of its own holiness.

An expression of this imbalance is seen in overly zealous "evangelistic" efforts which make no complementary effort to relate to the world or to meet the needs of those being evangelized. Here we find a church in conflict with culture, rather than one which brings a viable gospel to the world.

The characteristic pride prevalent in the "attack" mode also fails to recognize that God is present in the world. The perception of the church as an entity separate from the wider human community serves only to alienate the church and to undermine its mission in the world. This point was recognized in the "Faith and Order" papers at the World Council of Churches conference in Geneva (1986): "As soon as the Church tries to view its own life as meaningful in independence from the total human community, it betrays the major purpose of its existence."[16]

The second set of convergence outcomes involve those churches which emphasize cultural relevance at the expense of biblical orthodoxy. In an effort to achieve integration with the culture, these churches become trapped in accommodation. Excessive movement in this direction essentially converts the church into a secular organization, and leaves it with little spiritual substance.

Self-absorption

Self-absorption involves an emphasis on relevance at the expense of orthodoxy, coupled with an emphasis on community at the expense of outreach.

These emphases effectively reduce the church to the role of a secular self-help group. We recognize that many beneficial self-help groups use the facilities of local churches, and that often these programs are only a part of what these churches offer to their members. However, we also contend that if there is no specific orientation to Christian truth or to the assistance of others beyond the regular attenders, then self-help groups can be just as effective if they are held at the local community center.

Our intent is not to depreciate the value of group counseling or the coming together of interest groups to find solutions to shared personal concerns. Our point is that the Christian church really only functions **as the church** when it addresses problems with responses that draw upon its spirituality.

Community service

Community service represents another unbalanced portrayal of the church. It offers social programs without acknowledging a direct connection to God as the source of spiritual help.

This final convergence results from an over-emphasis on cultural relevance, combined with a view of outreach that minimizes Christian community. While the approach may be successful at securing government funding, if the dominant orientation is towards social problem solving, it depreciates the essence of being Christian.

At its extreme, this convergence allows the culture to determine how social problems are defined and solved. The church merely administers secular solutions to human problems. At this point, the church itself becomes extraneous to the dedicated efforts and fine work already being done by professional social workers.

Conclusion

Released from its excesses, the ministry model for effective churches, illustrated in *Figure 8.5*, provides a useful reference point for denominations and individual churches, allowing them to examine their own emphases in the light of the need for balance and the importance of resolving inherent tension issues.

Jesus' parable of the Prodigal Son reminds us of the dangers of excess. When the younger son squandered his inheritance, he became the victim of his excesses. More importantly, though, the parable raises the possibility of finding the road home. It holds out the promise of healing and restoration and an enthusiastic "welcome home."

In the biblical account, the father peers down the road daily, looking and hoping for the prodigal's return. The father knew which direction to look. He knew his son would return home on the same road he used for his departure.

The model of the four cornerstones suggests a number of possible excesses—a number of divergent roads upon which the church, or we as

Fig. 8.5
Ministry Mix for Effective Churches

Uplifting Worship

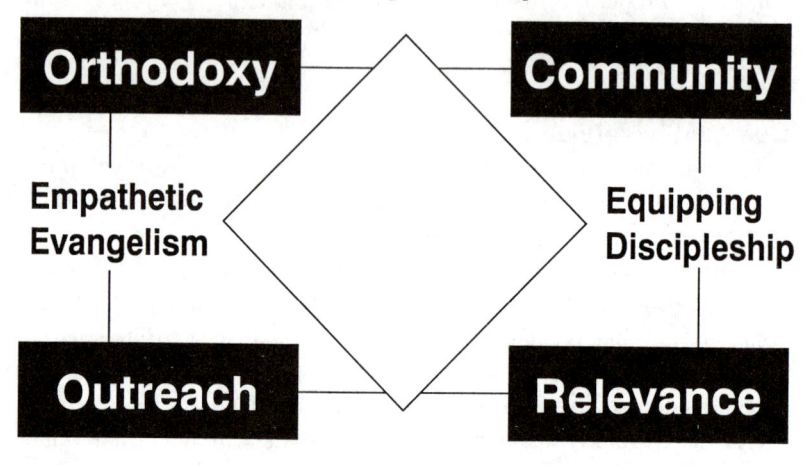

Orthodoxy — **Community**

Empathetic Evangelism — Equipping Discipleship

Outreach — **Relevance**

Contextual Social Action

individuals, can stray. But if we possess the will and desire to use it, the same road which took us in the direction of excess can also bring us back home.

By using the model of the four cornerstones, we hope that churches will be able to "locate" and assess themselves. If a church has drifted in the direction of excess, it will be important to take steps to adjust the ministry mix and move toward a balance that can lead to increased effectiveness.

The model can also be applied to one's personal life. At this level, it can provide a framework for achieving a more integrated and coherent life in Christ.

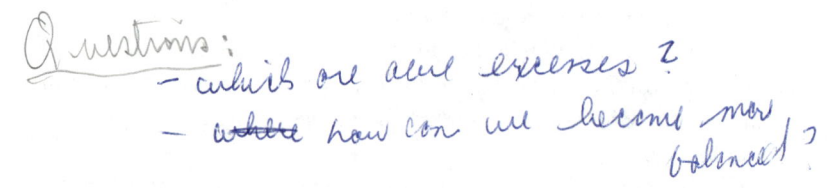

Effective Leadership Styles

Chapter Nine

Today's church leaders face a myriad of demands and expectations. The accumulation of historical roles along with the complex demands of contemporary life combine to create enormous expectations—especially for the clergy.

Church historian Bruce Shelley summarizes the triple roles that clergy have traditionally been expected to fulfil.

First, there is the **priest** role that places sacramental acts at the center of Christian ministry. Often called the "catholic" or "sacramental" view, the mediation of divine grace lies at the heart of priestly ministry. Performing ceremonies and sacramentalizing the rites of passage is a frequent priestly function.

The **minister** role emphasizes that pastoral service to people is central to the work of the clergy. The functions include counseling, comforting, visiting and healing. The minister is expected to be pastoral, empathetic, supportive and responsive to parishioner's needs.

The **preacher** role characteristically stresses the public declaration of the Word as central to the ministerial calling. Proclaiming the good news and expounding the scriptures are the primary task of the preacher.[1]

The priest, minister, and preacher roles are usually compatible or at least complementary to each other. However, as society has become more complex, more specialized and more professional, additional roles have been added to the traditional functions. To complicate matters further, the expectation of high competency levels in each of these expanding roles adds to the priestly, pastoral and preaching pressures on today's clergy.

For instance, as psychology matured and the demands for counseling increased among parishioners, expectations for ministers to understand their parishioners' psychological as well as the spiritual needs intensified. The **counselor** role became desirable.

Assumptions linked to continuing education also mean that pastors and preachers are often expected to hone their management skills, develop a business acumen and become experts in human relations. Whether it is realistic or not, the role of the clergy is tantamount to the president who reports to a board of directors in a business. Accordingly, the roles are now often expanded to **business manager** and **human relations specialist**. Because the newer roles can be in conflict with the traditional roles, tensions often result.

Some members of the clergy may resist the leadership expectations projected at them. They lament, "I didn't sign up for this kind of responsibility." They may even resent the assumption that their leadership is indispensable in fashioning an effective church.

But like it or not, the data supports the strong opinion of Episcopal priest and professor Howard Hanchey:

> Whether congregations are large or small, clergy leadership makes the most important difference in why some churches are spirited while others are not. Now again I say, this is not a pitch for a clergy-centred ministry. And I'm not suggesting that all lethargic congregations find their rest in clergy leadership...but clergy leadership makes all the difference.[2]

Lyle Schaller bangs the same drum: "Ministerial leadership is a far more influential factor...in all the characteristics that enhance congregational health and vitality."[3] This is echoed in our survey finding that three-quarters of the respondents felt that switching churches is justified if the clergy leadership style is inadequate. Only 3% felt that switching churches is "never justified" in such a case.

At the same time, being a good leader does not mean "doing it all yourself." Acknowledging the critical leadership role played by the clergy should neither demean nor lessen the importance of roles expressed by the laity and academics in creating effective churches. In fact, forming fresh leadership alliances between the prime players will be critical in the church of the future. Real progress will only be made when clergy, academics and the laity combine their gifts and complement each other's roles for the common purpose of fostering effective churches.

The survey questions on leadership acknowledge that there are various styles of clergy/pastoral leadership. Respondents were asked, "In your opinion, what styles of leadership are most effective for today's church?" An image of the effective church leader emerged as one who is focused on equipping others to develop their gifts; who seeks consensus but is not afraid to take risks; who meets people's needs rather than counting people as numbers; and who is ready to share authority.

Accordingly, this chapter uses the responses of the survey participants to profile what effective leadership in the 1990s looks like. And although members of the clergy are the central focus, these leadership dynamics also apply to laity and academics, elders, deacons and wardens, board members and session leaders. *(See Fig. 9.1a and Fig. 9.1b)*

Foster vision—then lead

History professor, Bruce Shelley, from Denver Seminary, observes that "most agree that leadership starts with vision...vision that serves as a bridge from the present conditions to future possibilities in ministry."[4]

A lay leader from Saskatchewan affirms the same message: "Effectiveness probably has more to do with church vision and a climate of acceptance than using the 'correct' strategies."

A Baptist minister from British Columbia asserts that, "The number one priority in choosing a church would be to determine what they seek to accomplish."

A Presbyterian minister from Ontario says, "Clergy leadership is critical—a leadership which helps people say 'yes' to vision/mission/ministry."

Proverbs 29:18 (KJV) pronounces the same message: "Where there is no vision, the people perish."

Leaders are people who know where they are going and who have the ability to take other people along with them. Today, we need women and men who can inspire others to keep moving in the direction God would like the Canadian church to travel.

A minister serving in the Christian Missionary Alliance church in Alberta sums up the section:
> There are two critical factors in effective church ministry, one is vision, a second is having a purpose and drive. These combined with vigorous, plural leadership can (under God) be instrumental in effective ministry.

Although leaders may not want the responsibility, and some clergy in particular may prefer to back away from the demands, visionary and pro-active leadership is essential in fashioning effective churches.

But along with the above encouragement a word of caution must

Where's a Good Church?

Fig. 9.1a

Preferred Leadership Styles

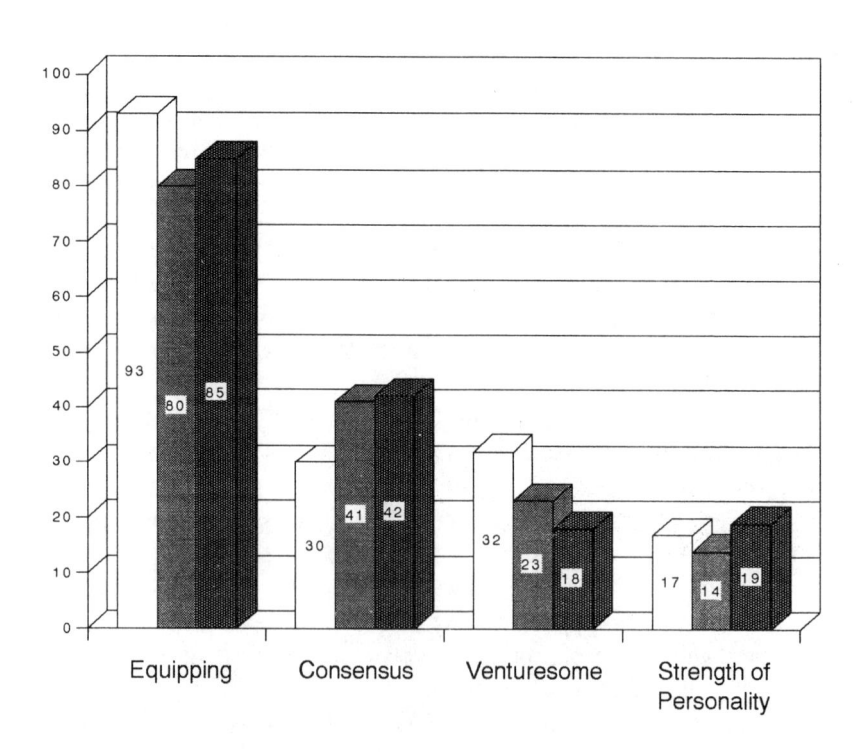

	Clergy	Academics	Laity
Equipping	93	80	85
Consensus	30	41	42
Venturesome	32	23	18
Strength of Personality	17	14	19

☐ Clergy ■ Academics ■ Laity

Graph shows percentage of respondents who ranked each leadership style as "very effective."

Fig. 9.1b

Preferred Leadership Styles

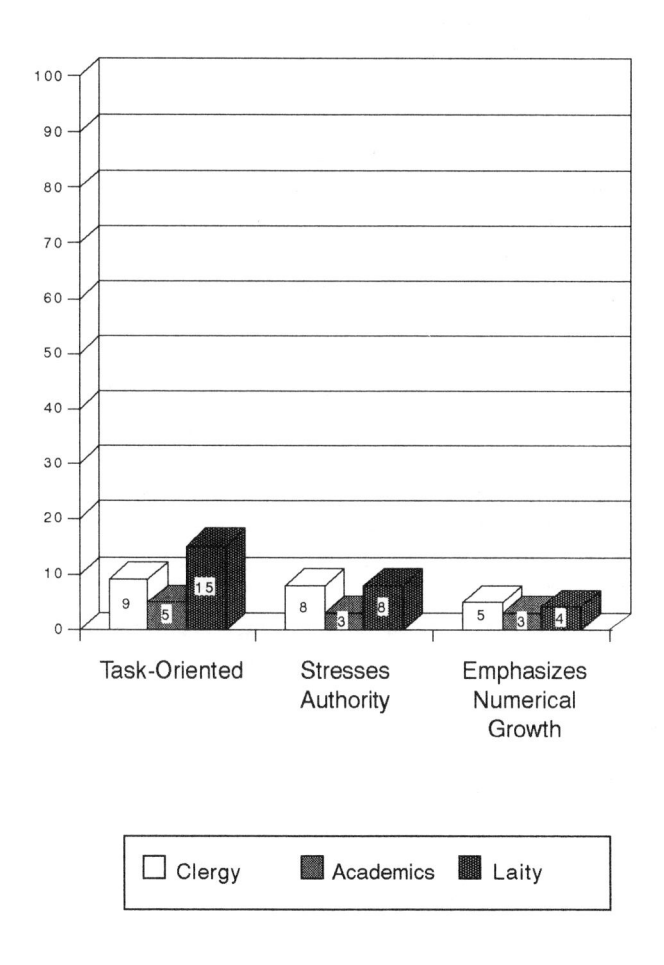

	Task-Oriented	Stresses Authority	Emphasizes Numerical Growth
Clergy	9	8	5
Academics	5	3	3
Laity	15	8	4

☐ Clergy ■ Academics ■ Laity

Graph shows percentage of respondents who ranked each leadership style as "very effective."

also be offered. When asked whether members of the clergy would be effective if they "lead with the strength of their personalities," just 18% endorsed the idea as "very effective." Canadians are nervous about giving their leaders too much prerogative. They have lived through too many past disappointments to hand out blank checks in the present. The public's awareness of scandals and repeated breaches of trust involving church leaders means it will be a long time before confidence in the clergy returns to former levels. As Bruce and Marshall Shelley have pointed out, today, "trust gained becomes trust guarded, ...leaders must be both consistent in their pursuit of moral principle, in their personal lives as well as in their ministries."[5]

Confirm compatibility—then lead

I was born into a Christian home. When the church doors were open, our family was present in the pew. As a child and a teenager, though I didn't always like the limits, I was well served by the church of my family heritage. I will always be indebted for the long-term impact of my early spiritual formation.

As a young adult, I became increasingly aware that I just didn't fit into the denominational mold of my heritage. After training for the ministry and serving seven stimulating years as a pastor in the denomination of my youth, the gulf between the denominational non-negotiables and my personal convictions was insurmountable. The theological, philosophical and methodological incompatibility were more than shared history and valued relationships could hold together. It was time for a denominational divorce.

When you have been raised and nurtured in a particular denomination, you never find an adequate replacement for your original spiritual roots. Still, the pain of severance is preferable to living with irreconcilable differences. In the long run, living and leading is impossible in the midst of incompatibility.

Every denomination has distinctives. Local churches also have their own sets of circumstances. Two churches from the same denomination, located in the same city, can vary greatly from each other.

Every member of the clergy has uniqueness too. Beyond theological convictions and liturgical and worship preferences, every leader has a specific temperament and definable style. Life in the church works best when there is a basic compatibility between the denominational ethos, the leader's style and personal vision, and the expectations of the members of the congregation.

There is enormous potential for incompatibility and conflict within the church. Can you imagine what would happen if the minister and lay person making the following comments were in the same church? Listen first to a lay member from a Mennonite Brethren congregation in British Columbia:

> Leadership in the church has been too focused on expectations imposed on the clergy. Churches seem to expect vision to emanate from someone they are pleased to call the senior pastor... Given the complexity of modern society, dependence on collective leadership is more sensible than searching out the increasingly elusive omni-competent senior pastor.

Contrast the implications of that perspective with those of a minister from an independent church in Nova Scotia:

> One of our main reasons for erosion in the church is that leadership is following the direction that is demanded by the [lay] people. Churches that are governed by the opinion of the people will not survive.

The independent minister and the lay member can both find a church where they can personally belong and contribute, but it will not be the same church. Geography is not all that makes these two respondents as far apart as British Columbia and Nova Scotia. Their under-

Fig. 9.2
Leadership Traits and Styles

Autocratic	Democratic	Laissez-faire
Acts without consulting	Consults then acts	Goes with the flow
Independent	Inter-dependent	Dependent
Incessantly intentional	Selectively intentional	Occasionally intentional
Task driven	Task concerned	Task aware
Active	Active/passive	Passive/active
Authoritarian	Authoritative	Compliant

standings about how life should work in a church community are simply incompatible.

The leadership grid above *(Fig. 9.2)* can assist members of the clergy to identify their dominant style as well as provide congregations with guidelines for selecting the kind of leader that will be compatible with their circumstances or appropriate for their current needs.

Strong compatibility between the leader and the group not only makes it relatively easy to find common ground, it reduces the potential for conflict. An analysis of the interplay around particular leadership styles illustrates the value of starting with compatibility or at least understanding what the other participants in the group prefer.

For example, focus on the implications of the differences when they apply to small churches. Although one-quarter of the national sample think that effective church leaders will take risks, in small churches less than half that number think that way. To further complicate matters, twice as many clergy as laity believe there is a link between risk taking and effective leadership. The ramifications are predictable. Particularly in small churches, leaders who are inclined to be venturesome and to take risks will meet resistance. And if they seek to initiate something new without first gaining a consensus, they will create havoc. At the same time, projecting the importance of getting the job done will be a welcomed leadership emphasis in small churches. The issues to monitor will revolve around the process of getting the job done. *(See Fig. 9.3)*

The data tell us that clergy are inclined to link taking risks with effective leadership, while laity are more prone to think that seeking consensus is important. Consequently, there is inherent distance. In all likelihood, incompatibility will arise between the primary players. Astute leaders will always close the distance before launching out in new directions. Leaders who don't stay close enough to the people they desire to influence not only start to feel lonely, they end up on their own. Except in those rare situations where a church has been built on the entrepreneurial energy and leadership style of one person, taking time to ensure that compatibility exists will preclude painful scenarios.

Share authority—then lead

Effective leaders in the 1990s will share authority. Only 8% of the survey group thought that "clergy leadership that stresses the leader's authority" would be "very effective." By contrast, over half said that leaders who stress their authority would be "basically ineffective" or "not effective at all."

Fig. 9.3
Clergy Leadership Styles
Comparison of Lay Members and Clergy Perceptions

	Small Church (under 75)		Medium Church		Large Church (500)	
	Lay (36) (%)	Clergy (21) (%)	Lay (300) (%)	Clergy (141) (%)	Lay (75) (%)	Clergy (51) (%)
Seeks Consensus	47	48	42	30	32	20
Venturesome	17	14	18	32	20	41
Strong Personality	22	5	12	17	19	22
Task-Oriented	25	10	15	9	11	8
Authority	8	10	8	8	7	12

Table shows percentage in each category who viewed each leadership style as "very effective."

The prevailing mood in society at large also resides in the church. Unless leaders have created a private kingdom, people who think they can wield power by virtue of their position, or for that matter can exert personal power in order to reach their objectives, are simply out of touch.

The data reveals little variance across mainline and conservative denominational lines. Only those in Pentecostal and Independent churches are a little more inclined to encourage their leaders to use an authoritarian style. *(See Fig. 9.4)*

Offering a positive prescription, a lay person from an Associated Gospel church in Quebec suggested that "Church leaders do not have to be authoritarian nor charismatic personalities, but [they must be people who are] full of compassion, who make talking, listening and getting to know people their top priority. This will naturally lend itself to church growth, numerically and spiritually."

Fig. 9.4
Use of Authority
Percentage in favor

Mainline	Conservative	Pentecostal	Independent
5	6	14	17

A lay leader from an Anglican church in British Columbia added this statement: "The priest is important but he/she is only part of the body of Christ, alone—nothing."

If there is a biblical leadership prototype for today, it is to be more like Barnabas than Paul. In a telling incident from the early years of the New Testament church, Paul and Barnabas argued about whether or not John Mark should be allowed to join them on their next missionary journey (Acts 15:36–41). The problem for Paul was that in his mind, "Mark was a quitter." And Paul was right. Mark did desert the team on the last mission. The problem for Barnabas was that he believed that people should have the right to fail and the freedom to begin again. In the end, "The disagreement became so sharp that they parted company; Barnabas took Mark with him and...Paul chose Silas and set out" (Acts 15:39–40, NRSV).

In that particular situation, Paul was more task driven than he was person centered. Barnabas, on the other hand, was more person concerned than he was task driven. Both Barnabas and Paul were strong and gifted leaders. In the history of their relationship, Barnabas had done the same thing for Paul that he was now doing for John Mark (Acts 9:27).

There will always be a need for Paul's leadership style in the work of the Kingdom, but at the moment, in the work of the local church, Barnabas' style of encouraging and believing in people is more compelling.

In the context of inviting leaders to share their authority, business leader Max DePree has this advice: "The first responsibility of a leader is to define reality. The last is to say thank you."[6]

Equip others—then lead

It follows naturally that if shared authority is a goal, then some effort must be made to equip people for leadership roles. The respondents came close to speaking with a single voice. A total of 87% said that "clergy leadership that encourages church members to develop their gifts to serve and lead" will be "very effective." In the life of the church, the call is for shared leadership.

A lay leader in a Mennonite Brethren church from Alberta said, "We are orientated far too much to the professional clergy and it is stifling lay-creativity and lay-ownership."

A woman minister from a Salvation Army church in Ontario used different language to convey the same message: "An effective church is one in which its members can discover and use spiritual gifts, grow in knowledge and practice of Bible principles."

While lay members were divided in their preference for lay leadership versus clergy leadership in the specific area of worship, the comments from the survey and focus group discussions represent a reaction to the professionalization of the church that confines all the work of spiritual ministry to the person being paid to do the job. The evidence supports the conclusion that "many laity are frustrated, feeling they are made of sterner stuff and called to greater things."[7] Clergy could breathe a sigh of relief and surrender some of their multiple roles to other members of the Body of Christ who have gifts and abilities to serve. George Barna offers complementary counsel: "If the church were to take the time and make the effort to identify their potential leaders' gifts, and permit them to use those gifts for ministry, there would be less volunteer burnout."[8]

A minister, from a Lutheran church in Alberta, leans in the right direction when he states, "Effective churches give people all of the 'tools' they need to grow in their faith. In other words, 'Come and listen very carefully to what the Word says to our world today—then go home and do what the Spirit leads you to do in response.'"

A lay member from a United church offered another perspective on liberating the laity: "The ego of [healthy] ministers is not threatened by the creative diversities of its members."

Stressing that leadership is an art, renowned business innovator Max DePree attests that the art of leadership is "liberating people to do what is required of them in the most effective and humane way possible."[9]

Along with many other writers, Catholic commentator Robert Greenleaf talks about leadership as "servanthood." Countering the idea that servant leaders simply do what they are told or act in ways that will make life easier for other people, Greenleaf contends that the best test of a servant leader is, "Do those served grow as persons? Do they, while being served, become healthier, wiser, freer, more autonomous, more likely themselves to become servants?"[10] In other words, the purpose of servant leadership is to develop the gifts and facilitate the growth of the people being served.

Again, Max DePree images that "A jazz band is an expression of servant leadership. The leader of a jazz band has the beautiful opportunity to draw the best out of the other musicians. We have much to learn from jazz-band leaders, for jazz, like leadership, combines the unpredictability of the future with the gifts of individuals."[11]

Extending the jazz band metaphor, members of the clergy who excel at playing their own instrument will do best when they step aside and let other members of the body move into the lead and play their instruments too.

A lay member of a Pentecostal church from Alberta summarized the messages from many respondents:

> There is a place and work for every believer…[and] the sooner we realize there is but one God and one body, though different abilities, the sooner we'll become a force to be reckoned with.

Build consensus—then lead

On another leadership issue, 38% said "clergy leaders that seek to gain the consensus of church members before acting" would be "very effective." A additional 41% said seeking consensus would be "somewhat effective." The picture is clear. Committed and involved church people want to be consulted before their clergy seek to lead. If ministers ever had the divine right to take their direction straight from God, it is certainly not the case today.

Reflecting a desire to personally participate, a lay leader from a Baptist fellowship in Ontario said, "Strong leadership must be balanced with a sincere concern for the opinions and concerns of the membership as individuals."

Understanding the dynamics of modern leadership, a Presbyterian member of the clergy from Ontario observed, "Leadership of the pastor needs to be visionary and enthusiastic. He/she must be able to enlist the following of the people toward an agreed upon goal."

A lay leader from a Baptist church in British Columbia said, "People cannot be pushed where they are not ready to go. The job of the leadership is to question and stretch the comfort zones of their congregation until the congregation is ready to move forward."

The danger of going too far in order to fashion a strong consensus is, of course, that life can fall to the level of the lowest common denominator. Too many compromises can result in a consensus that isn't worth pursuing into action. James Gillies, in his article, "Where Have All the Leaders Gone," says,

> Good leaders do not govern by polls or adjust their positions to every change in public opinion, which is always short term and greatly influenced by every new fad. They understand that sometimes they must offend some people, even their supporters, in order to move closer to the accomplishment of their goals.[12]

The point is that good leadership builds consensus. Often a leader is called upon to create consensus in the midst of conflict or disorder. Other times, the prevailing wishes are inconsistent with proper spiritual goals. A consensus-oriented leader with no discernment is no leader at all. Leadership is quite different from merely acting on whatever status quo happens to exist.

Prudent leadership doesn't wait to receive 100% endorsement before moving into action. But neither does wise leadership initiate action without the support of a strong group within the congregation. Building a group consensus is not the same as "asking permission." Young children go to their parents to ask permission. Leaders go to their groups to consult, solicit honest feedback, process plans and communicate vision.

Committed people in Canada's churches have some strong feelings about what should and should not be done in their churches. A lay leader from a Mennonite Brethren church said unambiguously, "We need to stop catering to baby-boomers and their supposed special needs, and instead challenge them to bring their self-centered special needs under the Lordship of Christ."

If the leaders of her congregation were to suddenly target their ministry toward "baby-boomers," without careful consultation, there would either be a conflict or her departure.

A lay attender from a Presbyterian church in Ontario did not cushion her words either: "Ministers need to continue to study and think with lay people... The laity I know are way ahead of the clergy leading them."

Business management consultant Lawrence Miller contends that "The highest-quality decisions are attained through consensus. Consensus is most valuable when it represents the collective wisdom of participants with diverse views and experience."[13] The same principle applies to life in the church. In this age, discerning leaders will build consensus—then lead.

Create community—then lead

The recipe for effective leadership is now predictable. Affirm people by equipping them and giving them opportunities to serve. Pay the price of constructing alliances of compatibility and build toward a strong group consensus. Share authority, and in doing so, create community. As well as giving people a place to serve and participate, give them a place to belong. Accordingly, 82% of mainline church participants and 86% of those who attend conservative churches claim that having a "sense of belonging" is "very important" in their criteria for what is an effective church.

By contrast, the recipe for being "ineffective" is to preclude a sense of community by asserting the leader's authority, being task driven and number centered. A mere 4% said that leadership that emphasized numerical gains would be "very effective" and only 12% said the same about leadership that was task driven. Unless leadership is people sensitive, the only place it can lead is to disaster.

A lay leader from a Baptist church in Nova Scotia offers a recommendation to colleges and seminaries who prepare their students for pastoral ministry: "Pastors being trained for ministry need a strong foundation in relating to the needs of others."

Today's world aches for pastoral touches. Everywhere we look, people have been wounded. Many of those same people are now ready to deal with the pain involved in repairing the damage. People's wounds seldom heal in isolation from other people. God created people for community. The support of others is especially crucial for people experiencing pain.

Many churches across the country have implemented small groups into their ministry structures. These groups provide places for people to share life together. When the survey asked if people were to choose another church, half of the participants indicated that the option of joining a small group would be a "high priority." When choosing another church to attend, conservative respondents were more likely than those attending mainline churches to look for small group options.

Small groups have the potential of serving a number of different purposes. Beyond offering individuals a place to be known and cared for, small groups are ideal structures for Bible studies, special interest discussion groups and prayer groups. Small groups can also encourage greater numbers of people to develop their leadership skills and pastoral gifts.

For more and more people, small groups provide the entry point into further involvement in the church. As a result, small groups create the possibility for numerical growth. As a minister from an Independent church in Manitoba observed, "If the pastoral care aspect of a church is not decentralized, the church will never grow beyond the pastor's ability to keep all the balls up in the air."

Involving people in the committees or activities of the church will not necessarily create community. Neither will programs designed specifically to bring people together so they can get to know each other. In the church, the basic building block for community is the people of God living out their shared life as followers of Christ. It's the combination of worshiping, praying, serving and mutually believing the truth of the gospel that creates community. Community is the result of weeping with those who weep and celebrating with those who celebrate. A common commitment to Christ's mission fosters shared and meaningful life.

Preach relevantly—then lead

The Sunday following the 1992 Los Angeles riot was troubling for me. The previous week, the Rodney King tape had been replayed incessantly on television. The "not guilty" verdict for the officers involved sent a message to black people everywhere that justice remains elusive. The disappointment with the verdict, combined with those images of Rodney King being beaten, the senseless deaths, the destruction by fire, the ethnic hatred and the ruining of so many lives, left my spirit in despair.

That same week, although there was no loss of life along Toronto's Yonge Street, the smashing of windows and the looting of stores left me feeling fragile.

As I went to church that morning, I longed for some sense of reassurance that God was aware of what was going on. My unspoken hope was that I might hear something that would help cushion the horror of what had happened during the week.

It wasn't that I expected an explanation, or a prescription that would prevent another outbreak of madness. But I did not expect the crisis to be ignored. Yet in that church, at least, not one word was mentioned, not one reference made to the events that had captured the attention of all of us during the week. Even the morning prayers were silent about the catastrophe.

As I walked out of the church, I was angry. I would have been better off staying at home or going for a walk.

When people were asked about what would be important if they were planning to switch churches, the highest response was in reference to "excellent preaching." Almost three-quarters of respondents said the quality of the preaching was a "high priority." Mainline and conservative respondents shared exactly the same view. In addition, two-thirds of those surveyed said that finding a church that was "in touch with the times" would also be very important.

A lay leader from a Pentecostal church in Ontario expressed the concern with penetrating insight:

> Effective church leadership presents the gospel accurately and fully in a culturally relevant manner focusing on the needs of the community. Ministers must have the ability to move from "shepherd" to "rancher." They need to be knowledgeable about cultural/social trends.

Karl Barth is famous for his insight that God's people must go into the world with the Bible in one hand and the newspaper in the other. In today's society, it is impossible to be in touch with the times without being informed about what people in the pew are watching on television. Because television both shapes and reflects modern culture, it is an indispensable source of input for relevance. Certainly it is possible to appeal to virtue and make a case for not watching television—but only at the cost of being culturally illiterate.

Jesus constructed his teaching material out of the stuff of life. His parables were about money, working for just wages, finding things that had been lost, and resolving conflict in the family. He taught that it was important to help people who were in trouble, even if it meant being late for a meeting. He talked with people about sex, and power, and the forces that control their lives. Jesus was tuned in to life around him. On one occasion he looked out across the city of Jerusalem, and wept. If Jesus was on earth today, he would grieve over violence in Toronto and death in Los Angeles and then he would lead his followers in a response.

For God's sake—lead

These are complicated days for leaders. The diversification of ministerial roles places new demands on everyone. Sometimes these demands are excessive. The marginalization of the Christian church in society means that instead of leading from positions of strength, clergy often find themselves in positions of weakness. In general, the prevailing attitude toward leaders in the country is more likely to generate criticism than to extend the benefit of the doubt. Too often, the expectations placed on clergy and the members of their families are inordinate. Still, we must not back away from the crucial difference that positive leadership can make. Kenneth Callahan makes this point in his book, *Twelve Keys to an Effective Church*:

> The time for leaders has come, the time for enablers has passed. In the churched culture of the 1950s, it was possible for the church to focus on developing enablers. In the unchurched culture of the 1980s it is decisively important that the church focus on developing leaders.[14]

Leaders are influencers. Leaders disrupt the status quo. And even though leadership in today's world is a complicated role to assume, people are still more inclined to look for people to follow than organizations to join. Just as there are many ways to enter the Kingdom, there are many ways to lead effectively:

Sometimes leaders support and encourage;
Sometimes leaders work alongside;
Sometimes leaders forge the way;
Sometimes leaders sit on people, slow down the pace, or counter the flow;
Occasionally leaders confront;
More often, leaders follow;
Leaders know the value of finding people who are out ahead of them.

Whatever expression of leadership is needed for the situation at hand, a Mennonite Brethren minister summarizes the importance of leadership in today's church: "Speed of the Leaders, speed of the Church!"

Marching Off the Map

Chapter Ten

The shoe-making industry provides wonderful insight into the speed and impact of change. From the middle ages until the beginning of the 20th century, shoe-making was the cobbler's domain. Working alone with skills handed down from master to apprentice, the cobbler individualized each pair of shoes. The same cobbler would cut the leather, sew the seams, pound the nails and polish the finished pair.

In the late 19th century, factory-made shoes became the norm. An assembly line of machines replaced the cobbler's bench; each worker on the line worked a machine to complete a single task, often touching a shoe only to pass it to the next station.

By the 1980s, the shoe assembly line was giving way to a new phenomenon: computerized robotic assembly. These automated assembly lines are run by a team of workers who never touch the shoe or the machines. Changes in shoe design and fashion are achieved by a team that collaborates to change the robot's program. The ability to change the robotics program allows each order to be specifically tailored to the buyer's requirements.[1]

What does the technological revolution in the shoe industry have to do with the characteristics of effective churches? Should churches become like factories? Should church programs, ministry, pastoral care and outreach be carried out with impersonal and robotic efficiency? Should church workers become like machines? Obviously not.

But think about the ways the church has functioned for the past 300 years. In the 1700s, priests stood behind pulpits to preach their sermons. In the 1800s, organs played the same tunes being played today. For the past 50 years, people across Canada have walked into their churches between 10:00 and 11:00 a.m. to sit in rows of pews. Next week, next month and next year people across Canada will walk into their churches between 10:00 and 11:00 a.m. to sit in rows of pews.

An 18th century cobbler walking into a modern shoe factory would be overwhelmed and fascinated, unable to sew a stitch. If a 19th century priest walked into a 1990s church, he could simply move to the pulpit and start preaching a sermon. The alarming reality is that he might even be able to pull out one of his 100-year-old sermons and not sound that much out of place. The church today looks and sounds very much as it did decades and even centuries ago.

Some of God's good people will look at the unchanging nature of the church and claim, "That's the way it should be. The gospel is for time and eternity. When the church changes, it gets itself in trouble." Others will counter and contend, "The resistance of the church to change is one of the reasons for its downfall. The refusal to keep up with the times turns the church into a historic relic. And when the church is irrelevant the gospel message is unbelievable."

Effective churches will remain faithful to their essence. At the same time, they will carefully distinguish "who they are" from "how they function." Without surrendering their message, they will adapt their methods. They will keep in touch with both the times and the truth. They will spend more time contextualizing their ministries to the specifics of their situations. They will give priority to the four cornerstones of effective churches: orthodoxy, community, relevance and outreach. They will know that relevancy and orthodoxy must co-exist. They will also keep in touch with the personal needs of the people in their congregations without neglecting the needs of others in the world around them. They will know that fostering a sense of community and extending themselves in outreach will create a vibrant spirituality. And as they seek to balance their activity, they will embrace creativity as an ally.

Encountering cultural commandments

The place of the church in the contemporary Canadian context is complicated and ambiguous. In some senses, the church is a routine part of everyday life, but in other ways, the church is simply ignored.

The annual *Maclean's/CTV* poll, by Decima, analyzes a broad spectrum of Canadian life. Following past patterns, the latest poll does not include a single reference to anything religious. The pole probes Canadians on such things as political views, social problems, concerns about the future, sports interests, and sexual practices. But the 47 separate survey items, involving over 100 variables, make no room for religion.

One question read as follows: "If you had a problem in your community, who would you turn to for assistance?" The options listed were politician, business leader, volunteers, neighbors, yourself.

Another question asked, "From your point of view, which one of the following groups has the most honesty and integrity?" The response options included doctors, scientists, university professors, business executives, journalists, lawyers and politicians—but there was no reference to religious leaders or members of the clergy.

Claiming to be an expression of the "Voices of Canada," the high-profile media poll, which filled 31 pages in *Maclean's* magazine, is tantamount to religious censorship.[2]

The absence of any religious reference in the *Maclean's* profile of Canadian life simply symbolizes the marginalization of formal religion in contemporary society. As noted in Chapter Five, the social and subsequent religious shifts in the culture have pushed religion to the sidelines.

Consequently, Christians shouldn't be surprised and neither should they think they are suffering from paranoia, when they suspect that there are cultural commandments that decree:

"Thou shalt not speak about thy faith in public."

"Thou shalt keep thy religion unto thyself."

And certainly, "Thou shalt not evangelize."

The paradox is that while the media sometimes censors religion out of the public square and while the current assumptions in the culture create difficulties for the faith, Canadians in general, are still interested in the spiritual aspects of life. Rather than denying the reality of the spiritual, they are open to God and supernatural phenomena. It's just that very few plan on pursuing their quest for the spiritual inside the country's churches. *(See Fig. 10.1)*

Still, the ambiguity for Canadian Christians persists, and unscrambling the mixed messages is complicated. On the one hand, declining participation in church life and the marginalization of formal faith as a cultural value sends the message that Canadians have written off God and the importance of the spiritual. On the other hand, the retained belief in God and the supernatural implies spiritual openness and potential interest.

Church leaders are left wondering why the majority of Canadians have absented themselves from regular involvement in institutional church life, when the evidence suggests that people are generally interested in pursuing what the churches purport to offer.

The next 20 years will be crucial for the longer-term future of the

Fig. 10.1
Beliefs
Percentage Agreeing

	Teens	Adults
God exists	81	83
Divinity of Jesus	80	75
Some people have psychic powers	69	59
Supernatural forces exist	66	*
Life after death	64	68
Evil forces exist	64	*
Astrology	53	34
Extrasensory perception	52	59
Contact with the spirit world	44	39
I have experienced God	34	46
I will be reincarnated	32	27

* figures unavailable
Sources: Project Teen Canada 1984, 1988, 1992; Project Can90 Bibby

church in Canada. Because the vast majority of Canadians still identify themselves as either Protestants or Catholics, some natural linkages remain intact. Church identification is clearly part of the Canadian consciousness.

There are other factors that signal a promising future for the church:
- many people express a readiness to experiment with life beyond the rational
- many people crave mystical and transcendent experiences
- many people seek practical help and direction in the midst of increasing complexity
- many people wrestle with profound loneliness and the pressures of meeting immediate needs
- many people come from or live in dysfunctional families
- many people struggle with addictive behaviors
- many people long for a sense of meaning in their lives, and recognize spirituality as an open door
- amidst all these people, there remains the Creator and Redeemer God to help people begin again.

These things point to opportunities for the church to make a comeback. Dennis Dwyer, who specifically interviewed people who have left the church, echoes similar reasons for hopefulness:

> Almost everyone I interviewed declared a need for some kind of smaller community where they would be accepted, challenged and cherished, where they could explore with others in an atmosphere of trust.[3]

One of the people Dwyer talked to had this to say:
> We live in times where people are increasingly desperate for something to believe in. Materialism has left us empty, politicians have betrayed our confidence, many people have experienced the heartbreak of a broken home, and the future problems faced by society would make anyone shudder.[4]

The challenge for churches will be to translate the brokenness of the times and the spiritual interest of Canadians into opportunities for organizational involvement.

"Mission" mindedness

One pattern is already entrenched. Church identification has become separated from participation for most Canadians. Canadians who are not at present actively involved in church life are not likely to start wandering in to places of worship on their own. Consequently, churches that passively wait for new people to enter their doors will have a certain future. They will decline. Unless they already possess an unusually positive reputation in their community, or have benefited from circumstances that are exceedingly unusual, their situation will deteriorate.

Accepting the fact that the age of Christendom is past in North America, Kennon Callahan computes the consequences:

> The professional minister movement, born in the churched culture of an earlier time, simply ceased to function on the mission field of the 1980s. The need today is for ministers who understand unchurched [North] America and ways to make the gospel clear in it. The hour demands missionary pastors.[5]

One might argue with Callahan and say that what the church needs is not only missionary pastors or priests, but missionary **people**. In any

Fig. 10.2
Characteristics of Ministry Styles

Mission Mindedness	Maintenance Mentality
God is acting	God exists
Seek and find	Come unto me
Increase	Survive
Expect extra-ordinary	Plan for the routine
People focused	Program focused

event, missionary priests, pastors, and lay people will live with a sense of mission. Rather than holding on to a maintenance mentality toward ministry and the church—a mentality that exists to preserve the status quo—they will intentionally seek to make gains for the sake of the gospel and the vitality of their churches. *(See Fig. 10.2)*

Howard Hanchey, an Episcopal professor of pastoral theology, distinguishes between ministry expressed in a maintenance mode and ministry that is motivated by a sense of mission. He contends that mission-minded clergy and churches know four important things:

1. The world belongs to God.
2. God is present in the world and is always stirring us to new visions of opportunity.
3. For eyes that can see, signs of God's ministry abound in the here and now of everyday life.
4. The capacity to speak about God's ministry without embarrassment, and in ways that generates interest for others, fuels a mission thrust.[6]

Hanchey continues:

> Growing congregations are marked mostly by what I have learned to identify as a mission mindset of hope. Declining congregations are marked mostly by a maintenance mindset; they are more concerned with repairs and programs than celebrating God's everyday presence and ministry, and they are mostly concerned with what they "ought" to do.[7]

Obeying God's "Great Commands"

Historically, the Christian church has found the basis for its "mission-mindedness" within two sets of scripture: the Great Commission, and the Great Commandment (Matthew 28:16–20 and Matthew 22:34–

40, Luke 10:25-27, John 15:12 respectively). A quick glance at Canadian churches, however, indicates that these two "commands" have not been appropriated to the same extent by all churches.

For many conservative or "evangelical" denominations, mission-mindedness has most often been focused on fulfilling the Great Commission. The injunction has been to go in the authority of Jesus and "make disciples of all nations..." (Matthew 28:16-20 NRSV). With commitment, vision and determination, obedience to the Great Commission has spawned an impressive missionary movement to the uttermost parts of the world. Today the church of Jesus Christ expresses its presence on all continents, in almost every country and among thousands of people groups.

Obedience to the Great Commission is propelled by a commitment to the cause of Christ to win the world. The challenge is to get the job done. Inherently, the Great Commission is flavored with a sense of the importance of the task.

At the same time, many mainline or "liberal" churches have been drawn to the Great Commandment to "...love the Lord your God with all your heart..." and to "...love your neighbor as yourself" (Matthew 22:34-39 NRSV; Luke 10:25-27; cf. John 15:12), as the basis for their own "missionary" enterprises.

For these churches, the neighbor who deserves our love has often been close at hand. The biblical injunction to "love your neighbor as yourself" has blossomed into a social consciousness and concern for social justice. Prison ministries and calls for correctional reform, food programs and day care, housing ministries and drop-in centers have all been ways in which these churches have tried to embody love of neighbor. These same churches have also taken a global perspective. They have extended a caring hand to victims of political oppression through organizations like Amnesty International; they have concerned themselves with issues of peace and disarmament; they have addressed issues of global economics and fought against corporate exploitation of developing-world populations.

Like their conservative counterparts, those who attend mainline churches understand the importance of the task set for them and feel the challenge of getting the job done.

Driven by relationships

In the 1990s, the majority of Canadians are not cause-driven people. We treasure relationships more than we value social activism. Because of this, it will be difficult for both of these emphases to flourish. Many of the social changes we have already described dictate that, in the 1990s, the Great Command "to love" will be more compelling than the Great Commission to "make disciples." The reasons are rather straightforward.

The command to love is framed within a relational motif. The mood of the age means that empathy is more persuasive than exhortation. Compassion is appealing. People who pontificate and make judgements are thought to be presumptuous and arrogant. Confrontation chases people away. Today, people are responsive to others in their lives who extend genuine care for them.

Accordingly, instead of using terms like "evangelism" or "witness" to describe the "outreach" cornerstone of effective churches, we have used the expression, "touching the needs of others."

How people are encouraged to participate in the mission of the church matters. In the 1990s, inviting people to partner in Christ's "ministry of reconciliation" will be more appealing than signing them up for "Evangelism Explosion." Training and motivating people to express the Great Command to love will receive a more positive response than utilizing the Great Commission motif. Both commands are still in effect, but motivationally, one will be more effective than the other.

Without letting the method overwhelm the mandate, a lay member from a Salvation Army church in Manitoba communicates the central conviction to affirm: "Many churches are ineffective because they have lost any central focus and mission."

Effective churches will mobilize their people into the mission to "love their neighbors." As they worship and work, there will be a healthy discontentment in their presence. While celebrating what God is doing, they will anticipate something more.

Practices to relinquish

In recent months, I was part of a weekend conference with several ministers and their people who all came from small churches in a rural setting. One of the pastors had recently returned from his denomination's annual conference. The conference had reviewed the past year's achievements and dealt with the normal quota of business resolutions. He showed me a summarized statement of the 60 or so churches in his region. The records included the normal attendance statistics and financial figures.

The pastor's denomination is one that follows the practice of holding both Sunday morning worship and Sunday evening services. What caught my attention was the difference between the number of people attending in the morning compared to the number of people attending in the evening. Following the Canadian pattern, only a few of the 60 churches had Sunday morning attendance that exceeded 300 people. Without exception, the evening attendance was less than half the morning attendance, and in numerous instances the ratios were one-fifth or even one-tenth. In several of the 60 churches, the evening attendance averaged fewer than 15 people.

I think about all the energy that goes into the preparation of those evening services. I wonder how often people who attend in the morning are exhorted and cajoled to "be sure to join us for the service tonight." My hunch is that those who attend often go out of a sense of duty, and when so few people are present, they wish they had done something else too.

Particularly in the conservative Protestant (evangelical) churches, the Sunday evening service was introduced when church activity was the only Sunday night show in town. The morning hour was the "worship" service for believers. The evening hour was the "evangelistic" service, especially aimed at people who were lost and outside the faith. At least 20 years have past, probably 30, since the Sunday evening service ceased fulfilling its original purpose. That is not to say that all those churches still holding Sunday evening services have stayed with their original emphases and purposes. But many congregations are hanging on to vestiges of life that take a lot more out of the available resources they have for ministry than they contribute.

In an analysis of the practice of holding Sunday evening "evangelistic" services, Reginald Bibby and Merlin Brinkerhoff remark on how this practice continues even though few, if any, outsiders ever attend or convert. Of the 20 churches they examined, all of which conducted regular Sunday evening evangelistic services, the congregations averaged less than two (1.3) converts per year. Bibby and Brinkerhoff ask the question, "If the goal is not actually being realized, why do such congregations continue year after year to use this particular means of outreach?" Part of the answer, they contend, lies in the symbolic value of conducting evangelistic services. "Holding evangelistic services even when the audience is predominantly Christian gives a church the appearance of 'preaching the gospel to the lost,' allowing a member to feel that he or she belongs to an 'evangelistic' church."[8]

Writing in a Mennonite Brethren periodical, Jim Holm stated, "I don't think the Sunday evening service any longer fills a clear purpose. Most of us don't need another sermon."[9]

A minister from a church in Alberta articulated the problem to be addressed: "Too many churches are structure-driven...rather than vision-driven."

In the book, *Prepare Your Church for the Future*, Carl George recommends a meta-model structure that might be helpful to churches evaluating their structures: "The two most visible elements of the Meta-Church are the small home-based group and the celebration-size-group."[10] The flexibility of the model may serve various sized churches if they aspire to be vision-driven.

No doubt everyone would agree that there is nothing sacred about structures. But churches that belong to the same denomination often look the same from coast to coast. One can only conclude that there is too much sameness and too little contextualization. Franchises for fast food outlets look the same from coast to coast in order to build a national client base and to maintain uniform quality standards. Churches in the same denomination will obviously share much in common, but when they turn out too much like franchises they have sacrificed some of their potential for local effectiveness.

A lay member from an Associated Gospel church in Ontario offers sound counsel: "Let's not get hung up on tradition, 'because we always did it that way,' but let's be able to be flexible and try some changes—as long as the Bible is the main source of teaching and direction."

A Baptist minister from Ontario said forcefully, "To be chained to tradition is deadly. We must implement changes if we desire to impact our world."

Sometimes structures and institutional practices **insulate** people from God. They may be proper and correct but, like an anesthetic, they have a numbing and dulling affect. Some programs take enormous amounts of energy and generate very little return. Other expressions of worship and program involvement spiritually **energize** people. They excite and enthuse people. They are like a divine injection. They release people into newness and the pursuit of the unknown.

Church leaders will be wise to relinquish some of those practices that insulate people from the God they want to love and replace them with initiatives that inject people with divine energy.

Innovations to pursue

Every denomination has their particular way of doing things. There is the "Anglican" way, the "Baptist" way, the "Presbyterian" way, the "Pentecostal" way and all the other denominational ways. One premise of this book is that there are many ways to do God's work on earth and faithfully pursue the purposes of the Kingdom.

There are also some principles and practices that override all of the denominational distinctives. For example, because all Christian organizations are subject to the rapid cultural changes swirling around them, simply taking a "business as usual" approach toward the future is untenable. Untenable, that is, unless they have a desire to limp their way "out of business."

The present position of the church in the culture, and the circumstances that will undoubtedly come with the future, require the church to experiment and to innovate. Those who have critiqued Ray Kroc, the founder of McDonald's, concluded that his genius was not in perfecting hamburgers, corporate strategy, financial management, or even in motivating people. His genius lay in creating a culture that continues to foster creativity and an aggressive commitment to its market. Rejecting numerous merger proposals and opportunities to enter into other business ventures, the key to McDonald's success has been coordinating strong and diverse personalities dedicated to a single mission.[11]

The combination of a sustained mission drive, creative innovation, and the continued expression of the diversity of denominationalism will be an adequate human contribution to enhance the future of the church.

In the past, in every denomination including independent churches, an inordinate amount of energy and resources has been invested in the institutional-program model of doing church. In other words, buildings have been erected, programs have been planned and operated inside the buildings, and people from the community have been invited to enter the buildings to avail themselves of the programs.

As long as the gravitational pull of society was toward the church, the strategy was successful. When the church doors were opened, people came in and participated. But when the gravitational pull began attracting people to other activities and interests, the institutional-program strategy became less and less effective.

Today, a total reliance on the strategy of the past will fail. Instead, what is needed is a multiple strategy. Designing the strategy of church life around the following three ministry models will be more fruitful:
- the people of God **gathered**
- the people of God **dispersed**
- the people of God **deployed**.

Fig. 10.3
Strategies for Modern Ministry

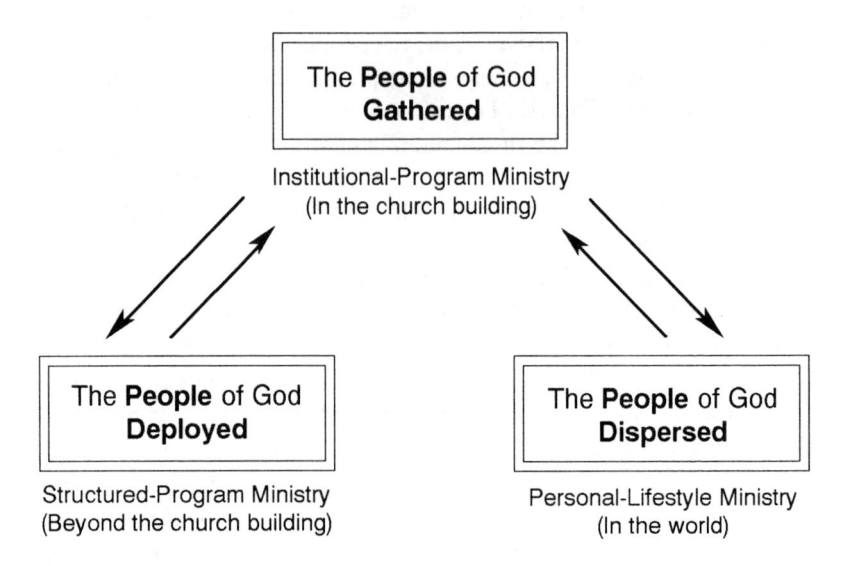

```
            ┌─────────────────────┐
            │  The People of God  │
            │      Gathered       │
            └─────────────────────┘
              Institutional-Program Ministry
                (In the church building)

┌─────────────────────┐          ┌─────────────────────┐
│  The People of God  │          │  The People of God  │
│      Deployed       │          │      Dispersed      │
└─────────────────────┘          └─────────────────────┘
 Structured-Program Ministry       Personal-Lifestyle Ministry
 (Beyond the church building)          (In the world)
```

The people of God gathered

The "people of God gathered" model is what has just been described as the institutional-program approach for doing church. Simply stated, the ministry of the church is fundamentally conceived to happen inside the church building. And even though a dependence on the old model done in the old way will be inadequate to assure a strong future, it will still remain as the central structure for the future.

From the beginning, the people of God came together to worship, to sing songs, to pray, to be taught and to partake of the sacraments. It is impossible to conceive of the church without these expressions of shared spiritual life.

But across the country, with increasing frequency, considerable numbers of congregations are re-tooling former forms of worship that have worn down and worn out.

Effective churches are choreographing worship as celebration and designing programs to respond to specific needs.

In many situations, local churches offer additional worship services that use contemporary music and adapted styles to appeal to people with non-traditional tastes. Dance and drama explore avenues of artistic expression that were formally off-limits inside these same churches.

Innovative churches are deleting some of their long-standing programs and replacing them with a range of new program options designed to respond to specific needs. The programs are still offered inside the church building, but they are meant for people who are not regular participants. They range from job and life skills programs for single mothers, to mornings out for nannies, from 12-step programs for those who have been abused, to recovery groups for the recently divorced.

Many churches have also been re-tooling the conventional Sunday morning worship service to create a fresh forum especially designed for spiritual "seekers."

Bill Hybels from the Willow Creek Community Church in the suburbs of Chicago has developed a prototype that has captured the imagination of a significant number of people, often from conservative Protestant churches, who want to reach the unchurched in Canada.

The Hybel's approach to ministry calls for both strategic and structural innovation. Instead of Sunday morning being a traditional worship service for the committed, that hour is designed for "seekers"—those people who are still figuring out where to place their faith and confidence in life.

If you were to attend a Sunday service at Willow Creek, you would join several thousand people in a theater-like building. You would focus your attention on a stage and be exposed to drama and modern music. The preaching would be engaging and would focus on felt needs. If you were present as a seeker or a visitor, when the offering plate was passed, you would be encouraged to keep your wallet in your pocket.

As **a regular** participant in the life of Willow Creek, you would attend a Saturday night worship service. You would decide whether or not to involve yourself in other community service programs and events during the week that are offered to those who have already made a Christian faith commitment.

David Brandon, pastor of the Alliance Church in Newmarket, Ontario, is a notable innovator who has used the Hybel's model with significant success. But for the gains that have been made in the past five years, there has also been a considerable amount of pain for those who have attempted to do church the Hybel's way. Too often, although intentions have been noble, the innovators have ended "up Willow Creek without a Hybels."[12]

The people of God dispersed

If the "people of God gathered" is institutional-program ministry inside the church building, the "people of God dispersed" is personal ministry expressed outside the church building. As a ministry model, it is characterized by the strategy to mandate ministry around individual gifts and interpersonal opportunities.

Many Canadians who attend church regularly find it difficult to talk about their personal faith with the people who naturally intersect their lives. Without inflicting guilt on those who feel that way, it should be recognized that they illustrate one of the tensions in the "four pillars" model. They stand in the middle of the inside/outside and community/outreach polarities. Many individuals and churches struggle with what British sociologist Bryan Wilson views as the tension between the values of separation from the world and the summons to go out into the world and preach the gospel.[13]

The scriptures teach that God's people have "different gifts according to the grace given." The gift list ranges from serving, teaching, prophesying, and healing, to leadership, encouragement, generosity and mercy (Romans 12:4–8; 1 Corinthians 12:4–11). In Ephesians 4, the list is expanded to people who are also graced with the abilities to be pastors, prophets, and evangelists. The strategy of the dispersed model encourages people to use their spiritual gifts as expressions of ministry in natural lifestyle ways during the week.

The "people of God dispersed" emphasis has been especially evident in those churches who urge their people to be involved in lifestyle evangelism. These churches use books and training sessions to teach members how to live in the world with evangelistic intentions. They encourage members to witness to the reality of faith in their lives by engaging people in spiritually related discussions. Because the majority of people no longer attend church, the marketplace becomes the center for their interpersonal ministry. For Christians who are so gifted and who have the temperament for interacting with people about spiritual concerns, lifestyle evangelism is both enjoyable and redemptive. Effective churches will both equip and encourage those who are able to be active in lifestyle evangelism.

The people of God deployed

The "people of God deployed" ministry model is a hybrid of the "people of God gathered" and "the people of God dispersed" models. The approach structures programmed ministry outside the church building. It is characterized by the strategy to **mobilize ministry around personal vision and shared interests.**

Frank Tillapaugh, former pastor of Bear Valley Baptist Church in Denver, Colorado, excelled at the "people of God deployed" model of ministry. Believing that lay people can be trusted with ministry, Tillapaugh espoused creating a church environment where individual members were encouraged and supported to begin ministries as an extension of their church's vision. Whether the vision involved various kinds of counseling, or ministry to street people, mothers of pre-schoolers, children of alcoholics, international students, or seniors, the strategy was to unleash the church.[14]

A complimentary but less ambitious approach involves holding church-sponsored events outside the church building. Designing a series of "Marketplace Lunches" on topics of interest gives an opportunity for business people to bring their colleagues to worthwhile events with spiritual content. Subjects like "ethics in business" and "balancing the demands of work and family" are life concerns that have implicit spiritual implications. "Family Forums" on subjects like "passing on values that last" or "parenting teenagers" or "helping your children make positive choices" can serve to both address community needs and make contact with people who would otherwise stay beyond the reach of the church's influence. Neutral settings such as community centers will increase the appeal of such programs.

Neighborhood Bible study groups provide a venue that allow people to express their ministries outside the church building. Re-channeling a portion of the churches' vision and program resources into the workplace, into creative events held around backyard barbecues and inside people's homes, will win for the Kingdom. When people curl or play golf together at church-sponsored tournaments and end up sitting beside each other listening to intriguing speakers at wind-up banquets, the future of the church will be enhanced. When groups of friends and neighbors participate in reading groups that discuss a range of books, some with religious titles, forums for wholesome faith discussions will naturally result. As the church creates more opportunities for people who go to church to enjoy time together with people who do not go to church, God will be pleased too.

Effective churches know that multiple ministry models contribute two critically important things to the health and well-being of churches: they provide alternative ways for people to participate, and they implicitly affirm a diversity of gifts. Wise leaders will not try to get an entire group to do the same thing. Instead they will involve people in ways that use their gifts and stimulate their interests.

Accordingly, effective churches will encourage people who are organizationally oriented and who work well within programmed structures to contribute their talents inside the institution where the people of God gather. Effective churches will affirm and equip persons who have the ability to communicate their faith in their everyday relationships as the people of God dispersed. Effective churches will support those who need more design and structure to express their sense of mission, but who are ready to try some new initiatives, by developing programs to be implemented outside the church building and by acknowledging them as the people of God deployed.

When people have places to participate and alternative ways to express their concern for the mission of Christ and the people in their lives, the church makes progress.

Right time for changes

Acknowledging the need for innovation and experimentation is one thing; surrendering the past in order to embrace the future is another. When all is said and done, churches have seldom been the first off the mark when it comes to initiating change. In fact, often for right reasons, churches have resisted and even feared change.

After a split vote at the Anglican General Synod defeated a canon (law) recommendation that had been in the making for 12 years, the news item that conveyed the action read, "Clergy licensing canon delayed for six years."[15] One can only hope that whatever is at stake doesn't matter very much. Eighteen years may not be very long in light of eternity, but it took only **eight** years to move from putting the first person in space to landing the first person on the moon.

Still, today is the time to initiate creative change in the church. There is a general acknowledgement that change must occur. The overwhelming evidence that the world is winning and that the church is losing ground not only lessens the resistance to change but demands that changes occur now.

The church is well-situated to take advantage of the prevailing mood in the culture. The openness to the spiritual and the supernatural is a window of opportunity for faith communities in Canada. Turn-of-the-century social theorist, Max Weber, interpreted openness to spiritual reality as a reaction against the confines of a technical-rational world devoid of mystery, imagination and hope.[16] Rationalism robs our spirit

of vision. Following this tradition, Bryan Wilson writes:
The search for the unprogrammed in an increasingly programmed society is a commentary on the limits of planning and rational organization...in an impersonal, calculating, instrumental and progressive society.[17]

A purely rational world also segments individuals into functions or roles in particular institutional contexts. Against the dehumanizing invasion of rationalism, the church can offer a place to belong, a place to be known as a whole person, a place to be free to express fears, hopes and vision.

As Rosabeth Moss Canter says, "The years ahead should be a good time for dreamers and visionaries...for the barriers to innovation, the roadblocks to inspiration and imagination, are being knocked down one by one."[18]

Meeting inside expectations

While dealing with the dynamics of change and the pressures of the age, churches can measure themselves by the maturity of the Christians they produce. What better criteria for evaluating spiritual maturity can there be than the Great Commandment.

In response to the lawyer's question, "Teacher, which commandment in the Law is the greatest?" Jesus replied: "'You shall love the Lord your God with all your heart, and with all your soul and with all your mind.' This is the greatest and first commandment. And the second is like it: 'You shall love your neighbor as yourself.' On these two commandments hang all the law and the prophets." (Matthew 22:35–40 NRSV)

The Great Commandment is multidimensional. First, it reveals the divine intent for all human creation to be in a close relationship with the Creator. Second, it affirms that the self-image of people who stand in close relation to God will be positive enough to allow self-love. Third, out of the life that flows from God, there will be regard and concern for the interests and needs of others. The invitation of the Great Command is to whole-person health; it is to be fully alive and to share that life with others.

The Great Commandment also frames a full-orbed faith that has both vertical and horizontal dimensions. There is love both for God and for others. People of faith are connected to God. They reach up to the God of the heavens who is greater and stronger than they are. But the

Fig. 10.4
Faith Types [19]

	Vertical God	Horizontal Others
Undeveloped	Low	Low
Vertical	High	Low
Horizontal	Low	High
Integrated	High	High

people of faith also reach out to others. Their world is not restricted to their own interests. They extend themselves to other people in their lives. Richard Niebuhr defines the purpose of the church and its ministry as "the Increase of the Love of God and Neighbor."[20]

We owe God faith, said Luther, not works. We owe our neighbor good works.[21]

Mature faith will express itself on both the vertical and horizontal axis. Love for God will not be isolated from love for people. And an active response to the needs of people will not preclude fostering a relationship with God. In so doing, faith will have both **personal** and **social** spheres to explore. And effective churches will not be satisfied until they stimulate new levels of life in both spheres.

Nurturing love for God

Few people would deny the social value of belonging to an effective church. Genuinely sharing life with people, carrying one another's burdens and celebrating each other's joys is what God designed for faith communities. But as rich as personal relationships can be, the primary purpose of the church is not to get people together. It is to get people in touch with God and then to nurture the life that flows between the Creator and those who are being re-created.

The results of our survey reveal that effective churches stimulate the life of faith in their people in several ways. As previously noted, love for God in effective churches is nurtured in people through the four cornerstones of orthodoxy (which also gains expression in worship), relevance, community, and outreach. In practical terms these cornerstones are expressed through:

- **uplifting worship** that invites people to release their inevitable preoccupation with themselves and to taste and see that the God of the heavens has not abandoned creation
- **orthodox teaching** that mines the scriptures for enduring truth that links the circumstances of yesterday with the complexities of today and the unknowns of tomorrow
- **relevant application** that links the historic faith with the realities of the modern Monday-through-Saturday world
- **experience in community** that in theory and practice counters the forces of individualism that parade so powerfully in our culture
- **family programs** that augment parents' desires to transmit the faith they treasure to the most important people in their lives.

Pursuing outside aspirations

While effective faith communities look inside and respond to the expectations of those who participate regularly, they also look outside and respond to the needs of others beyond their immediate boundaries. The survey findings affirm that outreach is an indispensable commitment of churches that are vitally alive.

Although Tom Sine addresses the church situation in the United States, the same patterns prevail in Canada:

> Mainline denominations are greying and declining, and these trends are beginning to limit seriously their ability to support mission projects overseas and at home. And there is every likelihood that the amount churches have to invest in mission is going to continue to decline as we enter a new century.
>
> More conservative Protestant churches are seeing some growth in both numbers and giving. The lion's share of the increased giving, however, is not invested in any form of mission for evangelism or social action. Rather, the increased income is being used principally to erect expensive edifices, finance overhead costs, or hire additional staff to service the needs of those within the church.[22]

Unless church decision makers alter their present course, the available financial resources will increasingly be invested in looking after ourselves. Many mainline congregations will be pressed to meet existing obligations and to pay for the cost of repairing older buildings. Conservative church congregations will put their money into expanded programs and additional personnel as well as their mortgages. Unless there is a shift in direction, less money will be allocated for external concerns.

Nurturing love for others

The issue of balancing the use of resources is raised in the comment from a lay leader from a Christian and Missionary Alliance church in Manitoba: "Many churches are so busy keeping the 'saints' happy that they have no time or energy to reach the lost—which is our mandate."

Although "reaching the lost" means something different to Christians in different denominations, there is a strong consensus that God's people are to reach out in love, in witness and care for others. Our research leads us to conclude that when churches meet the perceived needs of those participants who are already present in the pews, they do so with the expectation of equipping those same people to serve in the church and in the world.

Community service

Howard Hanchey states that mission-minded Christians have

> ...been taught to understand that in their daily occupations they help God take care of the world, their neighborhood and their community... Growing churches count it a joy to offer assistance and care to the surrounding community. Church facilities are regularly used by garden clubs, Alcoholics Anonymous, Al-Anon, Mothers Against Drunk Driving, and Sons Against Drunk Driving. There may be a day care program for working parents, or a kindergarten or school, and those not able to put bread on their table may be fed at a soup kitchen.[23]

Many churches across Canada have taken the initiative in extending assistance to the less fortunate in our society. The church has a long history of involvement in food banks, clothing distribution, and various forms of housing for those in need. The Salvation Army in particular stands out as a symbol of compassion to those who face extraordinary circumstances. NeighbourLink is a new social concern initiative sponsored by World Vision Canada. It works to mobilize volunteers from local churches to respond to the practical needs of people in their communities. Designed for ecumenical participation and in liaison with social services, local NeighbourLinks establish clearing houses that put people from churches in touch with people in their neighborhoods.

Efforts to transport people to medical appointments, tutor school dropouts, protect victims of abuse, offer financial counsel, baby-sit children of single parents, repair plumbing problems, and take people to shop for groceries, all work to express the love of God.

As governments face dwindling sources of revenue and as budgets continue to focus on spiralling deficits, allocations to social programs will continue to decline. As the government reduces its role in the provision of social services, there will be an opportunity for churches to increase their role in caring for the needs of Canadians. Effective churches will conduct needs assessments of their surrounding communities and respond in ways that send the message that people who love God also love their neighbors.

Inter-personal witness

Acting out the love of God will be a necessary part of making the message of Christianity believable in these times. But telling people about the love of God is also critical. Deeds and words must go together.

There is a story about a pastor who reported, with satisfaction, that he had mobilized his people to knock on doors and distribute Christian literature. In the first quarter of the year the sincerely motivated parishioners knocked on 2,000 doors.

Later, someone asked him, "What was the response? How many meaningful contacts did you make?"

"None," the pastor replied. "But we're going to redouble our efforts. Next quarter we're going to knock on 4,000 doors."[24]

Not too long ago, I ran into a pastor whose own experience paralleled, in part, the experience of the pastor in the story. He and his parishioners were working to establish their church in a suburban upscale neighborhood. Over lunch one day, he explained to me that they were a small group of people still meeting in a school facility. They had reasoned that inviting the community to their Easter Sunday service would be a good way to bring in new people, and so they prepared an attractive pamphlet announcing the details. The regular attenders banded together and delivered their invitation to 3,500 homes in the surrounding neighborhood. But when the doors opened on Easter Sunday, not one new person walked in for worship. Instead of celebrating the Easter event, the congregation was despondent.

The pastor was still downcast as he asked, "What went wrong?"

I tried to respond carefully: "The invitation was impersonal. In new neighborhoods, people rarely arrive inside a church unless they already have denominational ties or they already know someone who attends. And second, there is a social law of life that operates in Canadian society: people who live in $300,000–$400,000 homes do not come to school gymnasiums and sit on wooden chairs to worship."

In today's world, the personal is powerful. People usually start attending a church because they have been invited by someone they know and trust. Kennon L. Callahan contends that "People win people to Christ; programs do not. People discover people in significant relational groups, not in a merry-go-round of programs and activities."[25]

A survey of 6000 people who attend conservative Protestant churches reveals the importance of interpersonal witness and influence. When asked about the main influences in making a personal faith commitment to Christ, there was a significant shift between the dominant pattern prior to the 1980s when compared to those who claimed a faith experience in the 1980s. In earlier decades, the influence of the family or Christian upbringing was foremost (52%) while influence linked to personal witness was secondary (26%). During the 1980s, the influence was re-ordered. Personal witness was paramount (55%) and family influence was reduced (22%). During the same periods of time, evangelistic rallies and church services were identified as much lower sources of influence in prompting personal faith responses. *(See Fig. 10.5)*

Although mainline church attenders are not generally encouraged to verbalize the significance of their personal faith to the people who naturally intersect their lives, the cultural shift to the power of the personal deserves careful attention.

A convergence of the indicators forces the conclusion that dependence on an institutional approach to ministry in the future will destine local churches and their denominations to certain decline. Framing future ministry strategies so that they complement the historic strength of the institutional with the increasing influence of the personal will combine the vitality of the past with the power of the present.

Canadians are known for being excessively cautious in their conversations. However, one subject Canadians discuss frequently and with eloquence is the state of the weather; it is something we all have in common, and there is little risk of offending someone by bringing up the subject. When God's people can discuss their understanding of God's role in their lives with even a fraction of the ease with which they discuss the weather, the cause of the Kingdom will move forward.

Fig. 10.5

Main Influences in Making a Personal Commitment

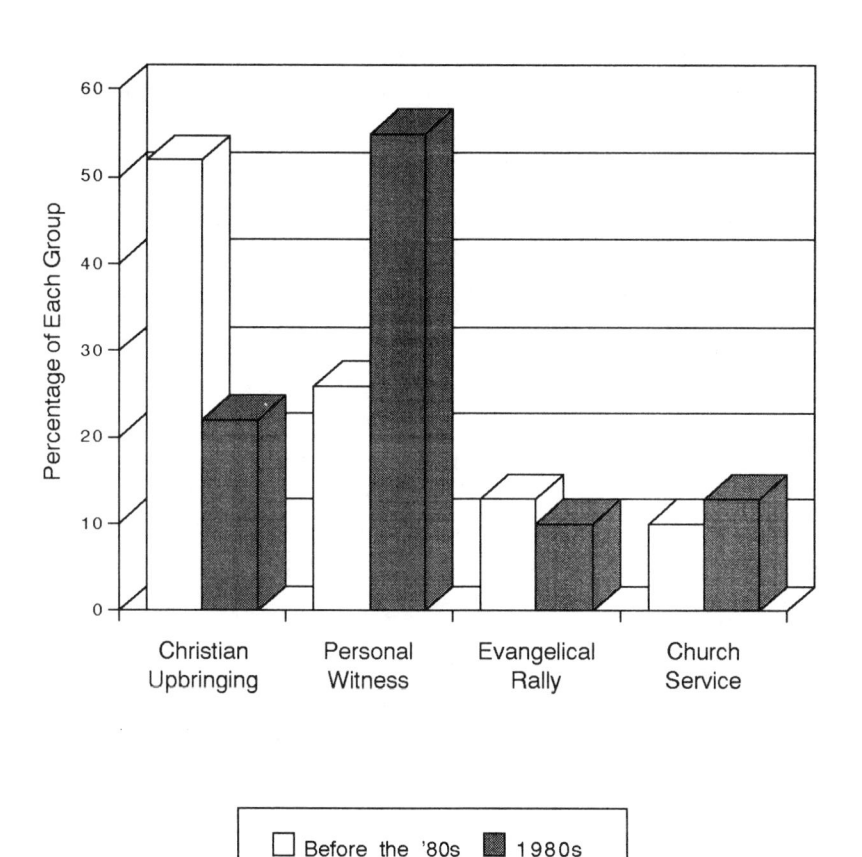

Percentage of Each Group — Christian Upbringing, Personal Witness, Evangelical Rally, Church Service

☐ Before the '80s ■ 1980s

Source: Arnell Mortz, *Reclaiming a Nation*, 1990.

Global compassion

The cause of the Kingdom will also advance as those who embrace the Christian faith are graced with global compassion.

Because God created the world, God's world is our world too. Accordingly, Christians are world citizens. As world citizens, created in the image of God and recreated in relationship with Christ, we carry two passports. We carry a national passport, and because we also belong to God's cosmic family, we carry a global passport.

Someone has written that for better or worse we have encased our planet in "a global electronic nervous system" from which we will never escape. Satellite dishes and fax machines, personal computers and cellular phones increasingly wire us together into one electronic global village.[26]

Although we may be wired together, we do not live together at the same level of peace and prosperity. In Canada, we have access to an inordinate amount of creation's resources. Mordecai Richler has observed that "Canada is an over-privileged country." Compared to the majority who live on planet earth, we are among the most fortunate. We are blessed. But still we complain. Sometimes we whine.

This acknowledgment of our favored status is not made with indifference to those people in Canada who are unemployed or who live in poverty. Neither is the motivation to arouse guilt because so many of us have so much. It is to call Canadian Christians to live with a sense of gratefulness. For Christians, the words "Praise God from whom all blessings flow" represent more than just the doxology; they express an attitude for living.

It is a spirit of gratitude that will propel Christians to cultivate a global awareness that is touched with compassion. Does that mean that it is necessary for Christians to understand the implications of global market economies or be conversant with structural adjustment programs? Does global citizenship require leaving one's own country to serve as a missionary in another culture?

Obviously not entirely, but surely it means that we shed our indifference to injustice in God's world and make a commitment to raise our awareness of injustice among God's family. Christian theology emphasizes that knowledge implies responsibility. News reports portray the tragedies of the developing world and take away our ability to hide in ignorance.

Surely world citizenship calls us to specific acts of "global sharing." At the very least, it calls us to individually and collectively share our money, our technology, our knowledge, and our friendship; to express our concern by praying that peace will prevail, that evil will be held in check, that the abuse of power will cease, that hungry people will have enough to eat, that wise leaders will serve their people and improve the future of their people.

Ethnocentricity is a sin for people who carry two passports. Views of the world and concern for life that stop at individual rights, at community concerns, at provincial borders, or at a single nation's priorities are too small for people with a global compassion.

Identifying herself as a lifetime church attender who is now over 65 years old, a Presbyterian lay member confessed the following:

> For the first time in my life I have found a church that to me exemplifies what the true church should be: a place that preaches the gospel; a place that cares for people and empathizes with those with physical and mental problems; a place that reaches out to the community and the world.

Marching Off the Map

There is a story from the first century B.C. that may be apocryphal or may be true. Either way, the story sends a crucial message to the modern church as it journeys into the unexplored territory of the future.

The incident happened when much of the world was unexplored and unknown. Not surprisingly, global map-making was a very rudimentary and inexact science. When map makers drew their maps, they represented the area outside of their knowledge with symbols of dragons, monsters and large fish. The message was clear: the uncharted and unknown territory was a fearsome place; it was a region touched with terror, a realm to be avoided.

One commander of a battalion of Roman soldiers was more adventurous than fearful. Eventually, he found himself beyond the territory that the map makers had drawn. Being a well-trained military man, he neither wanted to turn back, nor did he recklessly pursue his course without further instruction. Immediately, he dispatched a messenger back to Rome with the urgent request, "Please send new orders, we have marched off the map."[27]

Conclusion

The primary purpose for boarding an airplane is to take a trip. It is the most convenient way to travel from one place to another, especially in Canada where distances are great.

The purpose for going to church is to work out our lives with God. It is to open our humanness to the touch of the divine.

There are secondary decisions involved in taking an airplane trip. For a price, you can indulge in comfort and enjoy the privilege of traveling by flying executive class. The seating is roomier, the food is finer, and the service is more personalized.

Priority to the primary

Churches striving to be effective are often tempted to give primary attention to secondary considerations. A word of caution is appropriate. People go to church to hear from God. Keeping primary commitments primary is crucial.

Consider the priority that 40 Anglican bishops in England are giving to the support of the campaign against the fur trade, saying it is cruel to animals.

Contending that animal welfare should be a leading Christian issue, the bishops cite the immorality of killing animals for fashion, and the importance of good stewardship of animals.

In Canada, Bishop Christopher Williams of the Arctic should be commended for both his humor and understanding of spiritual priorities. The bishop wonders if all 40 of the English bishops are vegetarians, and suggests that "Their support is probably misplaced and their stand based on misinformation."

Signaling his concern for the well-being of **people**, Bishop Williams reasons that the gathering of seals and animals for food and skins by Inuit "is not more cruel than the killing of beef or pigs. In the end, the seal hunt in Canada had an extremely detrimental effect on the economy of native peoples and has driven many of them to the welfare lines."[1]

In the pursuit of good stewardship of limited resources, giving primary attention to Kingdom priorities will be increasingly critical in the years to come. As important as many causes may be, the core of Christianity is not first about church attendance or even about being involved in a lifestyle of good works. As Howard Hanchey states, "It is not a philosophical world view, and it is not a human yearning to simply know more. The core of Christianity is an announcement that God has intervened in the history of the world."[2] Bringing contemporary meaning to the purpose of the historic presence of Jesus Christ on planet earth is a Kingdom priority.

Writer Frederick Buechner underscores the point: "In the last analysis, you cannot pontificate but only point. A Christian is one who points at Christ and says, 'I can't prove a thing, but there's something about his eyes and his voice. There's something about the way he carries his head, his hands, the way he carries his cross—the way he carries me.'"[3]

Internal integrity

In our introduction, we noted that the books and literature dealing with church effectiveness inevitably link the topic to church growth. A concern for numerical growth is not only commendable, it is desirable. But numerical growth is not the whole story and, as we have pointed out, when quantitative increases become the goal for church activity, factors can emerge that will discourage people from both coming and staying.

Whenever the presence and influence of any organization or institution is in decline in a culture, great care must be taken to ensure a promising future. In human terms, when the church was center stage in Canadian society, it could afford to be complacent and even somewhat presumptuous. Being in a position of strength meant that errors in judgment or absence of deliberate strategies were not especially consequential. The 1990s do not afford such past luxuries.

At this stage in the history of the church in Canada, faith communities have to work harder and be more strategic simply to maintain present levels of attendance. Because the majority of Canadians are no longer involved in church life, internal integrity will of necessity have to accompany any aspirations for external influence.

The practices of the people of God will have to coincide with the proclaimed church dogma. The people who go to church will need to be the visible church in the world during the week. Keeping the church building in good repair and visible in the community will not be enough. Nor will a church's rich history and positive reputation in the neighborhood be enough to keep new people coming. Rather than depending on contributions of the past, the church of the future will have to carve out a present-tense credibility. And should it be any other way?

During the process of this study, I left my hotel room on a Sunday morning and stopped at the front desk to get directions to a church that had been highly recommended as an effective church. After the instructions were clearly drawn on a map, I asked the attendant, "Can I drive there in 20 minutes or so?"

The woman behind the desk winced a little and said, "Probably a little longer." Then she paused a moment and said, "But today is Sunday and there is no traffic. You can probably make it in that time."

The attendant was right; there was no traffic problem. That is, there was no traffic problem until I turned into the church parking lot and tried to find a vacant space. There weren't any. The lot was jammed. As I walked into the entry way of the church, people were talking and laughing and obviously enjoying each other. There was a sense of warmth in the atmosphere.

Some people were still finding their places as the worship began. I noted a wide range of dress codes in the audience. Families with young children sat alongside each other, there was a healthy multi-ethnic mix, the gender balance appeared to be fairly even, and there was even a group of teenagers sitting together in the balcony.

The tone of everything that happened was positive, not in a phoney way, but in a manner that had the ring of expectancy. People were invited to open themselves up to God. There were no exhortations. Even though 400 or 500 people were present, you were made to feel that your presence mattered. You were comfortable but not complacent. The calendar outlined a program model that was diverse. There were places for different members of the family to participate. During the week, people could be involved in several compassionate ministries in the community.

The denominational association of this local church was identified in the calendar in small print.

Music was important. There was an orchestrated blend of contemporary and traditional styles. People felt free to express their feelings. A few worshipers extended their hands as a statement of personal praise. Children were full-fledged participants. The whole congregation enjoyed the story that was just for the children. The birth of a new baby was acknowledged with the gift of a rose for the father who was present. And more than once, people laughed.

Throughout the service God was the frame of reference. There was a serious place for prayer and moments for quiet reflection. The Bible was obviously important to those who were present. The worship was carefully designed but there was no sense of being in a hurry. Everyone knew that someone was in charge.

The sermon was intellectually engaging. The preacher said some tough things about divorce that were obviously rooted in deep convictions, but there was tenderness in his spirit as he said them. He conveyed compassion toward families who were living life at a level that was less than God's best, because "we all live below God's ideals."

The whole worship experience was faith affirming. I walked out to the parking lot and found myself saying, "This is a good church."

It is not, of course, the only good church. Our point is not to focus on one particular church and say, "Do church this way." Neither is our intent to implicitly convey that it is necessary to be a large church in order to be effective. In fact, all the ingredients that are mixed into the composition of what is going on in that church are within the reach and resources of both small and large congregations.

Rather, our reason for focusing on one specific church is to state one clear conclusion.

Churches can be effective.

Appendices

Methodology

Appendix A

This study of effective churches used a research methodology involving both qualitative and quantitative components.

Qualitative focus groups and interviews

The qualitative component involved a series of 20 focus group sessions with lay persons. In addition, six focus group sessions and 75 personal interviews were held with clergy and Christian academics.

The purpose of the focus group sessions was to provide qualitative input into the design of a survey questionnaire. These sessions also provided qualitative insights into what constitutes a "good church," from the perspective of active lay members, clergy, and Christian academics.

Obtaining a denominational mix of active church participants was a key factor in the selection of the focus group participants. Sessions were conducted in five regions of the country (British Columbia, Prairie Provinces, Ontario, Quebec, and Atlantic Provinces). In addition to "general mix" focus group sessions, we conducted five specialized focus group sessions with youth, and three specialized focus group sessions with recent switchers, that is, active members who had recently switched church affiliations.

Survey research component

The survey component of the research involved the use of a mailed survey which was completed by 452 lay members, 214 clergy, and 95 Christian academics, for a total of 761 responses.

Sample design

In developing the sample for the survey component, two key considerations formed the basis of the sample design.

First, we wanted to include only active church attenders. Across denominations, the survey sample consisted of those who were active participants in the church. We were not interested in sampling those who identify with a particular denomination, but who have no active church participation. We reasoned that any assessment of the successful ingredients of effectiveness should come first from the users: what would normally be refered to as the "customer base" in marketing research.

The second key consideration was to obtain a sample of churches across a broad denominational spectrum. This sample would include both mainline and conservative churches, and would consist of churches which denominational leaders had identified as being effective. We asked denominational leaders to identify two churches from each of five regions across the country (British Columbia, Prairie Provinces, Ontario, Quebec, and Atlantic Provinces). A total of 15 denominations agreed to participate in the study.

a) Lay members and clergy

The sampling unit involved individual churches which denominational leaders had identified as reflecting "the vibrancy and life of a 'model' church in your denomination." Each church in the sample received a package addressed to the senior pastor. Each package consisted of seven individually packaged questionnaires and a set of instructions for questionnaire distribution. Questionnaires were to be completed by the senior pastor, another clergy staff member (where applicable), and five lay members:
- One youth (aged 15-19)
- Two adults aged 20-49; 1 male, 1 female;
- Two adults aged 50 or older; 1 male, 1 female;
- No duplication of immediate family members.

Each questionnaire included a self-addressed, postage-paid envelope for return to the Angus Reid Group for data entry and analysis. A total of 161 churches were sent questionnaire packets (for a total of 1,127 questionnaires distributed in this manner). Responses were secured from 128 different churches. By denomination, these included:

Mainline churches

Anglican	18 churches
Presbyterian	9 churches
United Church of Canada	13 churches
Lutheran	9 churches

Appendix A

Conservative churches

Evangelical Free	8 churches
Christian and Missionary Alliance	10 churches
Mennonite Brethren	9 churches
Evangelical Mennonite	3 churches
Church of the Nazarene	6 churches
Associated Gospel Churches	4 churches
Salvation Army	11 churches
Christian Reformed	9 churches
Baptist (Fellowship)	15 churches
Baptist (Convention)	11 churches
Pentecostal Assemblies of Canada	12 churches
Independent (non-denominational)	14 churches

Regionally, the distribution of churches was as follows:

British Columbia	29 churches
Prairie Provinces	48 churches
Ontario	45 churches
Quebec	20 churches
Atlantic Provinces	19 churches

The 1,127 questionnaires included 322 to clergy, and 805 to lay members. Of the 1,127 questionnaires distributed to churches, we received a total of 761 returned questionnaires, for an overall response rate of 59%. This included 214 responses from clergy, from 128 different churches. The clergy response rate was 66%. A total of 452 lay members, from 91 different churches, responded to the questionnaire, for a response rate of 56%.

b) Christian academics

The sample of Christian academics was developed from a sampling unit comprised of Christian colleges and theological seminaries. A total of 50 colleges and seminaries were selected. Academic deans were contacted in each college and asked to provide faculty lists out of which a random sample of 400 Christian academics was selected. A total of 95 responses were received, for a response rate of 23.75%.

Respondent characteristics

A total of 29% of the survey respondents were from mainline churches. This included 11% Anglican, 6% Lutheran, 7% Presbyterian, and 5% United Church attenders. Responses from within conservative churches (71%) included 15% Baptist, 13% Pentecostal, 9% Mennonite, 6% Christian Reformed, 5% Alliance, 5% independent, and 18% comprising smaller proportions of other denominations.

Regionally, the survey sample included:
British Columbia	19.3%
Prairie Provinces	27.8%
Ontario	27.1%
Quebec	14.2%
Atlantic Provinces	11.6%

By church size, the survey sample included:
Churches with less than 75 members	8.9%
Churches with 75-125 members	19.0%
Churches with 126-175 members	16.1%
Churches with 176-249 members	15.1%
Churches with 250-500 members	21.0%
Churches with over 500 members	19.9%

Questionnaire

The questionnaire was designed on the basis of input from focus group sessions and interviews.

Pre-testing of the questionnaire was undertaken in two stages. The first stage involved 25 pre-test interviews, followed by extensive revision of the instrument and the development of a second pre-test draft.

The second draft was administered to a second sample of 25 respondents, which included lay members, clergy, and Christian academics.

A copy of the final Questionnaire used in the study has been included (Appendix B).

A copy of the instructions to pastors which accompanied the mailed survey has also been included (Attachment A, below).

Data handling

All questionnaires were processed at the Angus Reid Group data entry facilities in Winnipeg and included double entry and verification of all completed questionnaires. The data were analyzed using the SPSSx statistical package. The overall sample of 761 respondents can be considered accurate within 3.6% at a 95% confidence level. Sampling error estimates for individual categories include 4.6% for lay members, 6.7% for clergy, and 10.0% for Christian academics.

Attachment A

Survey of Church Effectiveness
Instructions to Pastors

The package you received contains seven questionnaire packets. Each individual questionnaire package contains a questionnaire booklet along with a postage-paid envelope addressed to Angus Reid Group. The Angus Reid Group is the research consulting firm responsible for compiling the data from the questionnaire and for undertaking a statistical analysis of the responses.

We ask that the questionnaire packets be distributed as follows:
    One questionnaire packet for yourself.
    One questionnaire packet for a clergy staff member.
    Five questionnaire packets for lay members.

Selection of lay members is to be based on the following:
    1. One youth (aged 15-19)
    2. Two adults aged 20-49; 1 male, 1 female;
    3. Two adults aged 50 or older; 1 male, 1 female;
    4. No duplication of immediate family members.

In distributing the questionnaire packets to lay members, it is important to remind respondents that:

1. The responses they give are kept confidential. They are not asked to give their names, nor are we asking you to provide the names of respondents.

2. To further protect confidentiality, the questionnaire is to be returned directly to the Angus Reid Group for data collation. Please remind respondents that they are not required to "hand in" the completed questionnaire to the church office, but rather to mail it directly.

3. Their participation in the survey is voluntary. However, if someone decides that they do not want to participate in the survey, we ask that you give the questionnaire packet to another member of your church in the same age/gender respondent category.

4. There are no "right" or "wrong" answers to the survey questions. We want their frank and honest opinions. It is a research survey, and not a test. As pointed out in the cover letter to respondents, the results of the study will be reported as overall percentages and general categories and will not indicate who expressed which opinion, or what church they attend.

Survey

Appendix B

Survey of Church Effectiveness in Canada

We have included below some statements that have been made concerning church effectiveness. They represent opinions for which there is no right or wrong answer.

For each statement, please circle the number that best represents your personal opinion.

1. Please indicate the extent to which you agree or disagree with the following statements. (Circle the number which best represents your personal view.)

		Strongly Agree	Agree	Disagree	Strongly Disagree
A.	To be effective, churches must provide an opportunity for most members of the church to become involved in programs and activities	1	2	3	4
B.	Effective churches are more likely to focus on a particular ministry or target group, rather than reaching a broad spectrum of people	1	2	3	4
C.	It is difficult for churches to relate to the outside world without compromising their traditional biblical teaching	1	2	3	4

Where's a Good Church?

		Strongly Agree	Agree	Disagree	Strongly Disagree
D.	Effective churches are more likely than other churches to be open about addressing social problems such as domestic violence, child abuse, racism, and alcoholism from the pulpit	1	2	3	4
E.	Churches today must allow for a wide range of diversity in belief and practice	1	2	3	4
F.	A church is not worth attending unless it provides practical guidance for expressing one's faith in the world during the week	1	2	3	4

2. How important to you, personally, are each of the following aspects of church life:

		Very Important	Somewhat Important	Not Very Important	Not At All Important
A.	A church which gives people a sense that they "belong" to that particular church	1	2	3	4
B.	A church which places a strong emphasis and teaching about the value of the family	1	2	3	4
C.	A church which creates a sense of self-worth among members	1	2	3	4
D.	A church geared to meeting the emotional needs of people who attend	1	2	3	4
E.	A church which demonstrates a strong understanding of today's culture	1	2	3	4

Appendix B

2. (Continued) How important to you, personally, are each of the following aspects of church life:

		Very Important	Somewhat Important	Not Very Important	Not At All Important
F.	A church which gives equal status and leadership opportunities to men and women	1	2	3	4
G.	A church which places a strong emphasis on numerical growth	1	2	3	4
H.	A church which places a strong emphasis on God's power to heal and perform modern miracles	1	2	3	4

3. Each of the questions below describes a continuum. For each one, please circle one number that most closely represents your personal preference on how you would like your church to be:

		Very Much	Somewhat	In Between	Somewhat	Very Much	
A.	Traditional Worship/ Hymns, Liturgy	1	2	3	4	5	Contemporary worship/Choruses, experimental venues
B.	Expressive worship	1	2	3	4	5	Quiet, contemplative worship
C.	A congregation that provides clear rules for how to live and behave	1	2	3	4	5	A congregation that leaves decisions to personal choice
D.	Ministry which focuses on needs of congregation members	1	2	3	4	5	Ministry which focuses on needs of community outside the church building

3. (Continued) Please circle one number that most closely represents your personal preference on how you would like your church to be:

	Very Much	Somewhat	In Between	Somewhat	Very Much	
E. Services conducted by professional clergy	1	2	3	4	5	Services with extensive lay member involvement
F. A congregation that is comprised of a multi-ethnic mix	1	2	3	4	5	A congregation that is comprised of people who share the same ethnic background

4. There are various styles of clergy/pastoral leadership. In your opinion, what styles of leadership are most effective for today's church?

	Very Effective	Somewhat Effective	Basically Ineffective	Totally Ineffective
A. Clergy leadership that stresses the leader's authority	1	2	3	4
B. Clergy leadership that is venturesome and inclined to take risks	1	2	3	4
C. Clergy leadership that seeks to gain the consensus of church members before acting	1	2	3	4
D. Clergy leadership that is committed to the tasks of the church whether people are ready to follow or not	1	2	3	4
E. Clergy leadership that places a high priority on numerical growth	1	2	3	4

Appendix B

4. (Continued) In your opinion, what styles of leadership are most effective for today's church?

		Very Effective	Somewhat Effective	Basically Ineffective	Totally Ineffective
F.	Clergy leadership that encourages church members to develop their gifts to serve and lead	1	2	3	4
G.	Members of the clergy who lead with the strength of their personalities	1	2	3	4

5. People switch churches for a variety of reasons. We would like to know your opinion on whether you feel that certain reasons are justified or not justified for switching to another church.

		Mostly Always Justified	Sometimes Justified	Hardly Ever Justified	Not Justified At All
A.	The clergy leadership style is inadequate	1	2	3	4
B.	Church programs do not meet personal or family needs	1	2	3	4
C.	Wanting a church where there are more people like yourself, in areas such as age group, family composition education and income	1	2	3	4
D.	Wanting a church where there are more people like yourself, in terms of ethnic background	1	2	3	4
E.	Switching to a church that is closer to where you live	1	2	3	4
F.	The church you currently attend demands too much of your time, leaving you with not enough time to spend with your family	1	2	3	4

5. (Continued) We would like to know your opinion on whether you feel that certain reasons are justified or not justified for switching to another church.

	Mostly Always Justified	Sometimes Justified	Hardly Ever Justified	Not Justified At All
G. The church you attend is not friendly, and you don't particularly like the people there	1	2	3	4
H. The church you attend has unresolved conflict among its members	1	2	3	4
I. The church you attend places unrealistic financial expectations on its members	1	2	3	4

6. If you were planning to switch to another church, which of the following characteristics would you personally rank as high, medium, or low priority in terms of your decision as to what church to attend:

Priority:	High	Medium	Low
A. Denomination	1	2	3
B. Closeness to home	1	2	3
C. Excellent preaching	1	2	3
D. Size of congregation	1	2	3
E. Opportunity to become involved	1	2	3
F. Church "in touch" with the times	1	2	3
G. Strong commitment to world missions	1	2	3
H. Strong commitment to evangelism with the local community	1	2	3
I. Provides the option of joining a small/cell group	1	2	3

Appendix B

This section includes some questions about the church you attend and about yourself which are used for statistical purposes.

1. Which of the following best describes your position or area of involvement in the church you currently attend?

    ___ Minister/Pastor/Priest

    ___ Other clergy on multiple church staff

    ___ Lay leader (board member, deacon, elder, etc.)

    ___ Lay member

    ___ Attender

2. On an average Sunday morning, approximately how many people attend your church (including children)?

    ___ Less than 75   ___ Between 175 and 249

    ___ Between 75 and 125   ___ Between 250 and 500

    ___ Between 126 and 175   ___ Over 500

3. Which of these categories would you, personally, describe as the "ideal" church size for you?

    ___ Less than 75   ___ Between 175 and 249

    ___ Between 75 and 125   ___ Between 250 and 500

    ___ Between 126 and 175   ___ Over 500

4. What denomination or affiliation is the church you currently attend?

    _____

5. How long have you been attending your present church? ____/____
                                                                                     Years/Months

6. In an average week, how many worship services and other church events/meetings do you personally attend?

    ___ one   ___ three   ___ more than four

    ___ two   ___ four

7. In your lifetime, in your church attendance patterns, have you switched denominations? If so, please indicate those you have attended.

   _____

   _____

8. Was there ever a period of time in your life when you did not attend any church?

   ___ Yes   If yes, for how long? _____ Years/Months

   ___ No

9. What denomination or affiliation was the church you attended while you were growing up? (If you did not attend church while you were growing up, please enter "none".)

   _____

10. Which of the following best describes your current employment situation?

    ___ In a ministry capacity in a church or para-church organization

    ___ Teaching in a Christian college or seminary

    ___ Employed in a secular (not church/ministry-related) occupation

    ___ Retired, formerly in a position of church or para-church ministry

    ___ Retired, formerly employed in a secular occupation

    ___ A student

    ___ At home

    ___ Unemployed, but seeking employment

    ___ Other (please specify) _____

11. Which of the following categories does your age fall into?

    ___ 18 or younger   ___ 35–44   ___ 65 or older

    ___ 19–24   ___ 45–54

    ___ 25–34   ___ 55–64

Appendix B

12. Are you: Male _____
               Female _____

13. What is your city and province of residence:

    City: _____ Province: _____

14. As you reflect on the matter of church effectiveness, are there any other comments or observations you would like to add?

    _____

    _____

    _____

    _____

    _____

Thank you very much for your cooperation and contribution. Please place the completed questionnaire in the envelope provided and mail it to:

Angus Reid Group
1900–155 Carlton Street
Winnipeg, Manitoba
R3C 3H8

Survey Results

Appendix C

Table 1A
Agree/Disagree Attitude Statements
(clergy/academic/lay variances)

Base:	Total Sample (761) %	Clergy (214) %	Academics (95) %	Lay members (452) %

To be effective, churches must provide an opportunity for most members to become involved in programs and activities

Strongly agree	68	72	58	68
Moderately agree	28	23	37	29
Moderately disagree	3	4	4	2
Strongly disagree	1	1	1	0

Effective churches are more likely to focus on a particular ministry or target group, rather than reaching a broad spectrum of people

Strongly agree	6	8	9	5
Moderately agree	31	44	34	25
Moderately disagree	50	39	44	56
Strongly disagree	12	8	11	14
(not stated)	1	1	2	0

It is very difficult for churches to relate to the outside world without compromising traditional biblical teachings

Strongly agree	3	3	1	3
Moderately agree	10	7	3	12
Moderately disagree	37	36	39	37
Strongly disagree	49	52	56	46
(not stated)	1	2	1	2

Table 1A Continued
Agree/Disagree Attitude Statements
(clergy/academic/lay variances)

Base:	Total Sample (761) %	Clergy (214) %	Academics (95) %	Lay members (452) %

Effective churches are more likely than other churches to be open about addressing social problems such as domestic violence, child abuse, racism, and alcoholism from the pulpit

Strongly agree	25	23	26	26
Moderately agree	50	46	57	50
Moderately disagree	20	24	13	20
Strongly disagree	4	6	3	3
(not stated)	1	1	1	1

Churches today must allow for a wide range of diversity in belief and practice

Strongly agree	6	6	11	4
Moderately agree	22	21	37	21
Moderately disagree	42	47	41	39
Strongly disagree	27	23	8	33
(not stated)	3	3	3	3

A church is not worth attending unless it provides practical guidance for expressing one's faith during the week

Strongly agree	43	55	33	40
Moderately agree	41	36	52	41
Moderately disagree	13	6	15	16
Strongly disagree	2	2	0	2
(not stated)	1	1	0	1

Appendix C

Table 1B
Agree/Disagree Attitude Statements
(church affiliation variances)

Base:	Total Sample (761) %	Mainline (214) %	Conservative (394) %	Pentecostal (98) %
To be effective, churches must provide an opportunity for most members to become involved in programs and activities				
Strongly agree	68	69	67	76
Moderately agree	28	29	29	22
Moderately disagree	3	2	3	2
Strongly disagree	1	0	1	0
Effective churches are more likely to focus on a particular ministry or target group, rather than reaching a broad spectrum of people				
Strongly agree	6	3	7	6
Moderately agree	31	25	35	30
Moderately disagree	50	55	47	52
Strongly disagree	12	16	9	12
(not stated)	1	1	2	0
It is very difficult for churches to relate to the outside world without compromising traditional biblical teachings				
Strongly agree	3	3	3	2
Moderately agree	10	14	7	11
Moderately disagree	37	35	37	42
Strongly disagree	49	48	52	44
(not stated)	1	0	1	1

Table 1B Continued
Agree/Disagree Attitude Statements
(church affiliation variances)

Base:	Total Sample (761) %	Mainline (214) %	Conservative (394) %	Pentecostal (98) %
Effective churches are more likely than other churches to be open about addressing social problems such as domestic violence, child abuse, racism, and alcoholism from the pulpit				
Strongly agree	25	24	26	24
Moderately agree	50	50	50	49
Moderately disagree	20	21	20	20
Strongly disagree	4	5	4	3
(not stated)	1	0	0	4
Churches today must allow for a wide range of diversity in belief and practice				
Strongly agree	6	10	5	3
Moderately agree	22	26	23	8
Moderately disagree	42	40	43	44
Strongly disagree	27	22	26	40
(not stated)	3	2	3	5
A church is not worth attending unless it provides practical guidance for expressing one's faith during the week				
Strongly agree	43	40	45	45
Moderately agree	41	42	40	42
Moderately disagree	13	17	11	9
Strongly disagree	2	1	2	2
(not stated)	1	0	2	2

Table 2A
Perceived Importance of
Various Characteristics of Church Life
(clergy/academic/lay variances)

Base:	Total Sample (761) %	Clergy (214) %	Academics (95) %	Lay members (452) %

A church which gives people a sense that they "belong" to that particular church

Very important	83	88	74	82
Somewhat important	15	11	22	16
Not very important	2	1	4	2
Not at all important	0	0	0	0

A church which places strong emphasis on and teaches about the value of the family

Very important	68	66	46	74
Somewhat important	27	29	36	25
Not very important	4	4	17	1
Not at all important	1	1	1	0

A church which creates a sense of self-worth among members

Very important	69	73	59	69
Somewhat important	29	26	37	29
Not very important	2	1	4	2
Not at all important	0	0	0	0

A church geared to meeting the emotional needs of people who attend

Very important	55	55	39	58
Somewhat important	39	41	49	36
Not very important	6	3	11	6
Not at all important	0	1	1	0

Table 2A Continued
Perceived Importance of
Various Characteristics of Church Life
(clergy/academic/lay variances)

Base:	Total Sample (761) %	Clergy (214) %	Academics (95) %	Lay members (452) %
A church which demonstrates a solid understanding of today's culture				
Very important	53	62	68	46
Somewhat important	40	34	30	45
Not very important	6	4	2	8
Not at all important	1	0	0	1
A church which gives equal status and leadership opportunities to men and women				
Very important	43	44	57	39
Somewhat important	40	41	31	43
Not very important	12	12	7	12
Not at all important	5	3	5	6
A church which places strong emphasis on numerical growth				
Very important	7	8	6	7
Somewhat important	38	51	39	31
Not very important	42	34	41	46
Not at all important	13	7	14	16
A church which places strong emphasis on God's power to heal and perform modern miracles				
Very important	25	25	12	28
Somewhat important	39	46	29	38
Not very important	23	18	33	22
Not at all important	11	9	24	9
(not stated)	2	2	2	3

Appendix C

Table 2B
Perceived Importance of
Various Characteristics of Church Life
(church affiliation variances)

Base:	Total Sample (761) %	Mainline (214) %	Conservative (394) %	Pentecostal (98) %

A church which gives people a sense that they "belong" to that particular church

Very important	83	82	86	76
Somewhat important	15	15	12	21
Not very important	2	3	1	3
Not at all important	0	0	1	0

A church which places strong emphasis on and teaches about the value of the family

Very important	68	60	69	79
Somewhat important	27	29	28	21
Not very important	4	9	2	0
Not at all important	1	2	1	0

A church which creates a sense of self-worth among members

Very important	69	70	71	64
Somewhat important	29	28	27	34
Not very important	2	2	2	1
Not at all important	0	0	0	1

A church geared to meeting the emotional needs of people who attend

Very important	55	50	58	59
Somewhat important	39	43	37	36
Not very important	6	6	5	5
Not at all important	0	1	0	0

Table 2B Continued
Perceived Importance of
Various Characteristics of Church Life
(church affiliation variances)

Base:	Total Sample (761) %	Mainline (214) %	Conservative (394) %	Pentecostal (98) %
A church which demonstrates a solid understanding of today's culture				
Very important	53	48	58	41
Somewhat important	40	45	36	45
Not very important	6	6	4	13
Not at all important	1	1	2	1
A church which gives equal status and leadership opportunities to men and women				
Very important	43	49	41	34
Somewhat important	40	38	40	49
Not very important	12	9	13	14
Not at all important	5	4	6	3
A church which places strong emphasis on numerical growth				
Very important	7	7	7	8
Somewhat important	38	34	40	35
Not very important	42	45	42	42
Not at all important	13	14	11	15
A church which places strong emphasis on God's power to heal and perform modern miracles				
Very important	25	23	18	60
Somewhat important	39	36	42	35
Not very important	23	25	28	3
Not at all important	11	14	10	0
(not stated)	2	2	2	2

Appendix C

Table 3A
Preferences in Church Emphasis
(clergy/academic/lay variances)

Base:	Total Sample (761) %	Clergy (214) %	Academics (95) %	Lay members (452) %
Traditional worship	19	12	22	20
In between	41	45	43	41
Contemporary worship	40	43	35	39
Expressive worship	41	52	25	37
In between	43	41	45	45
Quiet worship	16	7	30	18
Clear rules for living	45	39	30	50
In between	28	33	34	26
Personal choice	27	28	36	24
Congregational-needs focus	27	28	18	27
In between	59	55	69	59
Outside-community focus	14	17	13	14
Clergy-led worship	29	21	16	36
In between	34	36	25	36
Extensive lay involvement	37	43	59	28
Multi-ethnic mix	58	57	56	59
In between	34	36	35	32
Ethnic similarity	8	7	9	9

Table 3B
Preferences in Church Emphasis
(church affiliation variances)

Base:	Total Sample (761) %	Mainline (214) %	Conservative (394) %	Pentecostal (98) %
Traditional worship	19	28	14	12
In between	41	44	42	29
Contemporary worship	40	28	44	59
Expressive worship	41	32	42	48
In between	43	49	39	39
Quiet worship	16	19	19	13
Clear rules for living	45	45	43	46
In between	28	26	28	30
Personal choice	27	29	29	24
Congregational needs focus	27	29	23	27
In between	59	61	58	51
Outside-community focus	14	10	19	22
Clergy-led worship	29	36	26	30
In between	34	38	31	34
Extensive lay involvement	37	26	43	36
Multi-ethnic mix	58	62	57	63
In between	34	34	34	24
Ethnic similarity	8	4	9	13

Appendix C

Table 4A
Perceived Effectiveness of Clergy Leadership Styles
(clergy/academic/lay variances)

Base:	Total Sample (761) %	Clergy (214) %	Academics (95) %	Lay members (452) %
Stresses leader's authority				
Very effective	8	8	3	8
Somewhat effective	37	40	32	37
Basically ineffective	41	42	46	40
Totally ineffective	10	8	14	9
(not stated)	4	2	5	6
Venturesome/risk-taking				
Very effective	24	32	23	18
Somewhat effective	58	59	67	56
Basically ineffective	11	6	2	16
Totally ineffective	3	0	1	4
(not stated)	4	3	7	6
Seeks congregational consensus				
Very effective	38	30	41	42
Somewhat effective	41	49	42	36
Basically ineffective	15	17	11	14
Totally ineffective	2	2	1	3
(not stated)	4	2	5	5
Task-oriented				
Very effective	12	9	5	15
Somewhat effective	31	31	25	32
Basically ineffective	42	50	47	38
Totally ineffective	10	9	15	9
(not stated)	5	1	8	6

Table 4A Continued
Perceived Effectiveness of
Clergy Leadership Styles
(clergy/academic/lay variances)

Base:	Total Sample (761) %	Clergy (214) %	Academics (95) %	Lay members (452) %
High priority on numerical growth				
Very effective	4	5	3	4
Somewhat effective	37	49	44	30
Basically ineffective	41	36	33	45
Totally ineffective	14	7	14	17
(not stated)	4	3	6	4
Encourages members to develop their gifts				
Very effective	87	93	80	85
Somewhat effective	9	6	14	8
Basically ineffective	1	0	0	1
Totally ineffective	0	0	0	1
(not stated)	3	1	6	5
Strength of personality				
Very effective	18	17	14	19
Somewhat effective	46	51	56	40
Basically ineffective	24	25	20	25
Totally ineffective	7	5	3	9
(not stated)	5	2	7	7

Table 4B
Perceived Effectiveness of
Clergy Leadership Styles
(church affiliation variances)

Base:	Total Sample (761) %	Mainline (214) %	Conservative (394) %	Pentecostal (98) %
Stresses leader's authority				
Very effective	8	5	6	14
Somewhat effective	37	31	39	48
Basically ineffective	41	48	42	26
Totally ineffective	10	12	9	6
(not stated)	4	4	4	6
Venturesome/risk-taking				
Very effective	24	24	24	20
Somewhat effective	58	60	59	50
Basically ineffective	11	10	10	20
Totally ineffective	3	1	4	2
(not stated)	4	5	3	8
Seeks congregational consensus				
Very effective	38	39	39	40
Somewhat effective	41	39	42	33
Basically ineffective	15	15	13	15
Totally ineffective	2	2	2	5
(not stated)	4	5	4	7
Task-oriented				
Very effective	12	10	13	14
Somewhat effective	31	33	28	37
Basically ineffective	42	46	43	41
Totally ineffective	10	7	13	2
(not stated)	5	4	3	6

Table 4B Continued
Perceived Effectiveness of Clergy Leadership Styles
(church affiliation variances)

Base:	Total Sample (761) %	Mainline (214) %	Conservative (394) %	Pentecostal (98) %
High priority on numerical growth				
Very effective	4	4	4	5
Somewhat effective	37	31	39	44
Basically ineffective	41	46	40	33
Totally ineffective	14	14	14	12
(not stated)	4	5	3	6
Encourages members to develop their gifts				
Very effective	87	83	89	83
Somewhat effective	9	12	7	9
Basically ineffective	1	0	1	2
Totally ineffective	0	0	1	1
(not stated)	3	5	2	5
Strength of personality				
Very effective	18	22	17	13
Somewhat effective	46	47	46	46
Basically ineffective	24	21	24	28
Totally ineffective	7	6	9	7
(not stated)	5	4	4	6

Appendix C

Table 5A
Perceptions of Whether Certain Situations/Conditions Justify Switching Churches
(clergy/academic/lay variances)

Base:	Total Sample (761) %	Clergy (214) %	Academics (95) %	Lay members (452) %

If clergy leadership style is inadequate, switching churches is:

Mostly always justified	11	7	4	13
Sometimes justified	63	66	67	60
Hardly ever justified	20	22	22	19
Not justified at all	3	2	3	4
(not stated)	3	3	4	4

If church programs do no meet personal and family needs, switching churches is:

Mostly always justified	31	23	24	38
Sometimes justified	55	67	63	47
Hardly ever justified	10	8	8	12
Not justified at all	2	0	3	3
(not stated)	2	2	2	0

When wanting a church where there are people more like yourself in areas such as age, family composition, education and income, switching churches is:

Mostly always justified	9	7	4	12
Sometimes justified	51	62	60	43
Hardly ever justified	27	26	25	28
Not justified at all	12	4	8	16
(not stated)	1	1	3	1

Table 5A Continued
Perceptions of Whether Certain Situations/Conditions Justify Switching Churches

(clergy/academic/lay variances)

Base:	Total Sample (761) %	Clergy (214) %	Academics (95) %	Lay members (452) %

When wanting a church where there are more people like yourself in terms of ethnic background, switching churches is:

Mostly always justified	4	4	2	5
Sometimes justified	42	51	47	36
Hardly ever justified	36	35	35	38
Not justified at all	17	10	15	20
(not stated)	1	0	1	1

When wanting a church that is closer to where you live, switching churches is:

Mostly always justified	21	21	32	18
Sometimes justified	62	65	57	62
Hardly ever justified	12	10	9	14
Not justified at all	5	4	2	6

When the church you currently attend demands too much of your time, leaving you with not enough time to spend with your family, switching churches is:

Mostly always justified	9	7	8	11
Sometimes justified	41	51	49	34
Hardly ever justified	34	34	29	34
Not justified at all	15	8	11	20
(not stated)	1	0	3	1

Appendix C

Table 5A Continued
Perceptions of Whether Certain Situations/Conditions Justify Switching Churches
(clergy/academic/lay variances)

Base:	Total Sample (761) %	Clergy (214) %	Academics (95) %	Lay members (452) %

When the church you attend is not friendly, and you don't particularly like the people there, switching churches is:

Mostly always justified	21	15	18	24
Sometimes justified	47	52	49	45
Hardly ever justified	22	26	22	20
Not justified at all	9	7	7	11
(not stated)	1	0	4	0

When the church you attend has unresolved conflict among its members, switching churches is:

Mostly always justified	14	10	9	17
Sometimes justified	56	58	53	55
Hardly ever justified	24	28	34	20
Not justified at all	5	4	2	8
(not stated)	1	0	2	0

When the church you attend places unrealistic financial expectations on its members, switching churches is:

Mostly always justified	15	10	11	18
Sometimes justified	47	57	54	40
Hardly ever justified	28	28	29	27
Not justified at all	7	3	4	10
(not stated)	3	2	2	5

Table 5B
Perceptions of Whether Certain Situations/Conditions Justify Switching Churches
(church affiliation variances)

Base:	Total Sample (761) %	Mainline (214) %	Conservative (394) %	Pentecostal (98) %
If clergy leadership style is inadequate, switching churches is:				
Mostly always justified	11	15	9	5
Sometimes justified	63	58	66	63
Hardly ever justified	20	20	19	22
Not justified at all	3	3	4	5
(not stated)	3	4	2	5
If church programs do no meet personal and family needs, switching churches is:				
Mostly always justified	31	33	34	17
Sometimes justified	55	55	53	65
Hardly ever justified	10	10	9	14
Not justified at all	2	1	3	2
(not stated)	2	1	1	2
When wanting a church where there are people more like yourself in areas such as age, family composition, education and income, switching churches is:				
Mostly always justified	9	9	10	3
Sometimes justified	51	46	53	53
Hardly ever justified	27	33	24	24
Not justified at all	12	10	12	19
(not stated)	1	2	1	1

Appendix C

Table 5B Continued
Perceptions of Whether
Certain Situations/Conditions
Justify Switching Churches
(church affiliation variances)

Base:	Total Sample (761) %	Mainline (214) %	Conservative (394) %	Pentecostal (98) %

When wanting a church where there are more people like yourself in terms of ethnic background, switching churches is:

Mostly always justified	4	3	5	3
Sometimes justified	42	36	43	52
Hardly ever justified	36	40	36	31
Not justified at all	17	20	16	14
(not stated)	1	1	0	0

When wanting a church that is closer to where you live, switching churches is:

Mostly always justified	21	15	26	19
Sometimes justified	62	59	60	66
Hardly ever justified	12	18	9	13
Not justified at all	5	8	5	2

When the church you currently attend demands too much of your time, leaving you with not enough time to spend with your family, switching churches is:

Mostly always justified	9	9	8	13
Sometimes justified	41	41	42	38
Hardly ever justified	34	32	34	32
Not justified at all	15	17	15	17
(not stated)	1	1	1	0

Table 5B Continued
Perceptions of Whether Certain Situations/Conditions Justify Switching Churches

(church affiliation variances)

Base:	Total Sample (761) %	Mainline (214) %	Conservative (394) %	Pentecostal (98) %

When the church you attend is not friendly, and you don't particularly like the people there, switching churches is:

Mostly always justified	21	29	20	15
Sometimes justified	47	48	47	39
Hardly ever justified	22	14	24	31
Not justified at all	9	6	9	15
(not stated)	1	3	0	0

When the church you attend has unresolved conflict among its members, switching churches is:

Mostly always justified	14	12	14	14
Sometimes justified	56	57	57	48
Hardly ever justified	24	25	24	29
Not justified at all	5	5	5	9
(not stated)	1	1	0	0

When the church you attend places unrealistic financial expectations on its members, switching churches is:

Mostly always justified	15	16	13	16
Sometimes justified	47	50	48	38
Hardly ever justified	28	22	31	34
Not justified at all	7	7	7	7
(not stated)	3	5	1	5

Appendix C

Table 6A
Priority of Various Factors in Selecting a New Church
(clergy/academic/lay variances)

Base:	Total Sample (761) %	Clergy (214) %	Academics (95) %	Lay members (452) %
Excellent preaching				
High	72	74	68	72
Medium	25	24	28	25
Low	3	2	4	3
Local evangelism				
High	70	80	61	66
Medium	26	18	35	29
Low	4	2	4	5
In touch with the times				
High	66	76	60	63
Medium	29	21	36	29
Low	5	3	4	8
Opportunity to become involved				
High	61	70	62	55
Medium	34	27	34	38
Low	4	3	4	7
Denomination				
High	52	51	61	50
Medium	30	28	31	32
Low	18	21	8	18

Table 6A Continued
Priority of Various Factors
in Selecting a New Church
(clergy/academic/lay variances)

Base:	Total Sample (761) %	Clergy (214) %	Academics (95) %	Lay members (452) %
Commitment to world missions				
High	49	50	55	48
Medium	44	44	43	45
Low	7	6	2	7
Option to join small/cell groups				
High	49	64	35	45
Medium	36	28	45	39
Low	15	8	20	16
Closeness to home				
High	20	16	34	19
Medium	60	62	52	61
Low	20	22	14	20
Congregation size				
High	4	5	5	3
Medium	48	55	56	45
Low	48	40	39	52

Appendix C

Table 6B
Priority of Various Factors in Selecting a New Church
(church affiliation variances)

Base:	Total Sample (761) %	Mainline (214) %	Conservative (394) %	Pentecostal (98) %
Excellent preaching				
High	72	74	74	69
Medium	25	24	25	29
Low	3	2	1	2
Local evangelism				
High	70	54	75	85
Medium	26	36	24	14
Low	4	10	1	1
In touch with the times				
High	66	58	69	64
Medium	29	34	27	31
Low	5	8	4	5
Opportunity to become involved				
High	61	61	62	56
Medium	34	34	34	37
Low	5	5	4	7
Denomination				
High	52	59	46	66
Medium	30	24	35	23
Low	18	17	19	11

Table 6B Continued
Priority of Various Factors in Selecting a New Church
(church affiliation variances)

Base:	Total Sample (761) %	Mainline (214) %	Conservative (394) %	Pentecostal (98) %
Commitment to world missions				
High	49	39	50	62
Medium	44	50	44	36
Low	7	11	6	2
Option to join small/cell groups				
High	49	44	55	39
Medium	36	37	33	47
Low	15	19	12	14
Closeness to home				
High	20	17	24	16
Medium	60	54	60	68
Low	20	29	16	16
Congregation size				
High	4	3	5	4
Medium	48	44	51	44
Low	48	53	44	52

Endnotes

Introduction

1. Thomas Oden, *Pastoral Theology* (New York: Harper & Row, 1983), 12.

Chapter One

1. Reginald Bibby, *Fragmented Gods* (Toronto: Irwin, 1987).
2. Bruce Shelley and Marshall Shelley, *The Consumer Church* (Downers Grove, Ill.: InterVarsity, 1992), 154.
3. Bibby, *Fragmented Gods*, 51.
4. Bibby, *Fragmented Gods*, 134.

Chapter Two

1. Herbert O'Driscoll, Convocation Address, Wycliffe College, Toronto, May 13, 1991.
2. Cal LeMon, "Surviving Sunday Morning Innovations," *Leadership* (Spring Quarter 1986): 88.
3. Eugene H. Peterson, *Reversed Thunder: The Revelation of John and the Praying Imagination* (San Francisco: Harper & Row, 1988), 70.
4. Reginald Bibby and Merlin Brinkerhoff, *Circulation of the Saints 1966–1990: New Data, New Reflections*. Paper presented at the annual meeting of The Society for the Scientific Study of Religion, Washington, November, 1992.
5. Peter Berger, *Invitation to Sociology* (Garden City: Doubleday, 1963), 27.
6. Kennon Callahan, *Twelve Keys to an Effective Church* (San Francisco: HarperCollins, 1983), xiii.
7. Win Arn and Charles Arn, "How to Use Ratios to Affect Church Growth," *Church Growth: The State of the Art* (Wheaton, Ill.: Tyndale House, 1986), 97–98.

8. Gregory Stone and Harvey Farberman, eds., *Social Psychology Through Symbolic Interactionism* (New York: John Wiley & Sons, 1970).
9. Gordon Aeschliman, *Cages of Pain* (Irving, Texas: Word, 1991).
10. Dietrich Bonhoeffer, *Life Together*, J. W. Doberstein, trans. (New York: Harper & Row, 1954), 22–23.
11. George Barna, *The Frog in the Kettle* (Ventura, Ca.: Regal, 1990), 7.
12. John R. W. Stott, *Christian Mission in the Modern World* (Downers Grove, Ill.: InterVarsity, 1992), 154.

Chapter Three

1. Theodore Levitt, *Innovation in Marketing* (New York: McGraw-Hill, 1962).
2. Lyle Schaller, *It's a Different World: The Challenge for Today's Pastor* (Nashville: Abingdon Press, 1987), 31.
3. Dean Kelley, *Why Conservative Churches are Growing* (New York: Harper & Row, 1972).
4. Reginald Bibby and Merlin Brinkerhoff, *The Circulation of the Saints:1966–1990: New Data, New Reflections*. Paper presented at the annual meeting of The Society for the Scientific Study of Religion, Washington, November, 1992.
5. Bibby and Brinkerhoff, *Circulation of the Saints*.
6. George Barna, *User Friendly Churches* (Ventura, Ca.: Regal Books, 1991), 161ff.
7. Barna, *User Friendly*, 50–51.
8. Leith Anderson, *A Church for the 21st Century* (Minneapolis: Bethany, 1992), 49.
9. James T. Richardson, "Paradigm Conflict in Conversion Research," *Journal for the Scientific Study of Religion* (24): 2.
10. Thomas Pilarzyk, "Conversion and Alternation Processes in the Youth Culture," *Pacific Sociological Review* 21 (1978).
11. James T. Richardson, "Conversion to New Religions: Secularization or Re-enchantment," *The Sacred in a Secular Age*, Phillip Hammond, ed. (Berkeley: University of California Press, 1985).
12. Peter Berger, *Invitation to Sociology* (Garden City: Doubleday, 1963), 52.
13. Gregory Stone and Harvey Farberman, eds., *Social Psychology Through Symbolic Interactionism* (New York: John Wiley & Sons, 1970), 237–248.
14. Meredith McGuire, *Religion: The Social Context* (Belmont, Ca.: Wadsworth, 1981), 59.

15. William Willimon, *What's Right with the Church* (San Francisco: Harper & Row, 1985), 9.
16. Dietrich Bonhoeffer, *Life Together*, J. W. Doberstien, trans. (New York: Harper & Row, 1954), 24.
17. Willimon, *What's Right*, 26.
18. David Read, *Overheard* (Nashville: Abingdon Press, 1969), 139–140.

Chapter Four

1. Richard Niebuhr, *The Social Sources of Denominationalism* (New York: Holt, 1929).
2. Lyle Schaller, *It's a Different World: The Challenge for Today's Pastor* (Nashville: Abingdon Press, 1987), 26–27.
3. Stanley Hauerwas and William Willimon, *Resident Aliens* (Nashville: Abingdon Press, 1989), 17.
4. Robert Bellah, *The Broken Covenant: American Civil Religion in Time of Trial* (San Francisco: Seabury Press, 1975), 109–110.
5. David Bosch, *Transforming Mission* (New York: Orbis Books, 1991), 349.
6. Bosch, *Transforming Mission*, 352–353.
7. Bellah, *Broken Covenant*, 109–110.
8. Elmer L. Towns, *An Inside Look at 10 of Today's Most Innovative Churches* (Ventura, Ca.: Regal Books, 1990), 248.
9. Leith Anderson, *A Church for the 21st Century* (Minneapolis: Bethany, 1992), 33.
10. George Barna, *The Frog in the Kettle* (Ventura, Ca.: Regal Books, 1990), 42.
11. Leith Anderson, *Dying for Change* (Minneapolis: Bethany House, 1990), 95.
12. Peter Berger, *The Sacred Canopy* (Garden City: Doubleday, 1969), 143–147.
13. Berger, *Sacred Canopy*, 151.
14. Douglas John Hall, *The Future of the Church: Where are We Headed?* (Toronto: United Church Publishing House, 1989), 99–100.
15. Berger, *Sacred Canopy*, 143–144.
16. Gregory Baum, *Religion and Alienation* (New York: Paulist Press, 1975), 150.
17. Cited by Anderson, *Dying for Change*, 86.
18. Donald Posterski, *Reinventing Evangelism: New Strategies for Presenting Christ in Today's World* (Downers Grove, Ill.: InterVarsity Press, 1989), 111.

Chapter Five

1. Mitchell, "Immigrants' Origins Increasingly Diverse," *The Globe and Mail*, December 9, 1992.
2. Angus Reid Group Inc., *Immigration Levels: Aspects of Public Opinion*. Report prepared for the Federal Government's Public Consultations on 1991–1995 Immigration Levels: Employment and Immigration Canada, 1990.
3. Reginald Bibby and Donald Posterski, *Teen Trends* (Toronto: Stoddart Publishing, 1992), 254.
4. Nicolass van Riju, "Not just for the boys: Scouts Canada finally goes co-ed," *The Toronto Star*, November 24, 1992.
5. Alain Baril and George Mori, "Leaving the Fold: Declining Church Attendance," *Canadian Social Trends* (Autumn, 1991).
6. Harold Fallding, "Mainline Protestantism in Canada and the United States of America: An Overview," *Canadian Journal of Sociology* (March 21, 1978).
7. C. S. Lewis, *The Abolition of Man* (New York: Macmillan, 1947).
8. Herbert O'Driscoll, Convocation Address, Wycliffe College, Toronto, May 13, 1991.
9. Reginald Bibby, *Mosaic Madness* (Toronto: Stoddart Publishing, 1990), 14.
10. Robert Bellah, et al, *Habits of the Heart: Individualism and Commitment in American Life* (New York: Harper & Row, 1985), 61.
11. Dana Flavelle, "Electronic Bonanza," *The Toronto Star*, December 20, 1992.
12. "More Kids Turning on to Television, Study Finds," *The Toronto Star*, April 15, 1992.
13. Peter Trueman, "Success of Vision TV is a Triumph of Decency and Quality," *Starweek*, October 24–30, 1992, 7.
14. Bibby and Posterski, *Teen Trends*, 52.
15. Reginald Bibby, *Fragmented Gods* (Toronto: Irwin, 1987), 80, 85.
16. Lorne Bozinoff and Peter MacIntosh, "Church Attendance Highest in Five Years," Gallup Report, June 6, 1992.
17. Jean-Louis Larochelle, "New Directions For The Future," Antoinette Kinlough, trans., study prepared for the Research Committee of the Assembly of Quebec Bishops on Local Christian Communities, 1992, 16.
18. Lesslie Newbigin, *Tell the Truth: The Gospel as Public Truth* (Grand Rapids: Eerdmans, 1991), 68.
19. Larochelle, "New Directions," 26.

20. Albert Beaudry, "Risk new future or die, report warns Quebec parishes," *Catholic New Times*, November 22, 1991, 14.
21. George Gallup, Jr., "Upon on Interfaith Dialogue, Emerging Trends," Address to a Jewish-Christian-Muslim consultation, November 1991, 2.
22. Bibby and Posterski, *Teen Trends*, 248.

Chapter Six

1. Cited in *Harper's Magazine* 286.1712, January, 1993, 26.
2. Pat Robertson, as quoted in *The Globe and Mail*, January 2, 1993, D1
3. Ron Graham, *God's Dominion* (Toronto: McClelland & Stewart Inc., 1990), 329.
4. James Sauer, "The Canadian Context," *The Practice of Ministry in Canada*, February 1985, 6.
5. Mark A. Noll, *A History of Christianity in the United States and Canada* (Grand Rapids: Eerdmans, 1992), 284.
6. Noll, *History of Christianity*, 55.
7. Noll, *History of Christianity*, 72.
8. Harold Fallding, "Mainline Protestantism in Canada and the United States of America: An Overview," *Canadian Journal of Sociology* III, 2 (1978): 144.
9. Seymour Martin Lipset, *Continental Divide: The Values and Institutions of the United states and Canada* (Toronto: C.D. Howe Institute, 1989), 80.
10. Quoted by Lipset, *Continental Divide*, 90.
11. Noll, *History of Christianity*, 276.
12. Noll, *History of Christianity*, 144.
13. Harry H. Hiller, "Continentalism and the Third Force in Religion," *Canadian Journal of Sociology* III, 2 (1978): 192.
14. Hiller, "Continentalism," 185.
15. Lipset, *Continental Divide*, 88–89.
16. Arnell Motz, *Reclaiming a Nation* (Richmond, B.C.: Outreach Canada Ministries, 1990), 65.
17. Reginald Bibby and Merlin Brinkerhoff, *The Circulation of the Saints: 1966–1990: New Data, New Reflections*. Paper presented at the annual meeting of The Society for the Scientific Study of Religion, Washington, November, 1992.
18. Hiller, "Continentalism," 191.
19. Lipset, *Continental Divide*, 89.
20. Lipset, *Continental Divide*, 77.
21. *Christianity Today*, 37.1, January, 1993, 46.

22. Hiller, "Continentalism," 191.
23. Harold Bloom, *The American Religion* (New York: Simon & Schuster, 1992), 197.
24. Bloom, *American Religion*, 197-198.
25. Bloom, *American Religion*, 197.
26. Bloom, *American Religion*, 223.
27. Bloom, *American Religion*, 191.
28. Hiller, "Continentalism," 191.
29. Sauer, "Canadian Context," 8.

Chapter Seven

1. Douglas Hall, *Thinking the Faith* (Minneapolis: Fortress Press, 1989), 206.
2. Hall, *Thinking the Faith*, 66.
3. Michael Griffiths, *God's Forgetful Pilgrims* (Grand Rapids: Eerdmans, 1978), 9.
4. Griffiths, *God's Forgetful Pilgrims*, 43.
5. John Frame, *Van Til the Theologian* (Pillipsburg: Pilgrim, 1976), 25.
6. Shoki Coe, "In Search of Renewal in Theological Education," *Theological Education* 9 (1973): 240.
7. Harvie Conn, *Eternal Word and Changing Worlds* (Grand Rapids: Zondervan, 1984), 176-205.
8. Samuel Escabor, in *Learning About Theology From the Third World* by William Dryness (Grand Rapids: Zondervan, 1990), 19.
9. For example, William Dryness, *Learning About Theology From the Third World*; John De Gruchy, *Theology and Ministry in Context and Crisis*; Rene Padilla, "Hermeneutics and Culture—A Theological Perspective," in *Down To Earth*, edited by John Stott and Robert Coote.
10. Ronald Wallace, *Calvin, Geneva and the Reformation* (Grand Rapids: Baker, 1987).
11. Hall, *Thinking the Faith*, 88.
12. Harvie Conn, *Eternal Word*, 229-235.
13. John Stott, InterVarsity Christian Fellowship USA—50th Anniversay address, July 28, 1991.
14. Avery Dulles, *Models of the Church*, 2nd ed. (New York: Doubleday, 1987), 19.

Endnotes

15. Paul Minear, *Images of the Church in the New Testament* (Philadelphia: The Westminster Press, 1960).
16. A. Motyer, *The Message of Philippians* (Grand Rapids: Eerdmans, 1987), 63.
17. The verb *politeuma* has solicited much debate in the theological literature. The Philippians lived in a unique city, administered by local magistrates elected by the local senate under Roman law. They were proud of their status and would have been very sensitive to the urban image that Paul used.
18. Acts 16:14.
19. Philippes Philip Collart, *Ville de Macedoine depuis ses origines jusqu'a la fin de l'epoque romaine* (Paris: Bocard, 1937).
20. Lake and Cadbury, *The Acts of the Apostles* (Grand Rapids: Baker, 1933), 324.
21. George Hunsberger, "The Changing face of Ministry: Christian Leadership for the Twenty-First Century," *Reformed Review*, vol. 44 no. 3 (Spring 1991).
22. Jack Kapica, "Praise the Lord, pass the chip dip," *The Globe and Mail*, October 17, 1992.
23. Paul Moloney, "Churches not fighting racism issue official says," *The Toronto Star*, January 10, 1993.
24. Michael McAteer, "Church members join anti-racism movement," *The Toronto Star*, January 31, 1993.

Chapter Eight

1. William Willimon, *What's Right With the Church* (San Francisco: Harper & Row, 1985), 46.
2. Willimon, *What's Right*, 91.
3. David Bosch, *Transforming Mission* (New York: Orbis Books, 1991), 382.
4. Abraham Maslow, *Toward a Psychology of Being* (New York: Van Nostrand Reinhold, 1986).
5. Emile Durkheim, *The Elementary Forms of Religious Life* (New York: Free Press, 1912, 1965).
6. George Forell, *Christian Social Teaching* (Minneapolis: Augsburg Publishing, 1966), ix.
7. Forell, *Social Teaching,* ix.

8. Gregory Baum, *Religion and Alienation* (New York: Paulist Press, 1975), 64.
9. Willimon, *What's Right*, 63–64.
10. Jim Wallace, *Call to Conversion* (New York: Harper & Row, 1982), 109.
11. Bosch, *Transforming Mission*, 378.
12. Howard Snyder, *Liberating the Church* (Downer's Grove, Ill.: InterVarsity Press, 1983), 11.
13. World Council of Churches, "Gathered For Life: Official Report, VI Assembly of World Council of Churches" (Geneva: WCC, 1983), 50.
14. Bryan Wilson, *Magic and the Millennium* (London: Paladin, 1975), 24.
15. Bosch, *Transforming Mission*, 378.
16. Gennadios Limouris, ed., "Church-Kingdom-World: The Church as Mystery and Prophetic Sign," Faith and Order Paper No. 130 (Geneva: World Council of Churches, 1986), 159.

Chapter Nine

1. Bruce Shelley and Marshall Shelley, *The Consumer Church* (Downers Grove, Ill.: InterVarsity Press, 1992), 7–8.
2. Howard Hanchey, *Church Growth and the Power of Evangelism* (Cambridge, Mass.: Cowley Publications, 1990), 28, 121.
3. Lyle Schaller, *It's a Different World: The Challenge for Today's Pastor* (Nashville: Abingdon Press, 1987), 80.
4. Shelley, *Consumer Church*, 221.
5. Shelley, *Consumer Church*, 221.
6. Max DePree, *Leadership Jazz* (New York: Doubleday, 1989), 9.
7. Harold Fallding, "Mainline Protestantism in Canada and the United States of America: An Overview," *Canadian Journal of Sociology (March 21, 1978)*.
8. George Barna, *The Frog in the Kettle* (Ventura, Ca.: Regal Press, 1990), 149.
9. Max DePree, *Leadership is an Art* (New York: Doubleday, 1989), 1.
10. Robert Greenleaf, *Servant Leadership: Journey Into the Nature of Legitimate Power and Greatness* (New York: Paulist Press, 1977), 13–14.
11. DePree, *Leadership Jazz,* 9.
12. James Gillies, "Where Have All The Leaders Gone?" *Inside Guide* (September/October 1992): 15.

13. Lawrence Miller, *Barbarians to Bureaucrats: Corporate Life Cycle Strategies* (New York: Fawcett Columbine, 1989), 180.
14. Kennon Callahan, *Twelve Keys to an Effective Church: Strategic Planning for Mission* (San Francisco: HarperCollins, 1983), 41.

Chapter Ten

1. Arthur Costa, et al., eds., *If Minds Matter, Volume One* (Illinois: Skylight Publishing Inc., 1992), 1–2.
2. "Voices of Canada," *Maclean's*, January 4, 1993, 14–45.
3. Joan Cadham, et al., *Bent But Not Broken: Today's Canadian Church* (Ste.-Anne-de-Bellevue: Shoreline Press, 1992), 65.
4. Cadham, *Bent But Not Broken*, 65.
5. Kennon Callahan, *Effective Church Leadership* (San Francisco: HarperCollins, 1990), 4–6.
6. Howard Hanchey, *Church Growth and the Power of Evangelism* (Cambridge, Mass.: Cowley Publications, 1990), 19.
7. Hanchey, *Church Growth*, 4.
8. Reginald Bibby and Merlin Brinkerhoff, "When Proselytizing Fails: An Organizational Analysis," *Sociological Analysis* (1976): 199.
9. Jim Holm, in *Mennonite Brethren Herald*, August 25, 1992.
10. Carl George, *Prepare Your Church for the Future* (Tarrytown, New York: Flemming Revell, 1991), 59.
11. Lawrence Miller, *Barbarians to Bureaucrats: Corporate Life Cycle Structures* (New York: Fawcett Columbine, 1989), 181.
12. This expression was first heard from Allan Dunbar, the pastor of Bow Valley Christian Church and the host of the television program, *To You With Love*, in Calgary, Alberta.
13. Bryan Wilson, *Magic and the Millennium* (London: Paladin, 1975).
14. Frank Tillapaugh, *Unleashing the Church* (Ventura, Ca.: Regal Books, 1982).
15. *Anglican Journal* (September 1992).
16. Max Weber, *The Sociology of Religion*, E. Fischoff trans. (Boston: Beacon, 1964).
17. Bryan Wilson, *Magic and the Millennium*, 504.
18. Rosabeth Moss Canter, *When Giants Learn to Dance* (New York: Simon & Schuster, 1989), 17.
19. Peter L. Benson, *Celebrating Possibility* (Search Institute, 1990), Video 1.
20. Richard Niebuhr, *The Purpose of the Church and Its Ministry* (New York: Harper & Row, 1956), 271.

21. William Willimon, *What's Right With The Church* (New York: Harper & Row, 1985), 86.
22. Tom Sine, "Shifting the Church into the Future Tense," *Perspectives,* March 1992.
23. Hanchey, *Church Growth,* 11–12.
24. C. Peter Wagner, *Leading Your Church to Growth* (Ventura, Ca.: Regal Books, 1984), 203.
25. Kennon Callahan, *Twelve Keys to an Effective Church: Strategic Planning for Mission* (San Francisco: HarperCollins, 1983), 39.
26. Sine, "Shifting the Church."
27. From an address by Stanley Mooneyham, delivered at an event celebrating the 40th anniversary of World Vision International, March 13, 1991.

Conclusion

1. "Religion Roundup," *The Toronto Star,* January 2, 1993.
2. Howard Hanchey, *Church Growth and the Power of Evangelism* (Cambridge, Mass.: Cowley Publications, 1990), 201.
3. Frederick Buechner, *Wishful Thinking: A Theological ABC* (New York: Harper & Row, 1973), 32.